T0250298

Network Anomaly
Detection
A Machine Learning Perspective

Network Anomaly

Detection

A Machine Learning Perspective

Dhruba Kumar Bhattacharyya

Jugal Kumar Kalita

CRC Press
Taylor & Francis Group
Boca Raton London New York

CRC Press is an imprint of the
Taylor & Francis Group, an **informa** business

A CHAPMAN & HALL BOOK

MATLAB® is a trademark of The MathWorks, Inc. and is used with permission. The MathWorks does not warrant the accuracy of the text or exercises in this book. This book's use or discussion of MATLAB® software or related products does not constitute endorsement or sponsorship by The MathWorks of a particular pedagogical approach or particular use of the MATLAB® software.

CRC Press
Taylor & Francis Group
6000 Broken Sound Parkway NW, Suite 300
Boca Raton, FL 33487-2742

© 2014 by Taylor & Francis Group, LLC
CRC Press is an imprint of Taylor & Francis Group, an Informa business

No claim to original U.S. Government works

Printed on acid-free paper
Version Date: 20130429

International Standard Book Number-13: 978-1-4665-8208-8 (Hardback)

This book contains information obtained from authentic and highly regarded sources. Reasonable efforts have been made to publish reliable data and information, but the author and publisher cannot assume responsibility for the validity of all materials or the consequences of their use. The authors and publishers have attempted to trace the copyright holders of all material reproduced in this publication and apologize to copyright holders if permission to publish in this form has not been obtained. If any copyright material has not been acknowledged please write and let us know so we may rectify in any future reprint.

Except as permitted under U.S. Copyright Law, no part of this book may be reprinted, reproduced, transmitted, or utilized in any form by any electronic, mechanical, or other means, now known or hereafter invented, including photocopying, microfilming, and recording, or in any information storage or retrieval system, without written permission from the publishers.

For permission to photocopy or use material electronically from this work, please access www.copyright.com (http://www.copyright.com/) or contact the Copyright Clearance Center, Inc. (CCC), 222 Rosewood Drive, Danvers, MA 01923, 978-750-8400. CCC is a not-for-profit organization that provides licenses and registration for a variety of users. For organizations that have been granted a photocopy license by the CCC, a separate system of payment has been arranged.

Trademark Notice: Product or corporate names may be trademarks or registered trademarks, and are used only for identification and explanation without intent to infringe.

Library of Congress Cataloging-in-Publication Data

Bhattacharyya, Dhruba K.
  Network anomaly detection : a machine learning perspective / authors, Dhruba Kumar Bhattacharyya, Jugal Kumar Kalita.
    pages cm
    Includes bibliographical references and index.
    ISBN 978-1-4665-8208-8 (hardback)
    1. Computer networks--Security measures. 2. Intrusion detection systems (Computer security) 3. Machine learning. I. Title.

TK5105.59.B474 2013
005.8--dc23   2013014913

Visit the Taylor & Francis Web site at
http://www.taylorandfrancis.com

and the CRC Press Web site at
http://www.crcpress.com

Dedication

This book is dedicated to my loving wife, Chayanika, who constantly encouraged, inspired and cooperated with me in the successful completion of this humble work.

Dhruba Kumar Bhattacharyya

This book is lovingly dedicated to my father (deuta) Benudhar Kalita, an accomplished author who passed away recently, and of whom I have fond memories, and my mother (maa), Nirala Kalita, a school teacher, who has been gone for sixteen years. They are surely looking down from heaven. It is also dedicated to my 7-year-old daughter Ananya Lonie, who I hope will grow to be a smart, thoughtful, compassionate and accomplished woman.

Jugal Kumar Kalita

Contents

List of Figures

List of Tables

Preface

With the rapid rise in the ubiquity and sophistication of Internet technology and the accompanying, increasing number of network attacks, network intrusion detection has become an important research area. During the past several years, many significant network defense mechanisms have been developed to thwart network attacks. The term *anomaly-based network intrusion detection* refers to the problem of finding exceptional or nonconforming patterns in network traffic data with reference to normal behavior. Finding such atypical patterns, usually referred to as anomalies, has extensive applications in areas such as intrusion detection for cyber security, fraud detection in credit cards, insurance or health care and military surveillance for enemy activities.

The book discusses networks and network anomalies. In particular, the book focuses on characterizing such anomalies and detecting them from a machine learning perspective. It includes discussion on the possible vulnerabilities a network faces at various layers due to weaknesses in protocols or other reasons. It introduces the reader to various types of layer-specific intrusions and modes of operation. This book presents machine learning techniques to counter network intrusion under categories such as supervised learning, unsupervised learning, probabilistic learning, soft computing and combination learners. A detailed pros and cons analysis of these method is also included to provide a clear understanding of the ability of each method. To describe attacks consistently, it presents a taxonomy of attacks. The reader will learn about anomalous or attack patterns and their characteristics, how one can look for such patterns in captured network traffic to unearth potential unauthorized attempts to damage a system or a network and to improve performance during attempts to locate such patterns. Looking for such patterns involves systems and programs that implement machine learning algorithms. We describe such algorithms and present applications in the context of intrusion detection in networks. The reader will learn the specifics of a large number of attacks, the available tools that intruders use to attack networks and how network defenders can use the knowledge of such tools to protect networks from attacks. The reader will also be exposed to additional current issues and challenges that need to be overcome to provide better protection to networks from such attacks.

Dhruba Kumar Bhattacharyya
Jugal Kumar Kalita

MATLAB® and Simulink are registered trademarks of The Math-Works, Inc. For product information, please contact:
The MathWorks, Inc.
3 Apple Hill Drive
Natick, MA 01760–2098 USA
Tel: 508–647–7000
Fax: 508–647–7001
E-mail: info@mathworks.com
Web: www.mathworks.com

Acknowledgments

This humble work would not have been possible without the constant support, encouragement and constructive criticism of a large number of people. Special thanks and sincere appreciation are due to our dedicated faculty members and Ph.D. students: Dr. Bhabesh Nath, Mr. Prasanta Gogoi, Mr. Monowar Hussain Bhuyan, Mr. Debasish Das, Mr. Swarup Roy, Mr. Hasin A. Ahmed, Mr. Nazrul Haque, Ms. Priyakshi Mahanta and Mr. R. C. Baishya.

We are grateful to the panel of reviewers for their constructive suggestions and critical evaluation. The constant support and cooperation received from our colleagues and students during the period of writing this book is sincerely acknowledged.

Abstract

Networked computer systems are deeply integrated into every aspect of our information-overloaded modern society. The mechanisms that keep our modern society flowing smoothly, with activities such as efficient execution of government and commercial transactions and services, or consistent facilitation of social transactions among billions of users, are all dependent on large networked computer systems. Today, every aspect of our lives is influenced by networked computer systems. The Internet, which provides transportation to all types of information including complex real-time multi-media data, is the universal network of millions of interconnected computer systems, organized as a network of thousands of distinct smaller networks. Recent growth of the Internet has been phenomenal and consequently, the computers and the networks that make the Internet hum have become the targets of enemies and criminals. Intrusions into a computer or network system are activities that destabilize them by compromising security in terms of confidentiality, availability or integrity, the three main characteristics of a secure and stable system.

Machine learning is used to extract valid, novel, potentially useful and meaningful pattern from a dataset, usually large, in a domain of interest by using non-trivial mechanisms. A machine learning algorithm attempts to recognize complex patterns in datasets to help make intelligent decisions or predictions when it encounters new or previously unseen data instances. To deal with unseen examples, a machine learning algorithm must be cognizant of this necessity and thus, when it learns it must make conscious and diligent efforts to generalize from examples it has seen. Good generalization from data is a prime activity a learner program must perform.

The book focuses on characterizing anomalies in networked computer systems and detecting them using machine learning. It includes discussion of the vulnerabilities networks face at various layers due to weaknesses in protocols or other reasons. It presents machine learning techniques to counter network intrusion under categories such as supervised learning, unsupervised learning, probabilistic learning, soft

computing and combination learners. Detailed discussion and analysis
of these methods are included to provide a clear understanding of the
abilities of each method. In addition to the technical description of
the algorithms, the book presents applications of these algorithms in
the context of intrusion detection in networks. The book also provides
specifics of a large number of attacks, the available tools that intruders
use to attack networks and also how network defenders can use the
knowledge of such tools to protect networks from attacks. Finally, it
exposes the reader to the current issues and challenges that need to be
overcome to provide better protection to networks from such attacks.

Authors

 **Dhruba Kumar Bhattacharyya** received his Ph.D. degree from Tezpur University in 1999 in cryptography and error control coding. He is a professor in Computer Science and Engineering at Tezpur University. Professor Bhattacharyya's research areas include network security, data mining and bioinformatics. He has published more than 180 research articles in leading int'nl journals and peer-reviewed conference proceedings. Dr. Bhattacharyya has written or edited 7 technical books in English and 2 technical reference books in Assamese. Under his guidance, six students have received their Ph.D. degrees in the areas of data mining and bioinformatics. He is on the editorial board of several international journals and also has been associated with several international conferences. More details about Dr. Bhattacharyya can be found at http://agnigarh.tezu.ernet.in/~dkb/index.html.

 **Jugal Kumar Kalita** teaches computer science at the University of Colorado, Colorado Springs. He received M.S. and Ph.D. degrees in computer and information science from the University of Pennsylvania in Philadelphia in 1988 and 1990, respectively. Prior to that he had received an M.Sc. from the University of Saskatchewan in Saskatoon, Canada in 1984 and a B.Tech. from the Indian Institute of Technology, Kharagpur in 1982. His expertise is in the areas of artificial intelligence and machine learning, and the application of techniques in machine learning to network security, natural language processing and bioinformatics. He has published 115 papers in journals and refereed conferences. He is the author of a book on Perl. He received the Chancellor's Award at the University of Colorado, Colorado Springs, in 2011, in recognition of lifelong excellence in teaching, research and service. More details about Dr. Kalita can be found at http://www.cs.uccs.edu/~kalita.

Chapter 1

Introduction

Networked computer systems play a vital role in every aspect of our information-overloaded modern society. The mechanisms that keep our modern society well-oiled and humming, with activities such as efficient execution of financial transactions and business processes, smooth and uninterrupted running of extensive government services or sustained facilitation of social transactions among a billion or more users, are all dependent on large networked computer systems. These days, there is not a single aspect of our lives that has not been significantly touched by computer systems. The highly interconnected computer systems that make all of this possible are in a state of constant flux as well. The hardware and software that constitute such systems are always changing at a rapid pace.

The Internet, which provides the underlay for all computer mediated activities, is the universal network of millions of interconnected computer systems, organized as a network of thousands of distinct networks. The Internet was designed to transport information of all types, starting from simple binary to complex real-time multimedia data, without any fuss or judgment. The number of Internet users is increasing dramatically across the world. A population distribution [92] of the number of Internet users across the world is shown in Figure 1.1. As the number of Internet users rises, constant efforts are underway to upgrade the Internet infrastructure as well. For example, collaborating partners Ciena[1], Cisco[2], Juniper[3], Indiana University[4] and Infinera[5] are developing an Internet technology termed *4th Gen Technology*, which will expand exponentially footprint, capacity and performance compared to the current network infrastructure. This new

---

[1]http://www.ciena.com/
[2]www.cisco.com
[3]www.juniper.net
[4]http://www.indiana.edu/
[5]http://www.infinera.com/

network has a capacity of 8.8 terabits with 100 gigabit Ethernet technology. Another way of looking at the growth of Internet users in terms

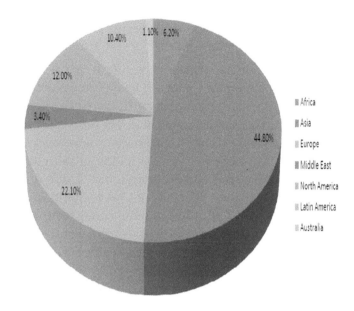

FIGURE 1.1:   Continent-wise Internet users statistics

of three geographical categories, i.e., global, developed and developing worlds (*source: http://www.internetworldstats.com*) is shown in Figure 1.2. It can be easily seen from the figure that the growth of Internet users for all these categories is increasing almost linearly. The explosive growth and consequent ubiquity has naturally made computers and networks the targets of enemies and criminals. The security of a computer system is compromised when an individual or a program enters a computer or a network in an unauthorized manner, possibly with plans to disrupt normal activities. Intrusions into or attacks on computer or network systems are activities that attempt to destabilize them by compromising security in terms of confidentiality, availability or integrity, the three main characteristics of a secure and stable system.

1.1   The Internet and Modern Networks

A network is created with individual physical and software components that interact in complex ways to provide people and machines with useful communication services. It is customary to think
of networks and networking functions in terms of layered architectures,
the two most prominent being the ISO/OSI (International Organization for Standardization/Open Systems Interconnection) model and the
TCP/IP (Transport Control Protocol/Internet Protocol) model. Each
layer in a model is responsible for a different facet of communication
in an independent manner, without affecting adjacent layers. Each individual entity inside a network layer is assigned a definite role to play
toward the collaborative behavior of the network. The primary reason
for layered representation of network communication is the inherent
complexity of the process. Layering makes it easier to understand.
However, with increased complexity, opportunities for malfunction or
malfeasance increase.

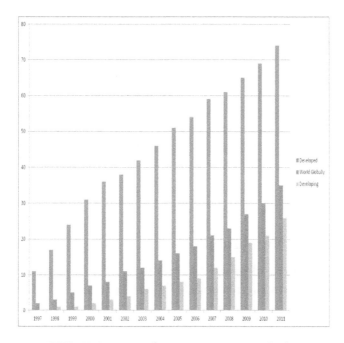

FIGURE 1.2:   Internet users statistics

An intrusion detection system (IDS) monitors events occurring in a computer system or network and analyzes them for signs of intrusion or unauthorized access or entry. A typical view of a network with the deployment of an IDS along with a protected local area network (LAN) and DMZ (demilitarized zone) is shown in Figure 1.3. A network-based IDS (NIDS) often consists of a set of single-purpose sensors or host computers placed at various points in a network. These units monitor network traffic, performing local analysis of that traffic and reporting potential attacks to a management process. Network based intrusion detection is broadly studied in two categories [221]: *rule based* and *anomaly based*. Rule-based (also called *misuse-based*) detection searches for specific patterns (or intrusion signatures or rules) in the data to effectively detect previously known intrusions. The rule-based approach usually does not generate a large number of false alarms since the rules are specifically designed to detect known intrusions. However, a rule-based approach fails to detect novel intrusions that do not have signatures or associated detection rules. Anomaly detection consists of analyzing and reporting unusual behavioral traffic patterns in computing systems. Network security has become a serious endeavor since organizations must protect their systems with confidential and valuable information from attacks at all costs or continuously provide revenue-generating services to clients without the slightest interruption. Traditional network security techniques, such as user authentication, encryption and firewalls, have been used to provide network security as the first line of defense, but these are not sufficient to prevent all attacks in the highly networked environment of today. Intrusion detection is often used as a second perimeter wall to provide for enhanced network security, and it has become vitally important.

1.2   Network Vulnerabilities

Why is a network vulnerable to attacks or intrusions from the outside or even from within the network? Vulnerabilities result from inherent weaknesses in the design, configuration or implementation of computer systems or networks that render them susceptible to security threats. Threats may arise from exploitation of design flaws in the hardware and software used to build computer network systems. For example,

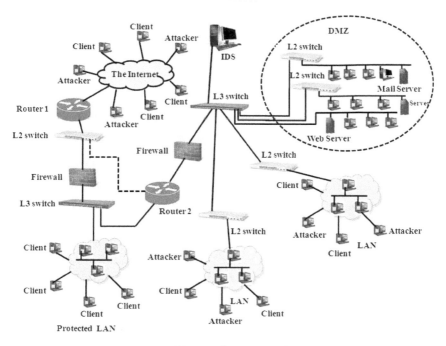

FIGURE 1.3: View of a network with a DMZ

systems may be incorrectly configured, and therefore vulnerable to attack. Such vulnerabilities may occur due to inexperience or insufficient training of responsible personnel, or half-done work by such individuals. Vulnerabilities also arise due to poor management of networked systems, such as the lack of adequate policies and procedures saying who has access to which resources and when, and insufficient or infrequent checks on traffic activities taking place within network systems.

1.3 Anomalies and Anomalies in Networks

Given a large dataset, nonconforming patterns are often referred to as anomalies, outliers, exceptions, aberrations, surprises, peculiarities or discordant observations in different application domains [63]. Out of these, anomalies and outliers are two of the most commonly used terms in the context of anomaly-based intrusion detection in networks. The statistics community has been studying the problem of detection of anomalies or outliers from as early as the 19th century [109]. Anomaly detection has extensive applications in areas such as fraud detection for credit cards, insurance or health care, intrusion detection for cyber security and military surveillance for enemy activities. An anomalous traffic pattern in a computer network could mean that a hacked computer is sending out sensitive data to an unauthorized host.

A computer network is formed when many individual entities are put together to contribute toward providing complex communication services. Things can go wrong with any of the interacting entities. Anomalies are network events that deviate from normal, expected or usual behavior, and are suspect from a security perspective. Anomalies in a network may occur due to two major reasons [367]: *performance related* and *security related*. A performance-related anomaly may occur due to malfunctions, such as network device malfunction, e.g., router misconfiguration. Security-related anomalies occur due to malicious activities that attempt to disrupt normal functioning of the network. Security-related anomalies are classified into six major categories [161, 387]: *infection, exploding, probe, cheat, traverse* and *concurrency*. The first category, infection, attempts to infect the target system by installing malicious files or by tampering with the system. Examples of this category are viruses and worms. Exploding anomalies attempt to overflow the target system with bugs. Buffer overflow is a common example of this category. The probe category of attacks mainly tries to gather information to identify the vulnerabilities of the system in various modes (e.g., $1:1$, $1:m$, $m:1$ and $m:n$). Port mappers (e.g., *nmap*) are common examples of this category of attack. A common characteristic of the fourth category of attack is the use of fake or abnormal callers. Internet protocol (IP) spoofing, media access control (MAC) spoofing, etc. are common examples of a cheating attack. The fifth category of attack attempts to compromise the target system by matching each possible key. Brute force attacks and dictionary attacks are commonly used attacks of this category. Finally, in concurrency attacks, the attackers attempt to victimize a system or a service by flooding or by sending mass requests, beyond the capacity of the system or the service. DDoS (Distributed Denial of Service) attacks are examples of this category. There are still some attacks which do not fall into any of these categories, like an attempt to infect the target system by exploiting the weaknesses or bugs in the system. Such attacks are mostly attempted by unskilled professionals.

According to Anderson [18], an intrusion or a threat is a deliberate and unauthorized attempt to (i) access information, (ii) manipulate information or (iii) render a system unreliable or unusable. For example, *Denial of Service (DoS)* attacks attempt to starve a host of its resources, which are needed to function correctly. *Worms* and *viruses* exploit other hosts through the network; *compromises* obtain privileged access to a host by taking advantage of known vulnerabilities.

1.4 Machine Learning

A computer, even if stand-alone, keeps track of logs of many activities that users perform on it. For example, there are records of users who log in and how long they are logged in, and there are records of system or application software updates. There are many other similar logs. A networked computer keeps records of a lot of additional activities. For example, there are records of which user has transferred which files to/from a system and when, and who has received e-mail from whom and when. Devices that facilitate and control communication activities can keep records of every bit of information (usually organized into chunks called *packets*) that comes to a machine or leaves a machine. The gist of this discussion is that there are potentially extremely large bodies of traffic and log information available on networked computer systems. Most activities are normal, but a very small fraction of activities may be outside the realm of what is usual or expected. It is possible that unusual activities are potential intrusions. Such abnormal activities may be found by matching logs and traffic datasets with patterns of known instances of abnormal activities that one has created a priori. However, traffic and log datasets are potentially very large, disparate and ever-growing. The patterns of intrusion may not be straightforward and easy to find. This is where ideas from machine learning may be able to help in a significant way in fishing out potential intrusion patterns, and provide warnings to network management personnel, when appropriate.

Machine learning aims to extract valid, novel, potentially useful and meaningful patterns from a dataset, usually large, in a domain by using a nontrivial learning mechanism. A machine learning algorithm attempts to recognize complex patterns in existing datasets to help make intelligent decisions or predictions when it encounters new or previously unseen data instances. A fundamental problem that a machine learning algorithm must address is the problem of generalization. When learning from data, it is possible that the learner simply memorizes what it has seen. If this is the case, a learner cannot process or react to data instances it has not seen before. To deal with unseen examples, a machine learning program must be cognizant of this possibility and thus, when it learns, must make conscious and diligent efforts to generalize from examples it has seen. This may necessitate estimating a probability distribution for what is acceptable and what is not. It may involve being able to detect examples which are sufficiently similar to or dissimilar from seen examples, usually using some mathematical approaches. Good generalization from data is a prime activity a learner program must perform.

At the gross level, machine learning algorithms can be primarily categorized into two types: *supervised* and *unsupervised*. A supervised algorithm requires a training dataset where data instances are labeled. This labeling is usually performed by humans and is expensive because it requires experts in relevant domains to spend precious time doing the labeling. An example of a label may be the class or sub-group a data instance belongs to. An unsupervised algorithm usually attempts to group data instances into categories or sub-groups based on inherent properties contained in them, using a measure or metric to compute similarity between an arbitrary pair of data instances. Alternatively, one can compute dissimilarity or distance between any pair of instances as well. There is also a third category of algorithms called *semi-supervised algorithms*. A semi-supervised algorithm may use a small number of labeled examples in addition to unlabeled examples. Some semi-supervised algorithms may use labeled examples from a limited number of categories. For example, if there are two possible labels, *yes* and *no*, we may have labeled examples from the *yes* class only.

Considering the mechanism used to group data objects, machine learning algorithms may also be categorized as either *classification* or *clustering* algorithms. A classification algorithm identifies to which one of a set of subclasses or subcategories or subpopulations a new instance belongs, on the basis of training on a dataset where class membership of each instance is known. Thus, classification algorithms are examples of supervised machine learners. An algorithm that performs classification is called a *classifier*. This does not mean that all supervised algorithms are classifiers. The idea of *clustering* or *cluster analysis* divides a set of data objects into groups that are formally called *clusters* such that objects within a cluster are more similar to each other than those in other clusters. Clustering is a type of unsupervised learning.

In addition to the above, in this book we also discuss probabilistic, soft computing, knoweldge-based and hybrid learning methods. Each of these methods can be supervised or unsupervised. They may be classifiers or clustering algorithms. Probabilistic algorithms use ideas from probability along with statistical computation to acquire patterns within the data. Soft computing methods can deal with uncertainty and brittleness better than other methods. They include approaches such as genetic algorithms, neural networks, fuzzy sets and rough sets. Knowledge-based methods encompass methods such as rule-based systems, expert systems and ontology-based systems. In other words, the system has prior knowledge about the domain of intrusion and this prior knowledge is encoded in a form useable by a detection program. Hybrid methods use a combination of two or more learning algorithms to obtain results.

1.5 Prior Work on Network Anomaly Detection

Network anomaly detection is a broad research area which already boasts a number of surveys, review articles, as well as books. Let us present some survey papers first. An extensive survey of anomaly detection techniques developed in machine learning and statistics has been provided by Hodge and Austin [169]. Agyemang et al. [10] present a broad review of anomaly detection techniques for numeric as well as symbolic data. Extended overviews of neural networks and statistics-based novelty detection techniques are found in [238, 239]. Exhaustive surveys on anomaly detection in several domains have been presented in [63, 245]. Patcha and Park [284] and Snyder [344] present surveys of anomaly detection techniques used specifically for cyber intrusion detection. Zhang et al. [419] present a survey of anomaly detection methods in computer networks. A good amount of research on outlier detection in statistics is found in several books [317, 35, 163] as well as survey articles [39, 29, 139].

A review of flow-based intrusion detection is presented by Sperotto et al. [350], who explain the concepts of flows and classified attacks, and provide a detailed discussion of detection techniques for scans, worms, Botnets and DoS attacks. An extensive survey of DoS and DDoS attack detection techniques is presented in [291]. Discussion of network coordinate systems, design and security is found in [102]. Wu and Banzhaf [386] present an overview of applications of computational intelligence methods to the problem of intrusion detection. They include various methods such as artificial neural networks, fuzzy systems, evolutionary computation, artificial immune systems and swarm intelligence.

There are several books that are similar and related to our book. Our search resulted in the following books.

- Jacobson, Douglas, *Introduction to Network Security*, CRC Press
- Cunningham, B., Dykstra, T., Fuller, E., Hoagberg, M., Little, C., Miles, G. and Schack, T., *Network Security Evaluation*, Syngress Publishing Inc.
- Endorf, C., Schultz, E. and Mellander, J., *Intrusion Detection and Prevention*, McGraw Hill
- Ghorbani, A., Lu, W. and Tavallaee, M., *Network Intrusion Detection and Prevention — Concepts and Techniques*, Springer
- Marchette, D. J., *Computer Intrusion Detection and Network Monitoring: A Statistical Viewpoint*, Springer
- Wang, Y., *Statistical Techniques for Network Security*, IGI Global
- Mirkovic, J., Dietrich, S., Dittrich, D. and Reiher, P., *Internet Denial of Service–Attack and Defense Mechanisms*, Prentice Hall
- Rehman, R. U., *Intrusion Detection with SNORT: advanced IDS techniques using Snort, Apache, MySQL, PHP, and ACID*, Prentice Hall, 2003
- Koziol, J., *Intrusion Detection with SNORT*, SAMS
- Yu, Z. and Tsai, J. J. P., *Intrusion Detection–A Machine Learning Approach*, Imperial College Press

Several of these books cover network security in a very general way, discussing various aspects of it. Several other books cover statistical techniques for intrusion detection in depth. Some of these books are professional books, covering the very well-known tool called SNORT for intrusion detection. Only the last book by Yu and Tsai is similar in spirit to our book. It is a small book with less than 200 pages that gives a brief overview of some of the topics we cover in this book. However, our coverage is more elaborate and we cover topics that are not covered by Yu and Tsai. We cover machine learning approaches and systems at a greater depth than Yu and Tsai, so that students can acquire a clear understanding of the state of the art. We provide a detailed discussion of a large number of feature selection algorithms, a topic not discussed by Yu and Tsai. We also present a discussion of a large number of practical tools for launching attacks in various modes, in addition to tools for capturing, packet or flow feature extraction, detection and analysis. We also have a detailed discussion on evaluation parameters and intrusion detection methods. Unlike Yu and Tsai, we provide material for hands-on experience development, so that students can code on a testbed to implement detection methods toward development of their own IDS. The particular contributions of this book are presented in more detail in the next section.

1.6 Contributions of This Book

It is clear by now that the book discusses networks and network anomalies. In particular, the book focuses on characterizing such anomalies and detecting them from a machine learning perspective. It includes discussion on the possible vulnerabilities a network faces at various layers due to weaknesses in protocols or other reasons. It introduces the reader to various types of layer-specific intrusions and modes of operation.

The book concentrates on presenting machine learning techniques to counter network intrusion under various categories such as supervised learning, unsupervised learning, probabilistic learning, soft computing and combination learners. A detailed pro and con analysis of these methods is also included to provide a clear understanding of the abilities of each method. To describe the attacks consistently, we present a taxonomy of attacks. The reader will learn about anomalous or attack patterns and their characteristics, how one can look for such patterns in captured network traffic to unearth potential unauthorized attempts to damage a system or a network and how to improve performance during attempts to locate such patterns. Looking for such patterns involves systems and programs that implement machine learning algorithms. The reader will be given a technical description of such algorithms and their application in the context of intrusion detection in networks. The reader will learn the specifics of a large number of attacks, the available tools that intruders use to attack networks and also how network defenders can use the knowledge of such tools to protect networks from attacks. The reader will also be exposed to additional current issues and challenges that need to be overcome to provide better protection to networks from such attacks.

Building on the discussion of the previous section, we claim that, unlike other relevant books on the market, this book provides a comprehensive discussion of the following topics in one single volume.

1. **Network and network anomalies:** This book aims to provide a background on network and network anomalies caused by performance-related or security-related reasons. It discusses possible vulnerabilities in a network at various layers due to weaknesses in protocols or other reasons. It also presents layer-specific intrusions and their behaviors.

2. **Machine learning focused:** A significant portion of this book is focused on how machine learning techniques are used to counter network intrusions. Methods and techniques are discussed under categories such as supervised learning, unsupervised learning, probabilistic learning, soft computing and combination learners. We provide enough technical and practical information on these methods in the context of their applicability to intrusion detection so that their comparative abilities and limitations become clear.

3. **Attack taxonomy:** This book provides a taxonomy of attacks based on their characteristics and behavior. This will help the reader describe the attacks consistently as well as to combat these and new attacks.

4. **Feature selection:** A network anomaly detection system has to deal with a huge volume of data which may contain redundant and irrelevant features, causing poor training and testing performance, significant resource consumption as well as degraded real-time detection performance. Therefore, selection of relevant features is considered an essential requirement in intrusion detection. This book introduces the concepts and discusses algorithms for feature selection, and also compares their performance.

5. **Evaluation of Intrusion Detection Systems (IDSs):** This book covers various methods and techniques to assess the accu-

racy, performance, completeness, timeliness, stability, interoperability, reliability and other dynamic aspects of a network intrusion detection system. It looks at accuracy with five important measures: sensitivity and specificity, misclassification rate, confusion matrix, precision and recall, F-measure and receiver operating characteristic (ROC) curves.

6. **Practical knowledge of attack-monitor-defense-evaluate:**
This book also aims to enable hands-on experience in launching attacks; monitoring, capturing and preprocessing packet or flow traffic; extracting basic, content-based, time-based and connection-oriented features; implementing methods to detect attacks; and finally to evaluate detection performance. Unlike other books, it includes discussion of a large number of tools and systems for different tasks at various levels during the development of a NIDS.

7. **Issues, challenges and prognosis for network intrusions:**
This book finally discusses important unresolved issues and research challenges. For example, it discusses how network intrusion patterns may change in the future. Another topic of discussion is the enhanced computational requirements necessary for a network defense mechanism to possess as changed motivations of attackers lead to more sophisticated attacks.

1.7 Organization

The book is organized in *three* major parts with a total of *nine* chapters and three appendices.

- *Part I* of the book contains three chapters. *Chapter 1* of the book, which is the current chapter, provides an introduction to modern computer networks and the problems they face in terms of anomalies in traffic and how these anomalies may affect performance, and the use of machine learning to detect such anomalies. *Chapter 2* delves deeper into concepts in networking including communication protocols, topologies, the open systems interconnection (OSI) model and types of networks, followed by a discussion of anomalies that may afflict modern computer networks, the reasons why networks are vulnerable to attacks, the motivations of attackers and the types of attacks. *Chapter 3* provides an introduction to approaches in statistical machine learning including popular supervised methods such as decision trees and Support Vector Machines (SVM); unsupervised methods such as clustering and association rule mining; probabilistic learning techniques such as Bayes networks, naíve Bayes and hidden Markov models; soft computing methods such as rough sets, fuzzy logic and artificial neural networks. This chapter also discusses knowledge representation in terms of logics and ontologies.

- *Part II* of the book covers five important topics, viz., system architecture, feature selection, application of machine learning methods to intrusion detection, performance metrics and tools for attacking, detection and monitoring. There are five chapters. *Chapter 4* aims to provide background on general issues in network anomaly detection, including system architecture, similarity measures, available datasets and issues in collecting private datasets. *Chapter 5* presents the need for feature or attribute selection, issues in feature selection and a catalogue of relevant feature selection methods with discussion of each. *Chapter 6* is the longest chapter in this part of the book with its presentation of machine learning methods researchers and practitioners use for network anomaly detection. We discuss a few popular or highly cited methods in detail whereas for other methods, we provide a high level overview of each. Our discussions are organized in terms of the categories of machine learning techniques discussed in *Chapter 3*, as far as possible. *Chapter 7* discusses various metrics for evaluating network anomaly detection methods. However, we go beyond the metrics to present a host of other topics such as quality, validity and reliability of the datasets. *Chapter 8* discusses a variety of tools for launching and detecting attacks. It also aims to provide a detailed taxonomy of attacks and associated tools.

- *Part III* of the book contains only one chapter. This chapter, *Chapter 9*, concludes the book with a discussion of research issues and challenges in network anomaly detection. It also includes a discussion on how network guardians should prepare as sophisticated and large-scale attacks become more commonplace in the future.

Chapter 2

Networks and Anomalies

To understand anomaly detection in networks, we must have a good understanding of basic network concepts. We also must understand how anomalies may arise in networks. This chapter provides the necessary background to both of these topics. The first part of the chapter discusses networking basics, components of networks, types of networks, scales of networks, topologies of networks and performance constraints. The second part introduces the concept of network anomalies, causes of anomalies, sources of anomalies and their precursors. It also presents a classification of network intrusions or attacks.

2.1 Networking Basics

A network is a complex interacting system, composed of many individual entities. Two or more computer systems that can send or receive data from each other through a medium that they share and access are said to be connected. The behavior of the individual entities contributes to the ensemble behavior of the entire network. In a computer network, there are generally three communicating entities: (i) *Users*: Humans who perform various activities on the network such as browsing Web pages and shopping, (ii) *Hosts*: Computers, each one of which is identified with a unique address, say an IP address and (iii) *Processes*: Instances of executable programs used in a client–server architecture. Client processes request server(s) for a network service, whereas the server processes provide the requested services to the clients. An example client is a Web browser that requests pages from a Web server, which responds to the requests.

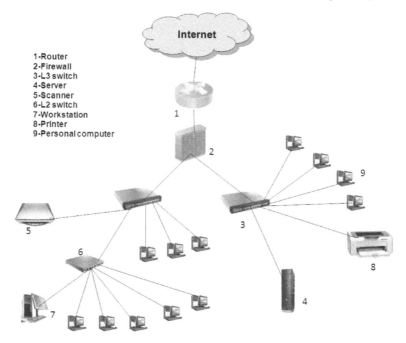

1-Router
2-Firewall
3-L3 switch
4-Server
5-Scanner
6-L2 switch
7-Workstation
8-Printer
9-Personal computer

FIGURE 2.1: A typical computer networking

2.1.1 Typical View of a Network

People usually think of a computer network as being composed of a number of computers and devices that communicate with one another, without much thought regarding how the communication takes place. In this simple view of a network, computers or devices are connected to each other using wires or media, or wirelessly so that they can exchange data. Figure 2.1 shows a typical view of a wired computer network. We see that computer nodes or servers or devices are connected using special devices such as switches, routers or hubs using appropriate communication media. Apart from the software used to support communication, the performance of data exchange among these nodes, servers or devices largely depends on the type of media and connecting devices used.

2.1.2 Communication Media

In the recent past, communication media technology has achieved remarkable progress in terms of speed, reliability and robustness. The function of communication media is to transport raw bit streams from

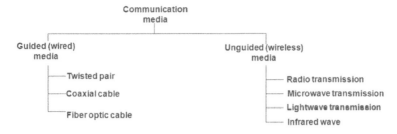

FIGURE 2.2: Classification of communication media

TABLE 2.1: Guided vs. Unguided Media: Comparison

Guided Media	Unguided Media
Contains the signal energy within a solid medium and propagates within the medium, i.e., in guided form	Signal energy is not contained and propagates in unguided form as electromagnetic waves
Point to point communication	Radio broadcasting in all directions
Discrete network topologies are relevant	Continuous network topologies are relevant
Attenuation or loss of energy depends on the distance exponentially	Attenuation is proportional to square of the distance
Scope for enhancing the transmission capacity by increasing the number of cables	No scope for enhancement
Installation may be costly and time consuming	Relatively less costly and less time consuming

one computer to another. We have several options for the selection of the appropriate communication medium for the actual transmission. The performance of these media types can be compared in terms of four crucial parameters: (i) bandwidth, (ii) delay, (iii) cost and (iv) installation and maintenance. We divide existing media types into two major categories [353, 364]: (i) *guided media* and (ii) *unguided media*. Figure 2.2 shows a basic classification of the existing popular communication media. A general performance comparison between the two types of communication media is given in Table 2.1. We see that both media types have their own merits and drawbacks.

2.1.2.1 Guided Media

As shown in Table 2.1, in guided media, signal energy is contained and guided within a solid medium and the communication is point to point. The three popular examples of this category of media are (i) twisted pair, (ii) coaxial cable and (iii) fibre optic cables.

2.1.2.1.1   Twisted Pair   This type of medium is built using two insulated copper wires (usually 1 mm thick) twisted together like a DNA molecule in a helical form. It uses the wires in a twisted form because the waves from different twists cancel out, so the radiation from the wires is low. The bandwidth of a twisted pair is dependent on two important factors: (i) the wire thickness and (ii) the traveled distance. Generally, in most cases, it allows several megabits/sec to travel for a few kilometers. The two major causes behind the popularity of twisted pair cable are that they provide adequate performance and they are inexpensive.

2.1.2.1.2   Coaxial Cable   *Coaxial cables* are popular for their simple structure and shielding mechanism, which enables them to provide a good combination of high bandwidth and excellent noise immunity. A coaxial cable is made of a stiff copper wire as the core, surrounded by an insulating material, encased in a cylindrical conductor like a closely woven braided mesh. A protective plastic sheath covers the outer conductor. Today, a coaxial cable has a bandwidth of approximately 1 GHz. This medium is widely used for cable television and metropolitan area networks.

2.1.2.1.3   Fiber Optic Cables   This media type is similar to coaxial cable, only without the braid. Figure 2.3 shows a sheath with three fibers. The center of the fiber cable is the glass core which allows it to propagate light. The diameter of the core varies based on the type of fiber used. In multi-mode fibers, it is typically 50 microns in diameter, whereas, in the single-mode fibers, it is 8–10 microns. A glass cladding with a lower index of refraction than the core sorrounds the glass core, to preserve all the light in the core. Finally, to protect the cladding a thin plastic jacket is used and the fibers are generally organized into groups of bundles, which are protected by using an outer sheath. The achievable bandwidth is in excess of 50,000 Gbps (50 Tbps). A commonly known signaling limit is about 10 Gbps, although, in the laboratories, 100 Gbps has already been achieved on a single fiber. A comparison of the three guided media is shown in Table 2.2.

2.1.2.2   Unguided Media

Unguided signals can travel from the transmitting end to the receiving end in several ways. Such media can propagate in all directions and

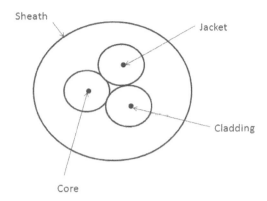

FIGURE 2.3: Fiber optic cable: end view of a sheath with 3 fibers

TABLE 2.2: Comparison of Guided Media

Media type	Data rate	Bandwidth	Repeater distance
Twisted pair	4 Mbps	3 MHz	2–10 km
Coaxial cable	500 Mbps	350 MHz	1–10 km
Fiber optic cable	2 Gbps	2 GHz	10–100 km

they are relatively less costly and their installation is also less time consuming. The three most popular unguided propagation methods are (i) ground wave propagation, (ii) sky propagation and (iii) space propagation. We will discuss four types of communication media, namely, (i) radio transmission, (ii) microwave transmission, (iii) lightwave transmission and (iv) infrared and millimeter waves.

2.1.2.2.1 Radio Transmission This unguided communication medium is commonly used for both indoor as well as outdoor applications because the signals can be easily generated, the signals can travel long distances and the signals can penetrate buildings easily. Unlike guided media, such waves are frequency dependent and can propagate in all directions (omnidirectional) from the source, which simplifies the task of alignment between the transmitter and the receiver. A radio wave with low frequency can pass through obstacles easily. However, with the increase in distance, the power falls off sharply. On the other hand, a high frequency radio wave can easily travel in straight lines and bounce off obstacles. Generally, frequencies in the range 30 MHz–1 GHz are referred to as the *radio range* and are typically suitable for any omnidirectional applications. Radio waves above 30 MHz can propagate through the ionosphere. As a result, the distant transmitters do not interfere with one another due to reflection from the atmosphere.

2.1.2.2.2 Microwave Transmission This type of unguided medium carries narrowly focused, high frequency (1 GHz–40 GHz) waves that travel in nearly straight lines. At these frequencies, it is quite possible for point-to-point microwave transmission to occur since the beams are highly directional. However, if the tranmitting towers are too far apart, there is every possibility that the earth will get in the way. As a result, it requires the use of repeaters periodically to strengthen the signals. With the increase in the height of towers, they can be placed apart accordingly. Microwaves cannot pass through buildings well. Although the beam is highly directional and focused at the transmitter, there is still some divergence in space. Microwave transmission is also used for satellite communications.

2.1.2.2.3 Lightwave Transmission This is an inherently unidirectional communication medium. It is used to connect networks in different buildings through roof-mounted lasers. Due to its unidirectional nature, each building needs to have its own laser as well as its own detection mechanism (e.g., a photodetector). This cost-effective medium is well known for its high bandwidth.

2.1.2.2.4 Infrared and Millimeter Waves These waves are widely used for short-range point-to-point and multipoint applications. Presently, almost all electronic devices such as televisions, video cassette recorders (VCRs) and stereos operate with infrared communication. The frequency range from 3×10^{11} to 2×10^{14} Hz is referred to as infrared. It is relatively directional, easy and convenient to use, cheap, and easy to build. However, a major limitation is that these waves cannot pass through solid objects.

2.1.3   Network Software

Hardware was the main focus during the initial development of computer networks and software was usually an afterthought. This is no longer true. Software is a lot more sophisticated and better put together now. In subsequent sections, we will discuss the structure of network software in some detail.

2.1.3.1 Layered Architecture

To reduce design complexity, most networks are organized in a layered fashion, where an upper layer is designed based on the layer below it. Each layer is designed to offer a set of predefined services to the layer above it, hiding details of implementation. During the conversation between two layers, say layer-n and layer-$(n-1)$, the rules and conventions used are collectively referred to as the layer-n protocol. A protocol represents an agreement as to how communications take place between two parties.

2.1.3.2 Connection-Oriented and Connectionless Services

Layers are designed to offer two types of network service: *connection oriented* and *connectionless*. In connection oriented service, the user (i) establishes a connection, (ii) uses the connection based on some mutually negotiated (among the sender, receiver and the subnet) parameters, e.g., maximum size of messages and the required quality of service and (iii) finally, releases the connection. In connectionless service, there is no logical connection through the network on which data flow can be regulated. As a result the data transfer becomes unreliable. Analogous to telegram service, an unreliable or unacknowledged connectionless service is referred to as datagram service. An example of datagram service is the request–reply service. According to this service, a sender sends a single datagram containing a request; the reply contains the answer. This request–reply service is very commonly used in the client–server model: the client sends a request and in response, the server sends the reply. Table 2.3 lists various types [364] of services and their examples.

2.1.3.3 Service Primitives

A service is specified by a set of primitives or simple operations. A user process can access these primitives to obtain the service. Connection-oriented service primitives are different from the primitives for connectionless service. Table 2.4 shows a list of service primitives used in a client–server environment to implement a reliable byte stream.

TABLE 2.3:   Six Different Types of Service

Service	Type	Example
Reliable message stream	Connection oriented	Sequence of pages
Reliable byte stream	Connection oriented	Remote login
Unreliable connection	Connection oriented	Digitized voice
Unreliable datagram	Connectionless	Electronic junk mail
Acknowledged datagram	Connectionless	Registered mail
Request–reply	Connectionless	Database query

TABLE 2.4:   Service Primitives

Name	Purpose and Action
LISTEN	to accept an incoming connection
	server process is blocked till connection request arises
CONNECT	to establish a connection
	client process is suspended till there's a response
RECEIVE	to receive the request from the client
	blocks and waits for a message
SEND	to send a message
	once packet reached, unblocks the server process
DISCONNECT	to terminate a connection
	once packet received, server acknowledges

2.1.3.4   Services and Protocols

A service refers to a set of operations provided by a layer to its immediate upper layer. A service also creates an interface between two consecutive or adjacent layers, where the lower layer serves as the service provider and the upper layer acts as the service user. A service related to the interface between two layers is illustrated in Figure 2.4. A protocol is a set of rules used to govern the meaning and format of the packets or messages exchanged between the entities within a layer. Entities on the same layer are called peer entities. Protocols are used by the entities to implement services. Entities are free to change the protocol as long as they are able to provide the required services.

2.1.4   Reference Models

We now discuss an important topic, that of network architecture or reference model and two well-known types: (i) the open systems interconnection (OSI) reference model and (ii) the transmission control protocol/Internet protocol (TCP/IP) reference model.

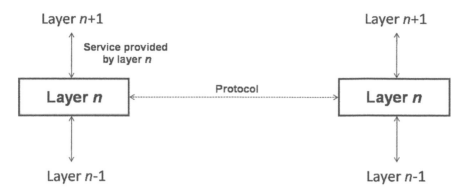

FIGURE 2.4: The relationship between service and protocol

2.1.4.1 The ISO OSI Reference Model

The OSI model was introduced by the International Organization for Standardization (ISO) as a reference model for computer protocol architecture and as a framework to develop protocol standards. This model comprises seven layers, as illustrated in Figure 2.5. We use dotted lines to represent virtual communication and solid lines for physical communication.

- **Application layer**: This layer provides users access (i) to the OSI environment and (ii) to distributed information services.

- **Presentation layer**: This layer provides independence to application processes from differences in data representation (syntax).

- **Session layer**: It provides the control structure for communication between applications. Establishment, management and termination of connections (sessions) between cooperating applications are the major responsibilities of this layer.

- **Transport layer**: This layer supports reliable and transparent transfer of data between two end points. It also supports end-to-end error recovery and flow control.

- **Network layer**: This layer provides upper layers independence from data transmission and switching technologies used to connect systems. It is also responsible for the establishment, maintenance and termination of connections.

- **Data link layer**: The responsibility of reliably transferring information across the physical link is assigned to this layer. It

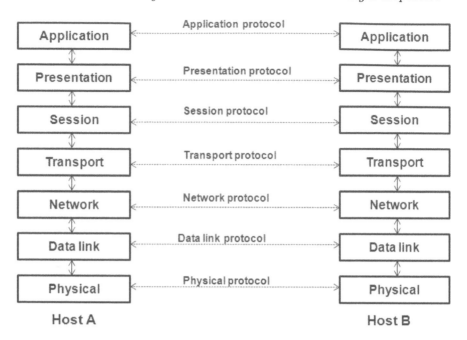

FIGURE 2.5:   The OSI reference model

transfers blocks (frames) with necessary synchronization, error control and flow control.

- *Physical layer*: This layer is responsible for transmitting a stream of unstructured bits over the physical medium. It must deal with mechanical, electrical, functional and procedural issues to access the physical medium.

The interfacing between each pair of adjacent layers is defined in terms of a set of predefined primitive operations and services made available by a layer to its immediate upper layer.

2.1.4.2   TCP/IP Reference Model

Although researchers have made several significant efforts to introduce variants (extended or compact versions) of the OSI reference model, the overall seven-layer model has not flourished. In an attempt to introduce a cost-effective version of the OSI model, the TCP/IP model [364] was introduced with fewer layers. The model has been widely accepted by the network community. The functions of the TCP/IP architecture are divided into five layers. See Figure 2.6. The

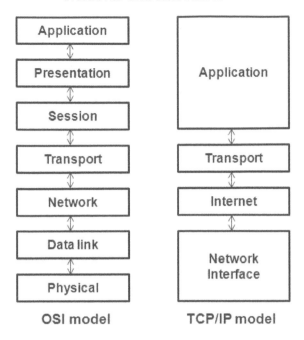

FIGURE 2.6: TCP/IP architecture

functions of layers 1 and 2 are supported by bridges, and layers 1 through 3 are implemented by routers, as shown in the figure.

The *application layer* is responsible for supporting network applications. As computer and networking technologies change, the types of applications supported by this layer also change. There is a separate module dedicated for each application, e.g., file transfer. The application layer includes many protocols for various purposes, such as (i) hyper text transport protocol (HTTP) to support queries on the Web, (ii) simple mail transfer protocol (SMTP) to support electronic mail and (iii) file transfer protocol (FTP) to support file transfer.

The *transport layer* is responsible for transporting application layer messages between the client and the server. This layer plays a crucial role in the network with the help of two transport protocols, TCP and user datagram protocol (UDP). These protocols support transportation of application layer messages. TCP supports a guaranteed connection-oriented service to deliver *application layer* messages to the destination. TCP also provides a congestion control mechanism by segmenting a long message into shorter segments, so that during network congestion a source can throttle its transmission rate. A connectionless, unreliable and non-guaranteed service of message delivery is provided by the UDP protocol to its applications by simply sending packets.

The *network layer* routes datagrams among hosts. It uses specialized hosts, called gateways or routers, to forward packets in a network. The router selects paths to forward packets toward their destination. The network layer supports the IP protocol (Internet protocol), which defines the fields in the IP datagram that determine the working of end systems and routers. To determine the routes for forwarding packets between a source and a destination, this layer also includes routing protocols. The TCP or UDP protocol in a source host forwards a transport layer segment and a destination address to the next layer protocol, i.e., IP. It is now the responsibility of the IP layer to deliver the segment to the destination host. On arrival of the packet at the destination host, the IP passes the segment to the transport layer within the host. The network layer performs the routing of a packet through a sequence of packet switches between a pair of source and destination.

The *network layer* depends on the services of the link layer when it forwards a packet from one node (host or packet switch) to the next. In particular, at each node, the network layer passes the datagram down to the link layer, which delivers the datagram to the next node along the route. At this next node, the link layer passes the datagram up to the network layer, depending on the specific link layer protocol that is used on the link. For example, a datagram may be handled by two different protocols at the two ends of a link, e.g., ethernet on one link and then PPP (point-to-point protocol) on the next link. The network layer receives a different service from each of these different protocols.

The *physical layer* moves the individual bits of a frame from one node to the other. The protocols included in this layer depend on the link and also on the physical transmission medium of the link (e.g., coaxial cable, twisted pair, etc.). For each communication medium type, ethernet has specific physical layer protocols. For example, the protocols for twisted-pair copper wire, coaxial cable or optical fibers are all different. Forwarding of a bit occurs across the link for each of these protocols in a different way.

2.1.5   Protocols

A protocol is a set of rules used to govern the meaning and format of packets, or messages exchanged between two or more peer entities, as well as actions taken when a message is transmitted or received, and

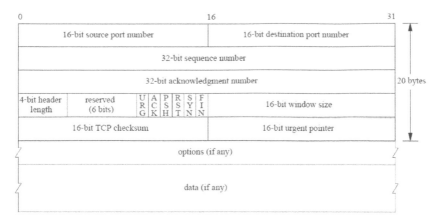

FIGURE 2.7: TCP header

in certain other situations. Protocols are extensively used by computer networks.

2.1.5.1 Transport Control Protocol

This transport layer protocol (TCP) supports a reliable connection for transfer of data between applications. A connection is a logical association established temporarily between two entities residing in two different systems. The logical connection or association is referred to by a pair of port values. To regulate the flow of segments properly and to recover from damaged or lost segments, an entity keeps track of TCP segments moving (both ways) to the other entity during the connection. A TCP header format is shown in Figure 2.7. The source port and the destination port shown at the top of the header are used to gather information about the applications running on the source and destination systems currently in communication. The other fields in the header such as *sequence number, acknowledgment number* and *window* fields are used for flow and error control. To detect occurrence of errors in the TCP segment, the checksum field (a 16-bit sequence) is used.

2.1.5.2 User Datagram Protocol

This connectionless protocol provides services such as message delivery, sequence preservation or duplicate protection. However, the user datagram protocol (UDP) does not guarantee these services. UDP supports a simplified protocol mechanism to enable a process to send mes-

FIGURE 2.8:   UDP header

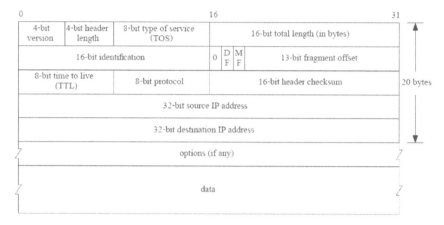

FIGURE 2.9:   IPv4 header

sages to other processes. This protocol is used by transaction-oriented applications. Due to its connectionless characteristics, it simply allows for port addressing, as in the simple UDP header shown in Figure 2.8. Like TCP, it also includes a checksum field (optional) to verify the occurrence of error(s) in the data.

2.1.5.3   Internet Protocol (IP)

This IP layer protocol is responsible for routing across multiple networks. An IP header for Internet protocol version 4 (IPv4) is shown in Figure 2.9. An IP packet or datagram is created by combining the header with the segment obtained from the transport layer. The source and destination addresses in the IP header are 32 bit. The header also includes a checksum field to help identify occurrence of errors in the header to avoid wrong delivery. The protocol field is used to indicate the higher-layer protocol using the IP. The ID, flags and fragment offset fields are used in the fragmentation and reassembly process.

2.1.5.4 SMTP

Simple mail transfer protocol (SMTP) is an integral component of the modern electronic mailing system. It offers a basic electronic mailing facility, which supports transfer of messages among hosts. Salient features of SMTP include (i) the ability to support mailing lists, (ii) sending back receipts for delivered messages and (iii) message forwarding from one user to another. Note that message creation is not under the control of the SMTP protocol. A user uses a local editor or an editor provided by the electronic mail system. Once a message is created, SMTP forwards the message with the help of TCP to an SMTP module on another host. The incoming message is received by the target SMTP module, which stores it in a user's mailbox by using a local mailing package.

2.1.5.5 SNMP

Simple network management protocol (SNMP) is an application-layer protocol that provides a facility to forward and receive management information among network devices. It facilitates the management of the entire network from a single point by assigning an IP address to each switch and by monitoring interfaces on that switch.

2.1.5.6 ICMP

Internet control message protocol (ICMP) provides a means for forwarding messages from a router or host to another host. It supports a feedback mechanism to gather information about problems in the communication environment. Here are some scenarios when the ICMP protocol is useful: (i) when a datagram is unable to reach its destination, (ii) a router lacks buffering capacity to transfer a datagram and (iii) when a router directs a station to forward traffic on a short-distance route. Generally, a message of this protocol is sent either by a router along the datagram's path or by the intended destination host, in response to a datagram. Figure 2.10 shows the format of an ICMP header. The header is at least 8 bytes long. Various fields of an ICMP header are (i) an 8-bit *type* to represent the type or category of an ICMP message, (ii) an 8-bit *type code* to specify parameters of the message that can be represented in a few bits, (iii) a 16-bit *checksum* for the entire ICMP message and (iv) a 32-bit *ICMP Data* field to specify lengthy parameters.

FIGURE 2.10:   ICMP header

2.1.5.7   FTP

File transfer protocol (FTP) is a commonly used protocol to transmit files from one system to another based on user command. FTP supports transmitting both text and binary files. It also facilitates controlled access for users. On invoking FTP for file transfer, a TCP connection is established with the target system to exchange control messages. This TCP connection transmits user ID and password. Then the user is asked to specify the file(s) to be transmitted and the desired file actions. If the file transfer is approved, the protocol initiates the set up of a second TCP connection for transferring data. Using the data connection, the desired file is transferred to the target system, without any overhead of headers or control information. Once the transfer is successfully finished, a completion signal is indicated by the control connection.

2.1.5.8   Telnet

Telnet is short for "Terminal Emulation". It provides users remote login capability. It enables a terminal user or a client to log in to a remote computer or server. Once logged in, the user can function as a directly connected user of that computer. This protocol allows the user to work as if in a local terminal with simple scroll-mode facility. Telnet is implemented in two distinct modules with distinct characteristics: (i) *user telnet*, which enables interaction with the I/O module of the terminal to communicate with a local terminal by mapping the characteristics of a real terminal to the network standard and vice versa; (ii) *server telnet*, which acts as a surrogate terminal handler to interact with an application, so that the behavior of the remote terminal looks like local to the application. Transmission of traffic between user and server telnets occurs using a TCP connection.

2.1.6 Types of Networks

There are many different kinds of networks, large and small. They are designed with different goals in mind, their sizes vary widely and they use different technologies.

2.1.6.1 Local Area Networks (LAN)

A LAN is a privately owned, limited area network that interconnects a number of computers within a single building, such as a home, an institution or organization, or a campus of up to say, 1 kilometer in size. LANs are commonly used to connect machines to share and exchange resources such as digital documents, printers or scanners. The three distinguishing features of a LAN are (i) the size of the coverage area, (ii) the communication technology used and (iii) the use of certain network topology. LANs may be developed using different (i) communication media types, such as guided or unguided media and (ii) network topologoies, such as star, ring or bus. With progress in computer and communication technologies, the speeds of networks are increasing at a phenomenal rate. The speed of a traditional LAN is between 10 Mbps and 100 Mbps, with minimum delay measured in microseconds or even nanoseconds. However, in recent LANs, the achievable speed has shot up to 10 Gbps, where 1 Gbps stands for 1,000,000,000 bits per second.

2.1.6.2 Wide Area Networks (WAN)

WANs are created by interconnecting a large number of machines or hosts spanning a broad geographical area, often a country or continent or a region by using communication subnets, private or public. The communication subnets may be structured based on two basic principles for transporting messages from one machine to another: *store and forward* or *packet switched*. Each subnet consists of two components: *switching components* and *transmission media*. Switching components are specialized, intelligent devices, referred to as routers. As discussed in Section 2.1.2, media can be of various types, such as coaxial cables, twisted copper wires, optical fibers or microwave transmissions to forward bits among the connecting machines. On arrival of packets on an incoming line, the switching component selects an outgoing line to forward the packet. Figure 2.11 shows a model of a WAN. In a WAN, a host may be either connected to a router directly or may be connected to a LAN on which a router is present.

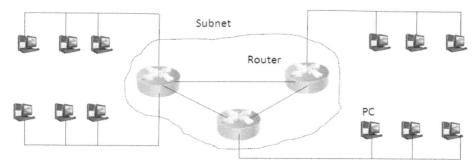

FIGURE 2.11:   Relation between hosts on LANs and the subnet

2.1.6.3   Metropolitan Area Network (MAN)

A MAN is created by connecting several local area networks spanning a township, city or a metropolitan area. Due to its wide area coverage requirement for sharing and exchanging resources, a MAN usually includes several routers, switches and hubs. To provide fast wireless Internet access these days, a MAN is created using the IEEE 802.16 standard.

2.1.6.4   Wireless Networks

Like wired networks, wireless networks can be of various types depending on their coverage area. The primary objective is to provide remote information transmission facilities by using unguided media such as radio waves. The three basic types of wireless networks are given below.

(i) *System interconnection*: This is an interconnection of the various components of a functioning computer such as monitor, keyboard, mouse and printer using short-range radio in a personnel area network.

(ii) *Wireless LANs*: In a wireless LAN, a system communicates with the rest of the systems within a building or an office area using a radio modem and antenna. Today, such wireless LANs are common in almost all modern low- and medium-scale corporate offices. Generally, a wireless LAN is convenient to create in places where installing ethernet is more troublesome.

(iii) *Wireless WANs*: This is an extended version of a wireless LAN in terms of scope and coverage area and is comparable to a WAN.

An example of a wireless WAN is a cellular network maintained by a cell phone company.

2.1.6.5 Internetworks

An Internetwork is created by connecting a network with several other networks, which may be incompatible, using specialized devices or machines, called *gateways*. In forming an Internetwork, designers must provide for adequate translation ability for the data from one network's format to the others', in terms of both hardware and software. A common example of an Internetwork is a WAN connected with a collection of LANs.

2.1.6.6 The Internet

The Internet is a worldwide network of computers, one that interconnects billions of users or computing devices spanning the globe. The computing devices may be desktop PCs, Linux or UNIX workstations and servers that provide support for storage, sharing and transmission of information. The Internet uses the TCP/IP protocol to connect its end systems or computing devices, although all applications may not use TCP. The end systems are interconnected via both guided and unguided transmission media. The transmission rate of a communication link is often referred to as the *bandwidth* of the link, which is usually measured in terms of *bits per second* or *bps*. All computing devices or end systems are interconnected indirectly through intermediate switching devices called *routers*. On the arrival of a chunk of information on one of its incoming links, the router can forward it to any of its outgoing links. The path chosen for forwarding the packet from the sending end to the receiving end system through a sequence of links and routers is known as the *route* or *path* across the network. For cost-effective utilization of resources while forwarding packets, the Internet uses a technique known as *packet switching* that allows sharing of the same path (or parts of a path) among multiple communicating end systems concurrently. To provide access to the end systems on the Internet, service providers, called Internet service providers (ISPs) facilitate end-user access. An ISP maintains a network of routers and communication links using a range of technologies. Different ISPs provide different types of network access to the end systems, including high-speed LAN access and wireless access. Figure 2.12 shows a schematic diagram showing

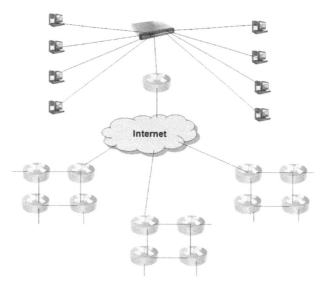

FIGURE 2.12:   A generic end system interconnection of the Internet

interconnections of systems to the Internet.

2.1.7   Scales of Networks

In addition to the network classifications presented earlier, another way to classify a network is its scale or comparative spread or magnitude. Based on the interprocessor distances and their span or coverage, networks can be classified into six distinct classes, as shown in Table 2.5. Small scale personal area networks, meant for single users are shown on the top row. An example of such a network is a wireless network connecting a computer with its keyboard, mouse and printer. Below personal area networks, various types of long-range networks are shown in the table. These networks are classified into three sub-classes based on their range or coverage: (i) local area networks or LANs, (ii) metropolitan area networks or MANs and (iii) wide area networks or WANs. A LAN may cover up to a 1 km range, whereas a WAN may spread over a country or a continent, i.e., may be up to a 1000 km range. The interconnection of several networks involving billions of users or computing devices spanning the globe is called an *Internetwork*. A well-known example of an internetwork is the worldwide Internet. Such a classification of networks based on distance is important, especially from the point of view of technologies used at various ranges.

TABLE 2.5: Classification of Interconnected Processors by Scale

Interprocess Distances	Processors Located in	Example Network
0.1 m	Same circuit board	Data flow machines
1 m	Same system	Personal area network
10 m–1 km	Same room, building or campus	Local area network
10 km	Same city	Metropolitan area network
100 km–1000 km	Same country or continent	Wide area network
10,000 km	Same planet	The Internet

2.1.8 Network Topologies

Network topologies are the arrangements or ways of interconnecting the end systems or computing devices attached to a network. Topologies can be of two types: *physical* and *logical*. The physical topology refers to the geometric shape of the layout of the physical media used in the network. The logical topology represents the way data flows from one end system to another in the network. The logical topology of a network may not be the same as its physical topology. Logical topologies can be dynamically re-configured using routers. Eight types of topologies are usually discussed in the network topology literature: (i) point-to-point, (ii) bus, (iii) ring, (iv) star, (v) tree, (vi) mesh, (vii) daisy chain and (viii) hybrid. In this section, we discuss four popular types of network topologies.

2.1.8.1 Bus

In the bus topology, all stations in the network are attached directly to a linear transmission medium or the bus through an appropriate hardware interface known as a tap. Data flows from the source machine to all other machines in both directions until the target recipient is found. Buses are of two types: *linear* and *distributed*. In a linear bus, the transmission medium has exactly two end points, and all nodes in the network receive the transmitted data simultaneously. In a distributed bus, there can be more than two end points, created by adding more branches to the main transmission medium. For simultaneous transmission of data by multiple machines, an additional arbitration mechanism is necessary to resolve conflicts. The operation of this mechanism may be centralized or distributed. For example, ethernet (IEEE 802.3) is a decentralized bus-based broadcast network operating within the range 10 Mbps–10 Gbps. An example of a bus

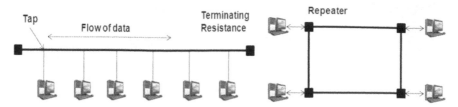

FIGURE 2.13:   Two broadcast network topologies: (i) bus, (ii) ring

topology is shown in Figure 2.13(a).

2.1.8.2   Ring

In this topology, a set of devices capable of receiving and transmitting data bit by bit are connected in a circular fashion by point-to-point links. These devices act as repeaters that help maintain signal strength. The transmission of data (frames) is unidirectional, either clockwise or anti-clockwise. As a frame moves in the circular path, the destination repeater recognizes its address and copies the frame into a local buffer. The transmission of the frame continues until it returns to the source repeater, where it is eliminated. Since the ring is shared by multiple stations, the medium access control mechanism has a responsibility to determine the time for each station to insert frames. Two common examples of this topology are (i) IEEE 802.5 token ring, which operates at 4–16 Mbps and (ii) fiber distributed data interface (FDDI) ring network. An example ring topology of a network is shown in Figure 2.13(b).

2.1.8.3   Tree

In a tree, the stations, which have unique addresses, are interconnected to a transmission medium with branches without a loop. The beginning point of the tree is referred to as the *headend*, from which multiple branching cables can be initiated, and each of these branches can have additional branches which may lead to a complex layout. Data is transmitted in small blocks, called *frames*, from any station toward all other stations throughout the transmission medium. Each of these frames has two components: (i) frame header, containing the control information and (ii) a portion of the data intended to be transmitted by a station. The header of a frame also includes the destination address for the frame. An example of a tree topology network is shown in Figure 2.14(a).

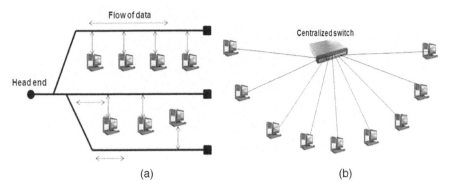

FIGURE 2.14: Two broadcast network topologies: (a) tree, (b) star

2.1.8.4 Star

In a star topology, there is a common central node that connects to all other stations in the network, as shown in Figure 2.14(b). The stations are attached to a central node using two point-to-point links for transmission as well as for reception. This topology allows two alternatives for the central node to operate: (i) operate in a broadcast fashion, where a frame transmitted from one station to the central node, often referred to as a *hub*, is retransmitted on all outgoing links and (ii) operate as a frame switching device, where the central node buffers an incoming frame and then retransmits it on an outgoing link to the destination station.

2.1.9 Hardware Components

A collection of software and hardware components is necessary to interface with the communication medium and to regulate the organized access to the medium.

2.1.9.1 Network Communication Devices

In this subsection we discuss five different hardware devices very commonly used in network communications.

2.1.9.1.1 Repeaters and Hubs The purpose of a repeater is to receive, amplify and retransmit signals bi-directionally. From a software point of view, connecting a series of cable segments in the physical layer makes no significant difference from using a single cable, although some additional delay may occur. By allowing multiple cables to connect with a repeater, we can create large networks.

Unlike a repeater, a hub does not usually amplify incoming signals. It includes several incoming lines joined electrically. It allows the frames arriving on an incoming line to transmit out on all the others. In case of collision, i.e., the arrival of two frames at the same time, the entire hub forms a single collision domain. An important requirement for a hub is that the speeds of incoming signals into a hub must be the same. The three basic types of hubs are (i) *Active hub*: It performs like a repeater, and can also regenerate or amplify signals. This type of hub requires electrical power to run and can cover up to 2000 feet. (ii) *Passive hub*: This kind of hub acts as a central device and forwards signals to other devices connected to it. It facilitates connecting multiple stations in a star fashion. A passive hub can cover up to 300 feet. (iii) *Intelligent hub*: This advanced type of hub also has management capability. In addition to signal regeneration, it is able to perform network management tasks and intelligent path selection. An intelligent hub has the ability to enforce flexible transmission rates to various devices.

2.1.9.1.2 Bridges A bridge works at the data link layer to provide connectivity among LANs. It supports routing by examining the data layer link addresses. A bridge can transport IPv4 or any other kinds of packets, as it does not examine payload fields. It minimizes processing overhead by enforcing the use of a single protocol. Without any additional burden on the communications software, this device can be used to extend a LAN. Bridges are of two types: (i) *Transparent bridge*: The presence and operation of this type of bridge are transparent to network hosts. They analyze the pattern of incoming source addresses from associated networks and gather knowledge of network topology. By using its internal table, a bridge forwards traffic. Bridges are standardized into the IEEE 802.1 standard and are popular in ethernet/IEEE 802.3 networks. (ii) *Routing bridge (RBridge)*: The operation of this device is based on the TRansparent Interconnection of Lots of Links (TRILL) protocol. This protocol (TRILL) supports (i) optimal pair-wise data frame forwarding service without configuration, (ii) safe forwarding even during periods of temporary loops and (iii) multipathing of both unicast and multicast traffic. To provide these services, TRILL uses a link-state protocol, referred to as the IS-IS (Intermediate System to Intermediate System) protocol. The IS-IS protocol supports broadcast connectivity to all RBridges, en-

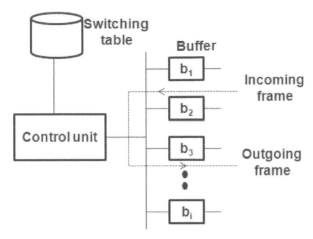

FIGURE 2.15: Working of a switch

abling the gathering of knowledge about one another and connectivity information. Based on such information, an RBridge can compute (i) pair-wise optimal paths for unicast and (ii) distribution trees for delivery of frames either to destinations or to multicast/broadcast groups.

2.1.9.1.3 Switches A switch works at the data link layer to provide a dedicated connection between ports. It minimizes transmission overhead by determining which ports are communicating directly and connecting them together. A switch interprets and operates upon the media access control (MAC) address field in received packets. On arrival of a packet at a port, this device makes a note of the source MAC address, associates it with that port and stores this information in an internal MAC table. If the destination MAC address is in its MAC table, the device forwards the packet to the respective port. If the MAC table doesn't include the destination MAC address, the packet is transmitted to all connected interfaces. If there is a match between the destination port and the incoming port, the packet is simply filtered. Figure 2.15 shows the working of a switch. The two basic types of switches are (i) *Store-and-forward switch*: Such a switch follows a three-step execution policy: accept, store and forward. It accepts a frame on an input line, buffers it, and then transmits it to the appropriate output line. (ii) *Cut-through switch*: This type of switch takes advantage of the occurrence of the destination address at the beginning of the MAC frame. It attempts to recognize the destination address by repeating the incoming frame onto the appropriate output line.

2.1.9.1.3.1 *Layer-2 switch* The operation of this category of switches is almost like a full-duplex hub. Such switches also provide the ability to include additional logic to use them as multiport bridges. By increasing the capacity of a layer-2 switch, several additional devices can be hooked up to it. It performs address recognition and frame forwarding functions at the hardware level, and can handle multiple frames simultaneously.

2.1.9.1.3.2 *Layer-3 switch* To address two important limitations of layer 2 switches, viz., (i) broadcast overload and (ii) lack of support for multiple links, a layer-3 switch came into existence. It breaks a large LAN logically into several subnetworks connected by routers. A layer-3 switch can be classified into two categories based on the nature of operation: *packet-by-packet* and *flow based*. The first category of layer-3 switch operates like a traditional router. The other category of switch attempts to improve performance by grouping IP packet flows with identical source and destination. Generally, layer-3 switches are interconnected at 1 Gbps and connected to layer-2 switches at 100 Mbps–1 Gbps.

2.1.9.1.4 **Routers** A router connects two networks by relaying data from a source to a destination end system using a routing table that includes lists for each possible destination network the next router to which the Internet datagram should be sent. The routing table can be either static or dynamic. In a static routing table, alternate routes are maintained to handle the unavailability of a particular router. A dynamic routing table provides more flexibility to respond to both error and congestion conditions. Such a router supports various types of network media, such as ethernet, asynchronous transfer mode (ATM), digital subscriber line (DSL), or dial-up. In addition to handling proprietary routers such as Cisco routers, a dynamic table can also be configured by using a standard PC with several network interface cards and appropriate software. Generally, routers are placed at the edge of multiple networks. Usually, they have a connection to each network. They can also take on other responsibilities in addition to routing. Many routers are equipped with firewall capabilities to filter or redirect unauthorized packets. Most routers can provide network address translation (NAT) services. Figure 2.16 shows a router in the TCP/IP model.

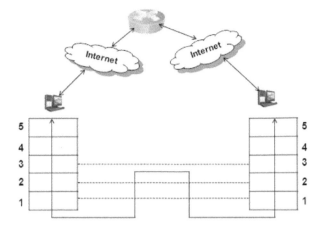

FIGURE 2.16: Router in the TCP/IP model

2.1.9.1.5 Gateway A gateway serves as a server on behalf of other servers which may not have direct communications with a client. Two major services provided by a gateway are (i) to provide server-side portals through network firewalls and (ii) to provide access to resources stored on non-HTTP systems as protocol translators. A gateway acts as an original server to receive requests from clients for the requested resources, without the knowledge of the client about it.

2.1.9.2 Network Interface Card (NIC)

This subsection will introduce four commonly used network interfacing components to establish connection between a station and a LAN.

2.1.9.2.1 Ethernet Card Ethernet is a well-accepted standard (officially called IEEE 802.3) for connecting stations on a LAN. It can also be used as an interface to connect a desktop PC to the Internet via a router, or an asymmetric digital subscriber line (ADSL) modem. A most commonly known Ethernet standard is 100baseT, which represents a transmission media type, viz., twisted pair cables with modular RJ-45 connectors on the ends, allowing transmission of data at the rate of 100 megabits/second. This standard supports the star network topology, with switches or hubs at the central node and the end devices. Each device connected to an ethernet network is assigned a unique MAC address given by the manufacturer of the NIC card. The MAC address functions like an IP address.

2.1.9.2.2   LocalTalk   This is a special kind of physical layer implementation of the AppleTalk networking system. It generally uses bus topology with the devices connected in a daisy chain fashion. LocalTalk uses the bus system provided by shielded twisted pair cabling, plugged into self-terminating transceivers, running at a rate of 230.4 Kbits per second. With the widespread popularity of ethernet-based networking, LocalTalk has become more or less obsolete.

2.1.9.2.3   Connectors   A connector is used to provide a physical link between two network components. To connect electrical circuits, an electrical connector, which is an electro-mechanical device, is used. A connection may be temporary or permanent. For portable equipment, the connection may be temporary, requiring quick assembly and removal. Depending on the requirement, connections may be of various types. Some features of connectors are shape, size, gender, connection mechanism and function. Some commonly found connectors are power connectors, USB connectors, D-subminiature connectors, 8P8C connectors and BNC connectors.

2.1.9.2.4   Token Ring Cards   In a token ring network, the token is allowed to move between the computers inside a logical ring and the physical layout of the cable ring passes through a hub. Users are connected to the ring via the hub. In special cases of implementation, a token ring network may use a star-wired ring topology with all computers on the network connected to a central hub. IBM's token ring implementation is an example. The transmitted frame moves around the ring until the intended destination station is reached. If a transmitted frame cannot find the destination station and reaches the sending station again, it is eliminated. It is the responsibility of the sending station to verify for the returning frame whether it was seen and subsequently copied by the destination or not. This architecture is able to handle high-bandwidth video conferencing and multimedia applications. The typical transmission speed of this standard is 4 Mbps or 16 Mbps.

2.1.9.3   Transceivers

A transceiver clamps around a cable securely so that its tap makes proper contact with the inner core. A transceiver is equipped with electronics to handle carrier detection and collision detection. On detecting a collision, a transceiver typically writes an invalid signal on the cable for other transceivers to realize that a collision has occurred. The cable of the transceiver is terminated on a computer's interface board, where the interface board includes a controller chip that transmits frames to, and receives frames from, the transceiver. Two major responsibilities of the transceiover are (i) to assemble data into the proper frame format and (ii) to compute checksums on outgoing frames to allow for verification on incoming frames.

2.1.9.4   Media Converter

A media converter supports connectivity between two dissimilar media types such as twisted copper wires with fiber optic cabling. In real-life networking applications, it is sometimes necessary to interconnect an existing copper-based, structured cabling system with fiber optic cabling-based systems. The device supports electrical-to-optical connectivity (with conversion) typically at the OSI layer-1, i.e., the physical layer, to bridge the difference between copper and fiber optic cabling. Media converters are widely used in enterprise networking.

2.1.10   Network Performance

In a network with hundreds or thousands of nodes or hosts, complex interactions with unforeseen consequences are common. Frequently, this complexity leads to poor performance and no one knows why. Therefore, it is absolutely necessary to tune crucial performance parameters. We discuss five important aspects of network performance, i.e. (a) Network Performance Constraints (NPC), (b)Network Performance Parameter Tuning (NPPT), (c)Performance Oriented System Design (POSD), (d) Protocols for Gigabit Networks (PGN) and (e)Faster Processing of TPDU (FPTPD), as shown in Figure 2.17.

2.1.10.1   Network Performance Constraints

Many times, the performance of a network suffers due to temporary resource overloads. A sudden increase in traffic arrival at a router, beyond its handling capacity, may cause congestion to build up, resulting in poor performance. Another important reason for network performance degradation is resource imbalance. For example, if a gigabit communication line is attached to a low-end PC, the poor CPU will not be able to process the incoming packets fast enough and some

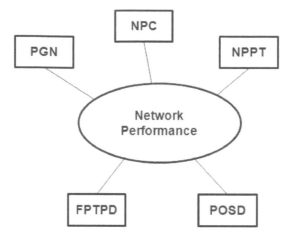

FIGURE 2.17:   Various aspects of network performance

will be lost. These packets will eventually be retransmitted, causing delay, wasting bandwidth, and resulting in reduced overall performance. Another reason for degraded performance constraints is lack of a proper parameter tuning. For example, if a transport protocol data unit (TPDU) contains a bad parameter (e.g., the port for which it is destined), often the receiver will suspect and send back an error notification. This is just a single instance. Now imagine what would happen if a bad TPDU is broadcast to a million machines! Each one might send back an error message, causing a broadcast storm, crippling the network.

2.1.10.2   Network Performance Parameter Tuning

To improve network performance, an administrator must observe the activities in the network using appropriate performance measurements. Once relevant parameters have been identified, one should try to understand the happenings in the network based on the parameter values. One can observe the goodness of network performance by changing parameter values incrementally. The process of observation and improvement can be repeated until no further improvement is possible.

2.1.10.3   Performance Oriented System Design

An iterative process, comprising (i) measurement of performance and (ii) tuning of parameters can help improve the performance of a network considerably. However, it cannot be the replacement for a well-designed network. When designing a network, the designer must take into consideration the following criteria: (i) prioritize higher CPU speed as being more important than network speed, (ii) reduce packet count to minimize software overhead, (iii) minimize context switching, (iv) minimize copying of data, (v) provide for higher bandwidth rather than lower delay, (vi) avoid congestion so that the system does not have to recover from it and (vii) avoid timeouts.

2.1.10.4 Protocols for Gigabit Networks

A major performance bottleneck in current networks is due to rapid increase in communication speeds compared to relatively lower CPU speeds. In such a scenario, a common assumption of the protocol designer that the time to use the entire sequence space would significantly exceed the maximum packet lifetime usually fails. Today the gigabit network designers should learn to design the network for speed, not for bandwidth optimization alone.

2.1.10.5 Faster Processing of TPDU

One can characterize the processing overhead of a TPDU in terms of two basic components, viz., (i) overhead per TPDU and (ii) overhead per byte. It is possible to improve TPDU processing performance by separating out the normal case and handling it specially. Once a sequence of special TPDUs is obtained to get into the *Established* state, TPDU processing becomes straightforward until one side closes the connection.

2.2 Anomalies in a Network

Anomalies are instances (e.g., points, objects, events, patterns, vectors, samples, etc.) in data that do not conform to an acceptable notion of normal behavior. Anomalies in a network also refer to circumstances [367] which cause network operations to deviate from normal behavior. Network anomalies may occur due to reasons such as overload in the network, malfunctioning of devices, network misconfiguration, malicious activities or network intrusions that capture and interpret normal network services. Anomalies in a network can be broadly divided into two categories: (i) network performance-related anomalies and (ii) security-related anomalies. We discuss each of these two categories of network anomalies and their sources and causes in detail. Performance-related anomalies may occur due to various network vulnerabilities.

2.2.1   Network Vulnerabilities

Vulnerabilities are inherent weaknesses in the design, implementation and management of a networked system. They render the system susceptible to threats. Existing known vulnerabilities are usually traced back to one of the following three sources.

(i) *Poor design*: A common source of network vulnerabilities is the presence of flaws in the design of hardware and software. An example of such a vulnerability is the *sendmail flaw* identified in earlier versions of UNIX. It enables hackers to acquire privileged access to hosts.

(ii) *Poor implementation*: Another important source of network anomaly is poor or incorrect system configuration. Such vulnerabilities usually result from lack of experience, insufficient training or sloppy work. As an example, a system may be configured without restricted-access privileges on critical executable files. This will enable an illegitimate user to easily tamper with these files.

(iii) *Lack of management*: Use of improper methods and inappropriate checks and balances is another source of network vulnerabilities. Improper monitoring and lack of proper documentation can also lead to network vulnerabilities. For example, a secure system must ensure that security steps are being followed and that no single individual can gain total control of a system.

2.2.1.1   Network Configuration Vulnerabilities

Vulnerabilities in a network may be caused by improper configuration. There are six major types of configuration vulnerabilities [356].

(i) *Weak network architecture*: Frequently, a small organization designs an initial, simple network with little emphasis on security. As the organization grows and its computer network becomes bigger, security holes may appear, providing potential backdoor entry for adversaries.

(ii) *Lack of data flow controls*: Absence or inappropriate use of data flow control mechanisms, such as an inadequate access control list (ACL) may enable illegitimate users or systems to access the network.

(iii) *Poor configuration of security equipment*: Use of default configuration for security equipment such as routers may lead to insecure open ports. In addition, unnecessary or unused network services running on hosts also may easily lead to security exploits. Improperly configured firewall rules and router ACLs can allow illegitimate traffic.

(iv) *Lack of backup of device configuration*: If an organization does not have established procedures for restoring network device configuration settings after an accidental or adversary-initiated security breach, it may be difficult to bring the system back up and to prevent loss of data. Well-documented backup procedures should be available to keep network failure time at a minimum.

(v) *Unprotected password transmission*: Transmission of unprotected passwords over insecure channels is susceptible to eavesdropping by adversaries. A successful capture of even one crucial password may allow an intruder to disrupt security operations or to monitor network activity.

(vi) *Use of passwords for long periods*: The use of passwords for long periods may allow an adversary to mount a successful offline dictionary attack. It may enable the adversary to disrupt security operations.

2.2.1.2 Network Hardware Vulnerabilities

Lack of appropriate protection and control mechanisms may lead to network hardware vulnerabilities. The following are the major causes of such vulnerabilities.

(i) *Inadequate physical protection of network equipment*: Appropriate monitoring and control of the network equipment can prevent damage or destruction.

(ii) *Insecure physical ports*: Use of insecure USB (universal serial bus) and PS/2 ports can be another major cause of unauthorized connection.

(iii) *Lack of environment control*: Inappropriate or loss of environmental control may lead to overheating or melting of the processors and consequently shutdown of operations to avoid damage.

(iv) *Inadequate physical access control mechanisms for equipment and network connections*: Unrestricted access and inappropriate use (or unauthorized manipulation of settings) of the network equipment may lead to theft or damage of sensitive data, software and hardware.

(v) *Lack of backup for critical networks*: Lack of periodic backup of critical network data may lead to sudden failure of the system.

2.2.1.3 Network Perimeter Vulnerabilities

The lack of a security perimeter and appropriate control mechanisms may lead to this special type of network vulnerability. The three major causes of this type of vulnerability are the following.

(i) *Lack of well-defined security perimeter*: If the control network does not have a well-defined security perimeter, it may be difficult to ensure necessary security controls in the network. This can lead to unauthorized access to systems and data.

(ii) *Improper configuration of firewall*: Improper configuration of firewalls can allow unauthorized or malicious data as well as software, including attacks and malware, to spread between networks, making sensitive data susceptible to monitoring or eavesdropping on the other network, and providing individuals with unauthorized access to systems.

(iii) *Use of networks for noncontrol traffic*: The purposes of and requirements of control and noncontrol traffic are different. Having both types of traffic on a single network makes it more difficult to configure the network so that it meets the requirements of control traffic.

2.2.1.4 Network Monitoring and Logging Vulnerabilities

Vulnerabilities in a network also may be caused by improper logging and inadequate firewall settings. Appropriate and accurate logging can be of significant help in identifying the causes of a security incident.

Regular security monitoring helps avoid the occurrence of unnoticed incidents or sudden damage to or disruptions of the network.

2.2.1.5 Communication Vulnerabilities

There are four major types of communication vulnerabilities.

(i) *Lack of critical monitoring and control path identification*: Unauthorized or illegitimate connections can leave a back door for attacks.

(ii) *Use of well-documented communication protocol*: Adversaries can exploit protocol analyzers or other utilities for well-documented and standard protocols to interpret the data. Such protocols include file transfer protocol (FTP), telnet and network file system (NFS).

(iii) *Lack of standard authentication of users, data or devices*: If users, data or devices are not authenticated properly, the possibility for replay, manipulation or spoofing of data or devices (e.g., sensors, user IDs, etc.) rises exponentially.

(iv) *Lack of integrity checking*: The lack of integrity checks may enable adversaries to manipulate communications undetected.

2.2.1.6 Wireless Connection Vulnerabilities

This type of network vulnerability may occur due to two major reasons.

(i) *Inadequate authentication*: The use of weak and biased mutual authentication between wireless clients and an access point may cause a legitimate client to connect to a rogue access point of an adversary. Such weak authentication may allow a new adversary to gain access to the system as well.

(ii) *Inadequate data protection*: Inadequate protection may allow the adversary to gain access to unencrypted data.

2.2.2 Security-Related Network Anomalies

In the preceding pages, we have discussed sources of network vulnerabilities, which may cause performance-related anomalies in a network.

Now we discuss the second category of anomalies, viz., security-related network anomalies, which are our prime concern. As mentioned earlier, anomalies are instances of data that do not comply with an acceptable notion of normal behavior. Anomalies in networks may occur due to several reasons: (i) network operation anomalies, (ii) flash crowd anomalies and (iii) flood anomalies or malicious activities. Of these, anomalies due to malicious activities are our main concern. Malicious activities in a network can be of various types, such as point anomalies, contextual anomalies and collective anomalies [63]. We briefly discuss each in terms of fraudulent credit card transactions.

(i) *Point anomaly*: Point anomalies are instances that are exceptional or anomalous with respect to the rest of the data. For example, an exceptional credit card expenditure in comparison to previous transactions is a point anomaly. Figure 2.18 shows an example of a point anomaly. Object O_1 is isolated from other group of objects C_1, C_2 and C_3. Object O_1 is a point anomaly.

(ii) *Contextual anomaly*: In a given context (e.g., within a given range), if an instance is anomalous or exceptional, such an instance is referred to as a contextual anomaly. An example is shown in Figure 2.18. Object O_2 is isolated in the context of the group of objects C_2. Object O_2 is a contextual anomaly.

(iii) *Collective anomaly*: With reference to a given normal behavior, if a group of instances is found to deviate anomalously, the entire group of anomalous instances is referred to as a collective anomaly. In Figure 2.18, group C_3 is different from groups C_1 and C_2 in terms of the *number of instances* and *compactness* (based on intra-instance distances) and hence C_3 can be referred to as a collective anomaly.

2.2.3   Who Attacks Networks

A computer network is a collection of interconnected systems running distributed applications. A network attack is a malicious attempt to exploit the vulnerability of a computer or network, attempting to break into or compromise security of the system. One who performs or attempts attack or intrusion into a system is an attacker or intruder. Anderson [18] classifies attackers or intruders into two types: *external*

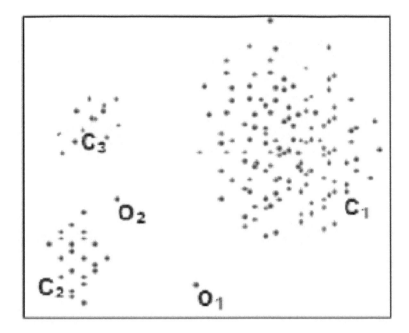

FIGURE 2.18: Point, collective and contextual anomalies

and *internal.* External intruders are unauthorized users of the systems or machines they attack, whereas internal intruders have permission to access the system, but do not have privileges for the root or super user. Internal intruders are further divided into masquerade intruders and clandestine intruders. A *masquerade intruder* logs in as another user with legitimate access to sensitive data, whereas a *clandestine intruder*, the most dangerous, has the power to turn off audit control. An attack or intrusion is perpetrated by an inside or outside attacker of a system to gain unauthorized entry and control of the security mechanism of the system.

2.2.4 Precursors to an Attack

Precursors to an attack are a series of events used to trigger an attack. A network attacker executes a sequence of steps to achieve the desired goal. The order and duration of these steps are dependent on several factors, including the attacker's skill level, the type of vulnerability to exploit, prior knowledge, and starting location of the attacker. The attacker's steps range from mapping the network via port scans, running exploits against the network, cleaning attack evidence and installing back doors to guarantee easy access to the network later. The four basic actions taken by an attacker prior to executing a computer attack are *prepare, exploit, leave behind* and *cleanup.* In the preparation step, the attacker attempts to collect network configuration information using port scanners to identify vulnerabilities in the network. It gathers information such as computer IP addresses, operating systems, open ports with their associated listening software types and versions. Once the vulnerabilities are identified, in the second step, the attacker attempts to exploit them. The attacker may execute multiple attacks during this step. After the successful launching of an attack, the attacker often installs additional software to enable accessing the network later. Such "leave behind" may include network sniffers or additional back-door network services. Finally, the attacker attempts to clean up any evidence left by the actions in the previous steps. This may include restarting daemons crashed during exploits, cleaning logs and other information, and installing modified system software designed to hide the presence of other software from normal system commands.

2.2.5   Network Attacks Taxonomy

An attack or intrusion is a sequence of operations that puts the security of a network or computer system at risk. Several classification schemes for network attacks are available in the literature [387, 161, 267, 228]. A taxonomy or classification of attacks aims to provide a consistent way to specify relationships among attacks, their classes and subclasses. Attacks can be classified into seven main categories based on how they are implemented, as shown in Table 2.6.

(i) *Infection*: This category of attacks aim to infect the target system either by tampering or by installing evil files in the system.

(ii) *Exploding*: This category of attacks seek to explode or overflow the target system with bugs.

(iii) *Probe*: This category aims to gather information about the target system through tools. Coordinated probes or scans are among the more serious attack of this category.

(iv) *Cheat*: Typical examples of this category include attempts to use fake identity.

TABLE 2.6: Taxonomy of Attacks

Main category	Subcategory
Infection	Viruses, Worms, Trojans
Exploding	Buffer Overflow
Probe	Sniffing, Port Mapping Security Scanning
Cheat	IP Spoofing, MAC Spoofing, DNS Spoofing, Session Hijacking, XSS (Cross Site Script) Attacks, Hidden Area Operation, and Input Parameter Cheating
Traverse	Brute Force, Dictionary Attacks, Doorknob Attacks
Concurrency	Flooding, DDoS (Distributed Denial of Service)

(v) *Traverse*: Common examples of this category include attempts to crack a victim system through a simple match against all possible keys.

(vi) *Concurrency*: This category of attack seeks to victimize a system or a service by sending a mass of identical requests which exceeds the capacity that the system or the service could supply.

(vii) *Others*: These attacks attempt to infect the target system by using system bugs or weaknesses directly. Such attacks are often trivial, without requiring any professional skills to mount.

Network attacks can also be classified as passive and active. Passive attacks have an indirect effect. These are launched by intruders for two major purposes: (i) to monitor and record traffic and (ii) to gather useful information for subsequent launch of an active attack. Since there is no overt activity, these attacks are not easily detectable. Packet sniffing, traffic monitoring and analysis are examples of passive attacks. On the other hand, active attacks are more dangerous and are usually more devastating to a network. Active attacks are classified into four categories in the defense advanced research projects agency (DARPA) intrusion detection evaluation plan [254]. The four categories are described in the following subsections.

2.2.5.1 Denial of Service (DoS)

DoS is a very commonly found class of attacks with many varieties. DoS attacks attempt to block access to certain resources [245] by making unavailable a particular network service such as e-mail, or by temporarily cutting off all network connectivity and services. In general, a DoS attack resets the target computer(s), or consumes resources extensively so that the intended service can no longer be provided. A DoS attack may also block access between intended users and the victim so that communication can no longer continue adequately between them. In some cases, a DoS attack may cut off access for millions of legitimate users from Web sites and compel the sites to cease operation temporarily. Successful DoS attacks often can spread very fast across branches of the network, and ultimately can lead to serious problems in the entire network. For example, if the total bandwidth between a router and a LAN is consumed, it may compromise not only the victim computer, but the entire network. Common forms of denial of service attacks are buffer overflow, ping of death (PoD), TCP SYN, smurf, neptune, teardrop and land.

2.2.5.2   User to Root Attacks (U2R)

This class of attack is very difficult to distinguish from normal traffic because it attempts to gain the system's superuser privileges. A U2R attack initially attempts to access a normal user account either by sniffing passwords or by dictionary attack. Once it is successful in stealing a legitimate user's password, it attempts to exploit weaknesses of the system to gain privileges of the superuser [245]. U2R attacks can be of various types: (i) *buffer overflow* attacks where the attacker's program copies large volumes of data into a static buffer without verifying the capacity of the buffer, (ii) other U2R attacks include *rootkit, loadmodule, Perl,* etc. A detailed discussion of these attacks is available in Chapter 8.

2.2.5.3   Remote to Local (R2L)

This attack class is similar to U2R attacks. It attempts to send packets to a remote machine or host over a network without being a legitimate user of that machine or host. For example, guessing passwords is an unauthorized access from a remote machine. Then, either as a root or as a normal user, the attacker tries to acquire access to the machine and execute malicious operations [211]. The two most common R2L attack examples are *buffer overflow* and *unverified input* attacks. They are either performed against public services (such as HTTP and FTP) or during the connection of protected services (such as POP and IMAP). The other common forms of R2L attacks are warezclient, warezmaster, imap, ftpwrite, multihop, phf and spy.

2.2.5.4 Probe

This class of attacks attempts to gain useful information about hosts, valid IP addresses, the sevices they offer, the operating systems used, etc., by scanning the network in various modes [45],[211]. The attacker uses this information to identify potential vulnerabilities of the system to launch attacks against machines and services. Some common probe attacks are (i) IPsweep, where the attacker scans the network for a service on a specific port of interest, (ii) portsweep, where the attacker scans through many ports to determine which services are supported on a single host, (iii) nmap, which is a tool for network mapping, etc. These scans are usually precursors to other attacks.

2.2.6 Discussion

In this chapter, we have introduced how computer networks work and how anomalies arise in networks. In the section on computer networks, we have included brief descriptions of various media types used in computer communication, reference models for layered architecture used in computer communications, protocols used in different layers of communication, various types of networks based on scale and requirements, different topologies of interconnections and physical components for network communications. In the section on anomalies in networks, we have classified network anomalies into two major classes: performance-related anomalies and security-related anomalies. We have described many vulnerabilities that exist in networks allowing bad players to exploit them to create anomalies under performance-related anomalies. Under security-related anomalies, we have mentioned sources of anomalies in networks, types of network intruders, steps in network attacks (including attack precursors) and types of attacks.

Many approaches have been developed for network anomaly detection. To test the performance of an approach, we must obtain input data to train the system and use appropriate evaluation metrics to measure performance. We will discuss various machine learning approaches and methods and their pros and cons in Chapter 3.

Chapter 3

An Overview of Machine Learning Methods

3.1 Introduction

Machine learning is the study of methods for programming computers to learn. Computers have been used to solve a vast array of problems, but in most cases, they are either routine tasks or tasks for which people with the appropriate background or expertise have been able to develop algorithms or detailed steps for solution. However, there are many tasks which are very difficult and neither human experts nor excellent but straightforward programming skills are sufficient to obtain satisfactory solutions. These tasks can be divided into several categories.

(i) Problems for which there exist no human experts. For example, in modern automated manufacturing facilities, there is a need to predict machine failures before they occur by analyzing sensor readings. It is extremely difficult or impossible to find human experts who can be interviewed by a programmer to provide the knowledge necessary to build a computer system. A machine learning system can study recorded data and subsequent machine failures and learn prediction rules.

(ii) Problems where human experts exist, but where they are unable to explain their expertise. This is the case in many perceptual tasks, such as speech recognition, handwriting recognition and natural language understanding. Virtually all humans exhibit expert-level abilities on these tasks, but none of them can adequately describe the detailed steps that they follow as they perform them. Fortunately, humans can provide machines with examples of the inputs and correct outputs for these tasks, and so machine learning algorithms can learn to map the inputs to the outputs.

(iii) Problems where phenomena are changing rapidly. In finance, for example, people would like to predict the future behavior of the stock market, of consumer purchases or of exchange rates. These behaviors change frequently, so that even if a programmer could construct a good predictive computer program, it would need to be rewritten frequently. A learning program can relieve the programmer of this burden by constantly modifying and tuning a set of learned prediction rules.

(iv) There are applications that need to be customized for each computer user separately. Consider, for example, a program to filter unwanted electronic messages. Different users will need different filters. It is unreasonable to expect each user to program his or her own rules and it is infeasible to provide every user with the assistance of a software engineer to keep the rules up to date. A machine learning system can learn which mail messages the user rejects and maintain the filtering rules automatically.

Machine learning addresses many of the same research questions as the fields of statistics, data mining and psychology, but with differences of emphasis. Statistics focuses on understanding the phenomena that have generated the data, often with the goal of testing different hypotheses about the phenomena. Data mining seeks to find patterns in the data that are understandable by people. Psychological studies of human learning aspire to understand the mechanisms underlying the various learning behaviors exhibited by people such as concept learning, skill acquisition and strategy change.

In contrast, machine learning is primarily concerned with the accuracy and effectiveness of the resulting computer system. To illustrate this, consider the different questions that might be asked about speech data. A machine learning approach focuses on building an accurate and efficient speech recognition system. A statistician might collaborate with a psychologist to test hypotheses about the mechanisms underlying speech recognition. A data mining approach might look for patterns in speech data that could be applied to group speakers according to age, sex or level of education.

Learning tasks can be classified along many different dimensions. One important dimension is the distinction between empirical and analytical learning. Empirical learning is learning that relies on some form of external experience, while analytical learning requires no external inputs. Consider, for example, the problem of learning to play tic-tac-toe, also called noughts and crosses. Suppose a programmer has provided an encoding of the rules for the game in the form of a function that indicates whether proposed moves are legal or illegal and another function that indicates whether the game is won, lost or tied. Given these two functions, it is easy to write a computer program that repeatedly plays games of tic-tac-toe against itself. Suppose that this program remembers every board position that it encounters. For every final board position (i.e., where the game is won, lost or tied), it remembers the outcome. As it plays many games, it can mark a board position as a losing position if every move made from that position leads to a winning position for the opponent. Similarly, it can mark a board position as a winning position if there exists a move from that position that leads to a losing position for the opponent. If it plays enough games, it can eventually determine all of the winning and losing positions and play perfect tic-tac-toe. This is a form of analytical learning because no external input is needed. The program is able to improve its performance just by analyzing the problem by solving repeated instances of the problem.

3.2   Types of Machine Learning Methods

Machine learning methods can be classified in many different ways. Quite frequently, we differentiate between supervised and unsupervised learning. In supervised learning, the learning program needs labeled examples given by a "teacher", whereas in unsupervised learning, the program directly learns patterns from the data, without any human intervention or guidance. The typical approach adopted by this method is to build a predictive model for normal vs. anomaly classes. It compares any unseen data instance against the model to identify which class it belongs to, whereas an unsupervised method works based on certain assumptions. It assumes [191] that (i) normal instances are far more frequent than anomalous instances and (ii) anomalous instances are statistically different from normal instances. However, if these assumptions are not true, such methods suffer from high false alarm rates. For supervised learning, an important issue is to obtain accurate and representative labels, especially for the anomaly classes. A number of

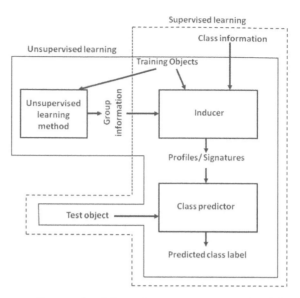

FIGURE 3.1:   Supervised learning vs. unsupervised learning

techniques have been proposed that inject artificial anomalies into a normal dataset to obtain a labeled training dataset [366].

3.3   Supervised Learning: Some Popular Methods

The input data in supervised learning can be represented as pairs of $< X, Y >$ where Ys are the actual labels of data elements in X. For example, each element $x_i \in X$ can be an image (a 400×400 matrix for a 400×400 pixel black and white image) and $y_i \in Y$ is a binary indicator showing if there is a cat in the image x_i or not. The goal would then be prediction of labels Y'_{new} for a new set of data X_{new} that are without labels.

Figure 3.1 depicts a framework to represent supervised and unsupervised learning mechanisms. In supervised learning (represented in inside the *dashed polygon*), the *inducer* module is fed the training data objects along with their class labels. The inducer generates a set of references or profiles corresponding to the available class labels, which are then used by the *class predictor* module to predict the class labels of a given test instance, whereas in unsupervised learning (represented inside the *solid polygon*), no class labels are provided to the *inducer*. The inducer in response generates a set of groups and/or profiles for the unlabeled input training data objects based on intrinsic properties of the objects as an individual or as a group. Finally, the *class predictor* module assigns class labels to these groups of unknown instances. There are many approaches within the paradigm of supervised learning. However, we discuss only two that are popular: decision and regression trees and support vector machines (SVMs).

3.3.1 Decision and Regression Trees

Decision trees are structures used to classify data. Each decision tree represents a set of rules which categorize data according to values of the attributes. A decision tree consists of nodes, leaves and edges. A node of a decision tree specifies an attribute by which the data is to be partitioned. Each node has a number of edges which are labeled according to a possible value of the attribute in the parent node. An edge connects either two nodes or a node and a leaf. Leaves are labeled with a decision value or label for categorization of the data. The approach begins with a set of cases or examples and creates a tree data structure that can be used to classify new cases. Each case is described by a set of attributes (or features) which can have numeric or symbolic values. Associated with each training case is a label representing the name of a class. Each internal node of the tree contains a test, the result of which is used to decide what branch to follow from that node. The leaf nodes contain class labels instead of tests. An example tree of depth $m+2$ of n objects is shown in Figure 3.2. The internal nodes represent a criteria and each branch represents a value of the criteria corresponding to the source node. The leaf nodes are the objects displayed in the oval shape. In classification mode, when a test case (which has no label) reaches a leaf node, a decision tree method such as C4.5 [304] classifies it using the label stored there.

Decision tree learners use a method known as divide and conquer to construct a suitable tree from a training set. The divide and conquer algorithm partitions the data until every leaf contains one case or example, or until further partitioning is impossible because two cases have the same values for each attribute but belong to different classes. Consequently, if there are no conflicting cases, the decision tree will correctly classify all training cases. This so-called *overfitting* is generally thought to lead to a loss of predictive accuracy in most applications.

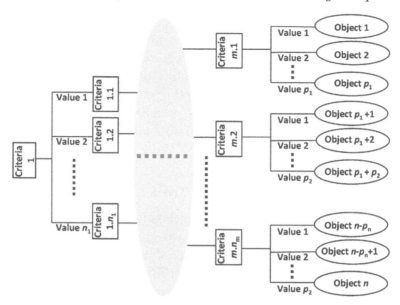

FIGURE 3.2:   An example decision tree

Overfitting can be avoided by a stopping criterion that prevents some sets of training cases from being subdivided (usually on the basis of a statistical test of the significance), or by removing some parts of the decision tree after it has been produced.

In the case of decision trees, the target attribute is discrete or nominal, whereas in the case of regression trees, the target attribute takes continuous values. Otherwise, regression trees are not different from decision trees. Classification and Regression Trees (CART) [52] are a method for creation of regression trees from data.

3.3.1.1   Classification and Regression Tree

CART [52] is a robust classifier for any real-life application described with numeric and categorical data. Based on training instances, it attempts to construct an optimal decision tree to classify new instances. To construct the decision tree it creates a sequence of *yes/no* questions, which help split the training data into components. For example, it may determine that *height* is the most appropriate attribute to ask a question at the top level. It then determines that the most appropriate relation to ask is $\geq$. Finally, it determines that the most appropriate value is 5 ft. Thus, it determines that the best possible question to ask at the top level to construct an efficient tree that performs well is "Is height $\geq$ 5 ft?" Thus, at every node the method attempts to determine the best possible split with reference to a given variable to decompose the tree into two parts. While splitting, it considers that within a part the homogeneity among the nodes is maximum. CART continues splitting each resultant part by considering a question for each node. A simple two-class decision tree constructed on the basis of CART's approach is shown in Figure 3.3. CART is able to handle hundreds of variables, which may be numeric as well as categorical. The other two major attractions of CART are (i) it can handle outliers efficiently. Any nonconforming or outlying instances can be easily isolated by CART based on nonfulfillment of conditions at the node level. (ii) The tree remains invariant with reference to any monotone transformations applied on independent variables. By substituting a variable, say x, in a node with either $\sqrt{x}$ or $log(x)$, one can validate the invariance of the structure of the tree.

Unlike decision trees, regression trees do not require preassigned class information. The response value of each observation is represented by a response vector Y in a variable matrix X. To construct the maximum regression tree one can use either the Gini splitting rule [138] or Twoing splitting rules. However, one can also use the SRM (squared residual minimization) algorithm, an alternative to the Gini index, to split the regression tree in order to minimize the expected sum variances for two resulting nodes.

Generally, for large datasets with the number of variables $\geq$ 100, the size of the maximum tree becomes too large and hence it is no longer cost effective during testing. Also, often such a tree contains a large number of nodes, where each node may not be significant in the context of the problem. Hence, the use of an appropriate technique such as minimization of objects in a node or cross validation is essential to optimize the size of the maximum tree by discarding the less significant nodes. Pruning by minimization of node(s) at a certain level depends on a user defined threshold, the α_{min}. By setting an appropriate value for α_{min} we can have a better tradeoff between tree complexity and the measure of tree impurity. Usually, a preferable range for α_{min} is $8\% \leq \alpha_{min} \leq 15\%$. However, based on dimensionality, the number of class labels and the data distribution pattern, α_{min} may vary.

Cross validation is another useful technique to prune insignificant nodes or even a tree component. It is well understood that the misclassification error (ME) on the training data is minimum (almost 0)

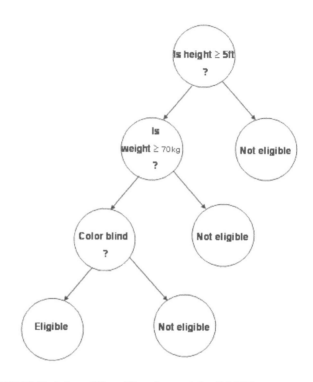

FIGURE 3.3:   Classification with CART

when the complete maximum tree is considered. With a decrease in the size of the maximum tree, ME increases. So, to achieve a better tradeoff between complexity and ME, CART uses a cost complexity function, defined as $ME_p(T) = ME(T) + \beta(T)$, where $ME(T)$ represents misclassification error of the tree T, $\beta(T)$ is the measure of complexity and β is heuristically found based on testing. Due to its iterative nature, cross validation is usually found to be expensive. The following are major advantages of CART.

(i) CART does not require specification of any functional forms, since it is nonparametric.

(ii) It can identify variables with high significance, so that users need not specify the variables in advance.

(iii) It can deal with both numeric and categorical data and can handle outliers efficiently.

(iv) Results generated by CART do not vary subject to monotone transformations of its independent variables.

(v) CART is cost effective and can adapt easily to a new environment or situation.

However, CART also suffers from the following limitations.

(i) If appropriate pruning is not applied, CART may not be cost effective in case of datasets with large variables.

(ii) While optimizing the size of the tree to make it cost effective during testing, interesting information may be lost.

In parametric regression analysis, we estimate the form of a relationship between the dependent variable and the set of independent variables. Such a form corresponds to a mathematical equation. In addition, parametric regression analysis needs to estimate values of a finite number of parameters or constants associated with the equation. Suppose the relationship between independent variable x and dependent variable y is represented by the linear equation $y = f(x) = mx + c$. For a given number of value pairs of variables x and y, the task of parametric regression involves finding the values of constants m and c that best fit the given value pairs. But in nonparametric regression, there is no prior knowledge of the relationship among the variables. So there is no prior form or equation available for the relationship. Hence, the predictor or model does not involve determination of parameter or constant values. That is why the term nonparametric is assigned to this category of regression analysis.

If the relationships among dependent variables and independent variables exhibit a form or equation throughout all possible values of variables for a set of parameter values associated with the equation, parametric regression can be used. But in most cases, the relationships among the variables are more complicated and subsets of the possible variable values exhibit different forms or similar forms with different parameter values. Let us consider a simple example of parametric regression, as shown in Figure 3.4. The diagram presents four points, $(1, 2)$, $(2, 2.5)$, $(3, 3)$ and $(4, 3.5)$, corresponding to independent variable x plotted on the x-axis and dependent variable y plotted on the

y-axis. The points fit to a line with the values of the parameters m and c equal to 0.5 and 1.5, respectively. But, now consider the case of a nonparametric regression, as shown in Figure 3.5. The points corresponding to the value pairs do not fit to a single line. Such a case cannot be handled by parametric regression. Nonparametric regression considers more than one form or equation by modeling a point with respect to its neighboring points instead of considering all the available points.

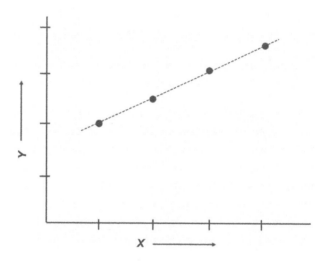

FIGURE 3.4:   A scenario of parametric regression

Kernel regression [52] is a widely used nonparametric regression analysis technique. Kernel regression builds a model that estimates the value of a continuous dependent variable by using a limited nearest set of local points that correspond to a set of known value pairs of dependent and independent variables. A kernel function is used to estimate the value of the dependent variable using information from local neighboring points. Some widely used kernel functions are the Nadaraya–Watson kernel estimator [265], the Priestley–Chao kernel estimator [300] and the Gasser–Muller kernel estimator [130].

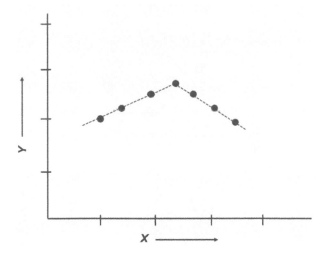

FIGURE 3.5: A scenario of nonparametric regression

3.3.2 Support Vector Machines

The support vector machine (SVM) is a powerful, state-of-the-art algorithm based on linear and nonlinear regression. The SVM is a supervised learning method [177, 375]. It performs classification by constructing an N-dimensional hyperplane that optimally separates the data into different categories. In binary classification, an SVM classifies the data into two categories. Given a training set of instances, labeled pairs (x, y), where y is the label of instance x, an SVM works by maximizing the margin between the two classes to obtain the best performance in classification.

SVMs are hyperplane classifiers based on linear separability. Suppose we have N training data points $(x_1, y_1), (x_2, y_2), \ldots, (x_N, y_N)$, where $x_i \in R^d$ in d-dimensional space and $y_i \in \{+1, -1\}$. Consider a hyperplane defined by (w, b), where w is a weight vector and b is a bias. We can classify a new object x with

$$f(x) = sign(w.x + b) = sign\left(\sum_i^n \alpha_i y_i (x_i.x) + b\right) \qquad (3.1)$$

Each training vector x_i occurs in a dot product and there is a Lagrangian multiplier [21] α_i for each training point. The Lagrangian multiplier value α_i reflects the importance of each data point. When a maximal margin hyperplane is found, only points that lie closest to the hyperplane have $\alpha_i > 0$ and these points are called support vectors.

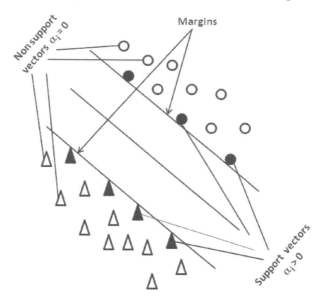

FIGURE 3.6: α_i for support vectors and nonsupport vectors

All other points have $\alpha_i = 0$ (see Figure 3.6). This means that only those points that lie closest to the hyperplane affect the behavior of the classifier. These most important data points serve as support vectors. Their values can also be used to obtain an independent bounding of the reliability of the hypothesis or the classifier. Figure 3.6 shows two classes and their boundaries, i.e., margins. The support vectors are represented by solid objects, while the empty objects are nonsupport vectors. Notice that the margins are only affected by the support vectors, i.e., if we remove or add empty objects, the margins do not change. Meanwhile any change in the solid objects, either adding or removing objects, could change the margins. Thus, the objective of the SVM [177, 375] is to define a decision hyperplane that separates the different classes with the largest margin from the nearest training examples. The support vectors, as shown in Figure 3.7, are the training examples that define the optimal hyperplane, which forms the perpendicular bisector of the support vectors. In essence, the support vectors represent the most informative patterns that allow one to best distinguish between the different classes. To define these support vectors, SVMs apply a transformation to the data so that the patterns represented by the data are linearly separable. This is possible because nonlinearly separable patterns can always become linearly separable in a sufficiently high dimensional representation. Thus, the data are

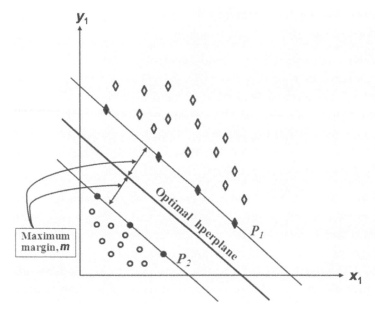

FIGURE 3.7: Optimal hyperplane and margins of a SVM

mapped by an appropriate (nonlinear) function to a higher dimension and optimization is performed to find the optimal separating hyperplane. Figure 3.7 shows two classes and their boundaries, i.e., margins P_1 and P_2. The support vectors are represented by solid objects, while the empty objects are nonsupport vectors.

3.4 Unsupervised Learning

Unsupervised learning, as illustrated in Figure 3.1, does not depend on the availability of prior knowledge or training instances with class labels. The inducer in an unsupervised learning module generates a set of groups and/or profiles for input instances based on intrinsic properties of the instances. The *class predictor* module assigns class labels to the group of unknown instances based on certain predefined criteria. Unsupervised learning tasks are categorized on the basis of types of models or patterns they find. Generally such tasks are of two types: predictive and descriptive. Predictive mining tasks perform inference on extant data to make predictions. Descriptive mining tasks characterize general properties of the data. Three major unsupervised mining tasks according to [156] are given below.

(i) *Cluster analysis*: Cluster analysis groups data objects based on characteristics that describe the objects and relationships among them. The goal of this task is to divide a set of objects into groups such that similar objects are grouped together and different groups contain objects with dissimilar characteristics. Good clustering is characterized by high similarity within a group and high differences among groups.

(ii) *Outlier Mining*: A dataset may contain objects whose characteristics are significantly different from the rest of the data. These data objects are known as outliers. Outlier identification finds smaller groups of data objects that are considerably different from the rest of the data. Outlier mining is used in fields such as telecommunication, financial fraud detection, rare gene identification and data cleaning. It is an important research area and is studied extensively by the data mining and machine learning communities [53], [156].

(iii) *Mining frequent patterns, associations and correlations*: Mining patterns that occur frequently in data lead to the discovery of interesting associations and correlations within the data. A typical application of association rule mining is market-basket analysis. In market-basket analysis, buying habits of customers are analyzed to find associations among the different items that customers place in their "shopping baskets". The discovery of such associations can help retailers develop marketing and placement strategies as well as plans for logistics or inventory management. In particular, items that are frequently purchased together by customers can be identified. An attempt is made to associate a product A with another product B so as to infer *whenever A is bought, B is also bought*, with high confidence, i.e., the number of times B occurs when A occurs is high.

Next we discuss each of these mining tasks and some methods in detail.

3.4.1   Cluster Analysis

During a cholera outbreak in London in 1854, John Snow used a special map to plot the cases of the disease that were reported [137]. A key observation, after the creation of the map, was the close association between the density of disease cases and a single well located at a central street. After this discovery, the well pump was removed, putting an end to the epidemic. Associations between phenomena are usually harder to detect than this, but the above is a simple and the first known application of cluster analysis. Cluster analysis is widely used in disciplines such as statistics, software engineering, biology, image processing and pattern recognition, anomaly detection, psychology and other social sciences to identify natural groups in large amounts of data.

Cluster analysis is an important task in unsupervised learning. It can be thought of as assignment of a set of objects into subsets called clusters so that objects in the same cluster are similar in some sense. The key idea is to identify classes of objects that are useful for the specific aims of the analysis. Unsupervised learning is used extensively in analyzing spatial data, network traffic data, satellite data and biological data, especially from DNA micro-array measurements. All these data, including network traffic data, may exist in various forms.

3.4.1.1 Various Types of Data

The attributes used to describe real-life objects can be of different types. The following are the commonly used types [156] of attribute variables.

(i) *Interval-Scaled Variables*: These variables are specified roughly on a linear scale. A variable of this type captures and represents intervals or differences between values. Some common examples of these variables are *weight, height, latitude, longitude* and *temperature*.

(ii) *Nominal Variables*: These variables distinguish an instance from another by having distinct names or values of attributes. Some common examples are *employee ID, fingerprint, zip codes* and *gender*.

(iii) *Binary Variables*: These variables can have only two states, 0 or 1, where 1 represents the variable is present and 0 means the variable is absent.

(iv) *Categorical Variables*: These variables can have more than two states. For example, *map colors, qualifications* and *intrusion classes*.

(v) *Ordinal Variables*: Like categorical variables, these variables can also have more than two states, but the states are ordered in a meaningful sequence. Some common examples are *grades* obtained in an examination (e.g., A+, A, B+, B, C+, etc.) and *height* (e.g., tall, medium and short).

(vi) *Ratio-Scaled Variables*: These variables are positive measurements on a nonlinear scale such as an exponential scale. Here both differences and ratios are meaningful. Examples are *temperature* in Kelvin, *length, time* and *counts*.

(vii) *Mixed-type Variables*: These variables are mixtures of variables of the types listed above.

The three influencing characteristics of data that may affect the performance of a clustering algorithm are [363] (i) *dimensionality*, i.e., the number of attributes in the dataset, (ii) *data distribution*, which may be of different types, such as uniform, nonuniform or skewed and (iii) *resolution*, e.g., properties of data obtained at different levels of resolution may be different i.e., a pattern visible at a fine level of resolution may disappear at coarse resolution.

3.4.1.2   Proximity Measures

Scientifically and mathematically, the distance between a pair of objects is a quantitative degree of how far apart the objects are. Similarity is a numeric quantity that reflects the strength of the relationship between two objects or two features. Similarities are higher for pairs of objects that are more alike. This quantity is usually in the range of either -1 to $+1$ or is normalized into 0 to 1. If the similarity between a pair of objects (O_i, O_j) is denoted by S_{O_i,O_j}, we can measure this quantity in several ways depending on the scale of measurement (or data type) that we have.

If $d(O_i, O_j)$ represents the normalized dissimilarity between a pair of objects (O_i, O_j), the relationship between dissimilarity and similarity [156] is given by

$$S_{O_i,O_j} = 1 - d(O_i, O_j) \tag{3.2}$$

where, S_{O_i,O_j} represents the normalized similarity between the pair of objects (O_i, O_j). When the similarity is one (i.e., two objects are exactly similar), the dissimilarity is zero and when the similarity is zero (i.e., two objects are very different), the dissimilarity is one.

3.4.1.3 Clustering Methods

In the past several decades, many significant clustering algorithms have been developed [156], [185]. The choice of an algorithm depends on the type of data, dimensionality of data it can handle and the purpose or application for which the algorithm was introduced. A well-regarded study categorizes the clustering algorithms into ten distinct classes: partitioning, hierarchical, densityn based, grid based, model-based, graph based, cluster ensembles, distributed, soft computing based and subspace clustering. We now discuss each of these classes, in brief.

Partitional Clustering Algorithms

A partitional clustering algorithm divides a given set of data objects into k (a user input) nonoverlapping (disjoint) clusters such that each object is in exactly one cluster. Partitioning methods can be of two types [156], *centroid based* and *medoid based*. In *centroid based* partitional clustering, each cluster is represented using the gravity center (mean) of the instances while in *medoid based* clustering, each cluster is represented by means of an instance closest to the mean. The k-means algorithm [162] is one of the most well-known centroid algorithms. It partitions the dataset into k subsets such that all points in a given subset are close to the same center. It randomly selects k of the instances to represent the cluster centers and based on the selected instances, all remaining instances are assigned to their nearest cluster center. k-means then computes the new cluster centers by taking the mean of all data points belonging to the same cluster. The process is iterated until some convergence criterion is met. The four important properties of k-means algorithm are (i) it is scalable, i.e., can handle large datasets, (ii) it often converges to a local optimum, (iii) it can identify clusters of spherical or convex shapes and (iv) it is sensitive to noise. A major limitation of this algorithm is that the number of clusters must be provided as an input parameter. In addition, choosing a proper set of initial centroids is a key step of the basic k-means procedure and results are dependent on it.

The k-medoid algorithm [194] is also an effective partitional clustering technique that clusters a dataset into k clusters and is more robust in the presence of noise and outliers than k-means. A medoid represents a most centrally located object in a given group of data. It can also be defined as an object of a cluster, with reference to which the average dissimilarity to all the objects in that cluster is minimal [156]. One of the most popular k-medoid clustering methods is the partitioning around medoids (PAM) algorithm. PAM begins with an arbitrary set of k objects as medoids out of a given set of objects. Each nonselected object is assigned to the cluster with the most similar medoid. Then a nonmedoid object, say O_i, is selected randomly and the total cost S_{cost} of swapping the initial medoid object with O_i is computed. If $S_{cost} < 0$, the algorithm swaps the initial medoid with the new one. The process of medoid selection and swapping is iterated until no further improvement in terms of cost is possible. Robustness and convergence to global optimum are two major attractions of the PAM algorithm. However, PAM suffers from scalability due to its $O(n^2)$ complexity.

The k-modes algorithm [179] is another significant algorithm in the partitioning approach. k-modes is based on a simple matching coefficient measure to deal with categorical attributes. For clustering problems described by mixed attributes, the k-prototypes algorithm [179] is another suitable algorithm. It is an integration of k-means and k-modes algorithms and uses a combined dissimilarity measure during clustering. In [407], a generalization of the conventional k-means clustering algorithm applicable to ellipse-shaped data clusters as well as ball-shaped ones is presented. This algorithm does not require the exact cluster number a priori.

Hierarchical Clustering Algorithms

Hierarchical clustering [156], [363] provides a nested sequence of partitions, represented graphically with a dendrogram. Each node (cluster) in the tree (except the leaf nodes) is the union of its children (subclusters) and the root of the tree is the cluster containing all the objects. Sometimes a leaf node consists of a single object and is termed a singleton cluster. Hierarchical methods are divided into two major subcategories: (i) *agglomerative methods*, which initiate cluster formation in a bottom-up fashion starting with an individual object in a separate cluster and attempt to merge them until all data instances belong to the same cluster and (ii) *divisive methods*, which initiate cluster identification by splitting up the dataset into smaller clusters in a top-down fashion until each cluster contains only one instance.

Both divisive and agglomerative algorithms exhibit the following properties.

- The clusters can be represented by dendograms.

- They do not require the number of clusters a priori.

- They are fast.

- The dendogram can be used to obtain a flat partition.

- The dendogram helps visualize the clusters as well as associations among them.

A major limitation of these two methods is that they cannot perform adjustments once a merging or splitting decision has been made. Hierarchical clustering techniques use various criteria to decide locally at each step which clusters should be merged (or split for divisive approaches). To merge or split clusters, the distance between individual objects is generalized to the distance between subsets. Such a derived proximity measure is called a linkage metric. Major intercluster linkages include [185]: *single-link*, *complete-link* and *average-link*.

Single-link similarity between two clusters is the similarity between the two most similar instances, one in each cluster. Single link is good at handling nonelliptical shapes, but is sensitive to noise and outliers. *Complete-link* similarity is the similarity between the two most dissimilar instances, one from each cluster. Complete-link similarity is less susceptible to noise and outliers, but can break large clusters inappropriately, and has trouble with convex shapes. *Average-link* similarity is a compromise between the two.

In the past several decades, many significant hierarchical clustering algorithms have been introduced. Some of such important algorithms are balanced iterative reducing and clustering using hierarchies (BIRCH) [422], Clustering Using REpresentatives (CURE) [148] and CHAMELEON [192]. BIRCH creates a height-balanced tree of nodes that summarise data by accumulating its zero, first and second moments (known as the cluster feature, CF statistic). It uses a hierarchical data structure called CF tree for partitioning the incoming data objects in an incremental and dynamic way. A CF tree is a height-balanced tree which stores clusters. It is based on two parameters: branching factor B_f and threshold T_h, which refers to the diameter of a cluster.

A CF tree is built as the data is scanned. When inserting each data object, the CF tree is traversed, starting from the root and choosing the closest node at each level. When the closest leaf cluster for the current data object is finally identified, a test is performed to see that the insertion of the data object to this candidate cluster will lead to a new cluster with a diameter that satisfies the user threshold. If it fits the leaf well and if the leaf is not overcrowded, CF statistics are incremented for all nodes from the leaf to the root. Otherwise a new CF is constructed. Since the maximum number of children per node (B_f) is limited, one or several splits can happen. When the tree reaches the assigned memory size, it is rebuilt and T_h is updated to a coarser one. The outliers are sent to disk and refitted gradually during tree rebuilds. It is capable of identifying noise effectively. Moreover, because BIRCH has linear time complexity, it is cost effective and hence it can be used as a more intelligent alternative to data sampling in order to improve the scalability of other clustering algorithms. However, it may not work well in identifying clusters of nonspherical shapes because it uses the concept of radius or diameter to control the boundary of a cluster. In addition, it is order sensitive as it may generate different clusters for different orders of the same input data. Bubble and Bubble-FM [128] clustering algorithms are extensions of BIRCH to handle categorical data.

In CURE [148], multiple well-scattered objects (representative points) are chosen to represent a cluster. These points usually capture the geometry and shape of the cluster. The first representative point is chosen to be the point farthest from the cluster center, while the remaining points are chosen so that they are farthest from all previously chosen points. This ensures that the representative points are naturally relatively well distributed. The number of points chosen is a parameter, but it has been found that a value of 10 or more works well. CURE uses an agglomerative hierarchical scheme to perform the actual clustering. Unlike centroid- or medoid-based methods, CURE is capable of finding clusters of different shapes and sizes and is also capable of handling noise. However, CURE cannot handle large datasets and as a result, it works on sample data points.

ROCK [149], is a categorical data clustering algorithm which (i) uses the Jaccard coefficient as a measure of similarity and (ii) links the concept to denote the number of common neighbors for any two objects. ROCK initially draws a random sample from the dataset and performs clustering of the data with links. Finally the data in the disk is labeled. It accepts as input the sampled set S to be clustered with points drawn randomly from the original dataset, and the number of desired clusters k. ROCK samples the dataset in the same manner as CURE.

CHAMELEON [192] uses a two-phase approach to cluster the data. In the first phase, it uses a graph partitioning algorithm to divide the dataset into a set of individual clusters. It generates a k-nearest neighbor graph that contains links only between a point and its k-nearest neighbors. During the second phase, it uses an agglomerative hierarchical clustering algorithm to find the genuine clusters by repeatedly merging these subclusters. None of the clusters formed can contain less than a user specified number of instances. Two clusters are merged only if the interconnectivity and closeness (proximity) between two clusters are high relative to the internal interconnectivity of the clusters and closeness of items within the clusters. Therefore, it is better than both CURE and ROCK as CURE ignores information about interconnectivity of the objects while ROCK ignores information about the closeness of two clusters.

Density-Based Clustering Algorithms

Density-based clustering identifies clusters based on the notion of density of data objects in a region in the space of objects. The key idea is that the core object of a cluster must contain in its neighborhood of a given radius (ϵ) at least a minimum number of objects (*MinPts*), where ϵ and *MinPts* are two input parameters. One of the most well-known density-based clustering algorithms is DBSCAN [114], which expands regions with sufficiently high density into clusters. DBSCAN recognizes data objects in three classes, viz., *core, border* and *noise*, as illustrated in Figure 3.8. The neighborhood within a distance of ϵ of an object p is called the ϵ-neighborhood of p. If the ϵ-neighborhood of p contains at least *MinPts* number of objects, p is a core object. DBSCAN's definition of a cluster is based on the notion of density reachability. The three basic concepts used in this density-based clustering are density-reachability, directly density reachability and density connectivity. An object q is directly density-reachable from another object p if it is within the ϵ-neighborhood of p and p is a core object. An object q is called density-reachable from p if there is a sequence of objects $p_1, p_2, \ldots, p_n$ such that $p_1 = p$ and $p_n = q$

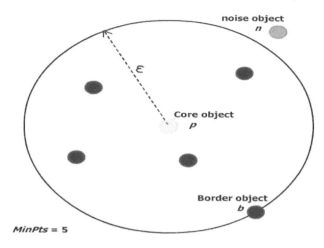

FIGURE 3.8:   An example of core, border and noise objects

where each p_{i+1} is directly density-reachable from p_i. The relation of density-reachability is not symmetric since q may lie on the edge of a cluster, having an insufficient number of neighbors for q to be core. Two objects p and q are density-connected if there is an object o such that both p and q are density-reachable from o. A cluster can therefore be defined as a subset of the objects that satisfy two properties: (i) all objects within the cluster are mutually density-connected and (ii) if an object is density-connected to any point of the cluster, it is part of the cluster as well.

DBSCAN can identify arbitrarily shaped clusters and can handle noise effectively. A major limitation of DBSCAN is its high computational requirements since the time complexity is $O(N^2)$. DBSCAN overcomes this drawback by using spatial index structure such as R or R^* tree during cluster expansion based on the identification of the ϵ-neighborhood of an object O_i. Another limitation of DBSCAN is that it cannot detect clusters of variable density.

The algorithm called ordering points to identify the clustering structure (OPTICS) [19] can detect clusters of variable density by creating an ordering of the dataset that represents its density-based clustering structure. OPTICS considers a minimum radius (ϵ') that makes a neighborhood legitimate for the algorithm. OPTICS is consistent with DBSCAN, but goes a step further by keeping the same two parameters ϵ, MinPts and introducing the concept of core-distance ϵ', which is the distance from a point to *MinPts* nearest neighbors when it does not exceed ϵ, and undefined otherwise. OPTICS covers a spectrum of all $\epsilon' \leq \epsilon$. With each point, OPTICS stores only two additional fields, the so-called core- and reachability-distances.

OPTICS is sensitive to its three parameters and experimentally, it exhibits runtime performance roughly equal to 1.6 times DBSCAN runtime. An incremental version of DBSCAN, which yields the same results as DBSCAN, is presented in [115]. A clustering algorithm (GDBSCAN) generalizing DBSCAN for both numerical and categorical attributes is presented in [319]. Distribution-based clustering of large spatial datasets (DBCLASD) [393], which eliminates the need for ϵ and *MinPts*, incrementally augments an initial cluster by its neighboring points as long as the nearest neighbor distance set of the resulting cluster still fits the expected distance distribution. DBCLASD relies on a grid-based approach and implements incremental unsupervised learning. Another density-based algorithm is DENCLUE [167]. It models the overall point density analytically as the sum of influence functions of the data points. The influence function describes the impact of a data point within its neighborhood. Then, by determining the maximum of the overall density function, one can identify the clusters present. DENCLUE introduces a compact mathematical description of clusters in high-dimensional datasets. It is fast and can identify clusters of any shape. DENCLUE can also handle noise effectively. The shared nearest neighbors (SNN) [111] algorithm blends a density-based approach with the idea of ROCK. SNN makes the similarity matrix sparse by only keeping k-nearest neighbors and uses them to derive the total strength of links for each object. In the past decade, several additional significant efforts have been made [127, 185, 430] to develop efficient density-based clustering algorithms. However, most algorithms still happen to be variations of DBSCAN.

Grid-Based Clustering Algorithms

Grid-based clustering quantizes the data space into a finite number of cells (hyper-rectangles) and then clusters the cells in the quantized space. Cells that contain a certain number of points are treated as dense and these dense cells are united to form clusters. We present a few grid-based clustering algorithms, viz., the statistical information grid-based method (STING) [379], WaveCluster [339] and clustering in quest (CLIQUE) [6]. STING [379] adopts a multi-level clustering approach by dividing the space into rectangular cells in order to form a hierarchical structure. The cells at a higher level are an aggregation of the cells at the lower levels. Each cell has four (default) children and stores a point count, and several attribute-dependent measures such as mean, standard deviation, minimum, maximum and distribution type. Measures are accumulated starting from bottom level cells and are propagated to higher level cells. STING is fast and effective, but it suffers from two major limitations: (i) the performance of STING relies on the granularity of the lowest level of the grid structure and (ii) the resulting clusters are all bounded horizontally or vertically, but never diagonally. CLIQUE [6] is another method based on the grid density approach. It attempts to find all dense areas in the one-dimensional spaces corresponding to each attribute. CLIQUE then generates the set of two-dimensional cells that might possibly be dense, by looking at dense one-dimensional cells, as each two-dimensional cell must be associated with a pair of dense one-dimensional cells. The dense units are then connected to form clusters. It uses the a priori algorithm [9] to find dense units. Generally, CLIQUE generates the set of n-dimensional cells that might possibly be dense by looking at dense $(n - 1)$ dimensional cells. CLIQUE is order independent and can find clusters in all subspaces of the original data space.

WaveCluster [339] works with numeric attributes and uses an advanced multi-resolution step. Initially it quantizes the feature space. Next a discrete wavelet transform is applied to the quantized feature space and new units are generated. Corresponding to each resolution of the wavelet transform, there is a set of k clusters, where at coarser resolutions, the number of clusters is usually fewer. In the next step, WaveCluster labels the units in the feature space included in the cluster. WaveCluster performs well with relatively high dimensional spatial data and can successfully handle outliers. It works in linear time for low dimensions, but with the increase in number of dimensions its complexity grows exponentially.

Model-Based Clustering Algorithms

A well-known model-based clustering algorithm is SOM [205]. The SOM is based on a single layered neural network. It organizes the data objects with a simple two-dimensional grid structure. Each neuron of the network is associated with a reference vector, and each data point is mapped to the neuron with the closest reference vector. In the process of running the algorithm, each data object acts as a training sample, which directs the movement of the reference vectors toward the denser areas of the input vector space, so that the reference vectors are trained to fit the distributions of the input dataset. Once training is complete, clusters are identified by mapping all data points to the output neurons. SOM is robust, can handle outliers easily and also can deal with missing values. However, it may not work well in all domains. It also requires the number of clusters and grid structure as input and the result is largely dependent on these parameters.

AutoClass [66], another well-known algorithm, uses the Bayesian approach. It starts with random initialization of the parameters and adjusts the parameter values incrementally to find their maximum likelihood estimates. AutoClass performs well on numeric data and can identify clusters of all shapes. However, it suffers from all the limitations found in SOM.

Graph-Based Clustering Algorithms

Graph-based clustering represents a problem in terms of a graph and tries to find clusters as a set of strongly connected components in the graph where the nodes of a component have high affinity or attraction. The cluster affinity search technique (CAST) [40] is based on the concept of a clique graph data model. CAST assumes that the true clusters among the data points are obtained by a disjoint union of complete subgraphs where each clique represents a cluster and where a cluster is a set of high affinity elements subject to a threshold. CAST discovers clusters one at a time. It performs well on datasets with variable density. Another advantage of this algorithm is its low dependency on input parameters. AUTOCLUST [219] is a graph-based algorithm that automatically extracts boundaries based on Voronoi modeling and Delaunay diagrams. Here, parameters are estimated (not user inputs) from the proximity structures of the Voronoi model, and AUTOCLUST calculates them from the Delaunay diagram. This removes human-generated bias and also reduces exploration time. Simlarly, cluster identification via connectivity kernels (CLICK) [336] identifies clusters as a highly connected component in a proximity graph based on a probabilistic assumption. CLICK is cost effective, and in addition to identifying disjoint clusters, it also detects intersecting clusters. Other advantages of this method are (i) it is effective in identifying clusters of different densities and (ii) it can identify multiple bridges linking clusters.

Ensemble of Clustering Algorithms

In an ensemble approach, the outputs generated by different clustering techniques are combined in order to provide a consensus output value [176]. The aim is to use the best features of each individual technique and improve the overall performance in terms of accuracy or precision. According to [159, 158], clustering ensembles are formed by the combination of a set of partitions previously produced by several runs of a single algorithm or by a set of algorithms. In unsupervised learning, sophisticated strategies are needed to combine partitions found by different algorithms or different runs of the same algorithm in a consensus partition. To generate the best possible consensus based on the outputs of multiple clustering algorithms is a complex task.

According to [357], cluster ensembles can be formed in a number of different ways, such as (i) the use of a number of different clustering techniques as base classifiers, selected either arbitrarily or based on past performance, (ii) the use of a single clustering technique with different initial conditions and (iii) the use of different partial subsets of features or patterns. In [121], a split-and-merge strategy is followed. In the first step, the k-means algorithm is used to generate small, compact clusters. An ensemble of clustering algorithms is produced by random initialization of the cluster centroids. Data partitions present in these clusterings are mapped into a new similarity matrix between patterns, based on a voting mechanism. This matrix, which is independent of data sparseness, is then used to extract the natural clusters using the single-link algorithm. In [26], multiple clustering algorithms are combined based on a weighted shared nearest neighbors graph method. In [409], multiple crossover repetitions are used to combine partitions created by different clustering algorithms. Each pair selected for a crossover operation should present a high overlap in the clusters. The initial population comprises all clusters created by the clustering algorithms used in the ensemble. This method, called heterogeneous clustering ensemble (HCE), differs from other ensemble approaches by taking characteristics from the individual algorithms and the dataset into account during the combinination of outputs of the individual clustering algorithms.

Distributed Clustering Algorithms

Distributed clustering analyzes large volumes of data (with a large number of instances with high dimensionality) in minimum time without compromising quality. It assumes that the objects to be clustered reside on different sites. Instead of transmitting all objects to a central site (also known as the server) where we can apply standard clustering algorithms to analyze the data, the data are clustered independently on multiple local sites. The central site finally updates the global clusters based on the feedback (i.e., cluster results) received from local sites. The following are the common scenarios observed in distributed clustering.

(i) *Feature-Distributed Clustering* (FDC) combines a set of clusters obtained from a clustering algorithm that has partial view of the data features.

(ii) *Object-Distributed Clustering* (ODC) combines clusters obtained from a clustering algorithm that has access to the whole set of data features and to a limited number of objects.

(iii) *Feature/Object-Distributed Clustering* (FODC) combines clusters obtained from a clustering algorithm that has access to a limited number of objects and/or features of the data.

Researchers have introduced several significant methods for distributed clustering. The parallel k-means algorithm was proposed in [97]; a parallel DBSCAN, called PDBSCAN that uses a shared-nothing architecture with multiple computers interconnected through a network was presented in [394]. PDBSCAN offers nearly linear speed-up and has excellent scale-up and size-up behavior. Additional approaches to parallel density-based clustering are reported in [186, 47]. Both perform satisfactorily on large spatial data without compromising the quality of clustering.

Soft Computing-Based Clustering Algorithms

Traditional clustering approaches discussed so far can identify disjoint groups or clusters. On the other hand, in many real-life datasets, clusters may not be well separated or disjoint, they are rather overlapping in nature. As a result, often the traditional hard computing approaches for cluster analysis are inadequate in handling such datasets. Fuzzy clustering is an attempt to handle this situation by associating each instance with a cluster using a membership function. A larger membership value indicates higher confidence in the assignment of the instance to the cluster. One widely used fuzzy clustering algorithm is the fuzzy c-means (FCM) algorithm [43], developed based on k-means. FCM attempts to identify the most characteristic instance in each cluster as the cluster center. Then it computes the degree of membership for each instance in the clusters. In [377], a density-based clustering using the roughset approach, called Rough DBSCAN, is presented. It aims to obtain results similar to DBSCAN, but in significantly less time ($O(N)$).

Researchers also have made significant contributions in performing clustering using neural networks. Some examples are self-organizing feature map (SOFM) [205] and adaptive resonance theory (ART) [368]. SOFM attempts to visualize a high dimensional input pattern with prototype vectors in a 2D lattice structure of neurons. The nodes, i.e., the neurons are connected to each other via adaptable weights. During the training process, the neighboring input patterns are projected into the lattice corresponding to adjacent neurons. The advantages of SOFM are (i) it enjoys the benefits of input space density approximation and (ii) it is input order independent. The disadvantages are (i) like k-means, SOFM needs to predefine the size of the lattice (the number of clusters) and (ii) it may suffer from input space density misrepresentation. ART [368] is a large family of neural network architectures, capable of learning any input pattern in a fast, stable and self-organizing way. The basic advantage of ART is that it is fast and it exhibits stable learning and pattern detection. The disadvantage is its inefficiency in handling noise and higher dimensional representation for clusters.

Genetic algorithms (GA) [144] are also effective in cluster analysis. GA-based clustering uses randomized search and optimization based on the principles of evolution and natural genetics. Several GA-based clustering algorithms are found in the literature [175, 32, 247, 31]. GAs have been used in real-coded variable string length genetic fuzzy clustering in [247]. Evolutionary techniques rely on certain parameters to empirically fit data and have high computational costs that limit their application in data mining. However, the use of combined strategies (e.g., generation of initial guess for k-means) has been attempted. GA-based clustering, although used extensively recently, is not always free from the local optima problem.

Some researchers perform cluster analysis by using the expectation-maximization (EM) algorithm [94]. They assume an underlying probability model with parameters that describe the probability that an instance belongs to a particular cluster. A limitation of such algorithms is that they tend to be computationally expensive. This approach also suffers from overfitting. Many researchers adopt a fully Bayesian approach to solve this overfitting problem by (i) reducing the number of input parameters and (ii) by generating the appropriate number of clusters.

Subspace Clustering Algorithms

Subspace clustering [6] analyzes higher dimensional numeric data over a subset of dimensions, based on a measure referred to as a *measure of locality* representing a cluster. Subspace clustering is performed in two ways: *top-down* and *bottom-up*.

Bottom-up subspace clustering exploits the downward closure property of density to reduce the search space. It estimates the locality by creating bins for each dimension. These bins are finally used to form a multidimensional grid using two approaches, (i) the *static grid-sized* approach and (ii) the *data driven* approach. CLIQUE [6] and ENCLUS [71] are two popular subspace clustering algorithms which follow the static grid-sized approach. MAFIA [143], CBF [72] and DOC [301] are some example subspace clusering algorithms based on the data driven approach.

CLIQUE [6] finds clusters within subspaces using a grid-density clustering approach and is capable of identifying arbitrarily shaped clusters in any number of dimensions without needing to be given the number of clusters a priori. The clusters identified by CLIQUE may be in the same space or in overlapped or disjoint subspaces. CLIQUE scales well with the number of instances and dimensions in the dataset. This method is not without its disadvantages. The grid size and the density threshold are input parameters that affect the quality of clusters. Small but important clusters can sometimes be eliminated during the pruning stage. ENCLUS [71] adopts a bottom-up approach to define clusters based on an entropy measure and can locate overlapped clusters of various shapes in subspaces of different sizes. ENCLUS's scalability with respect to the subspace dimensions is poor. The merging of adaptive finite intervals algorithm (MAFIA) [143] is a variant of CLIQUE and uses an adaptive, grid-based approach with parallelism to improve scalability. MAFIA can locate clusters of various sizes and shapes, and it is faster than CLIQUE owing to its parallel nature. Furthermore, it scales up linearly. However, the running time grows exponentially as the number of dimensions increases. Cell-based clustering (CBF) [72] is another bottom-up subspace clustering algorithm, which, unlike CLIQUE and MAFIA, creates partitions optimally to avoid exponential growth of bins with the increase in the number of dimensions. Like MAFIA, it can also identify clusters of various sizes and shapes, and scales up linearly with respect to the number of records in a dataset. Due to the use of an enhanced index structure for storing the bins, CBF is efficient. However, its performance is dependent on (i) the threshold used to determine the appropriate bin frequency for a dimension and (ii) the threshold used to determine the number of data points in a bin. Density-based optimal projective clustering (DOC) [301] is a hybridization of bottom-up and top-down approaches. It is based on the notion of an optimal projective cluster. The running time for DOC grows linearly with the number of instances. However, it is sensitive to input parameters and is able to identify mostly hyper-rectangular shaped clusters. In addition, its running time grows exponentially with the increase in the number of dimensions in the dataset.

Top-down subspace clustering is initiated with an approximation of clusters in an equally weighted full feature space. Then it follows an iterative procedure to update the weights and accordingly reforms the clusters. It is expensive, especially when used over the full feature space. However, the use of sampling can improve performance. The number of clusters and the size of the subspace are the most critical factors in this approach. PROCLUS [4] is a sampling-based top-down subspace clustering algorithm which randomly selects a set of k-medoids from a sample and iteratively improves the choice of medoids to form better clusters. Three limitations of this method are (i) it is biased toward hyper-spherical shaped clusters, (ii) the quality of clusters depends upon the size of the sample chosen and (iii) it is sensitive to input parameters. ORCLUS [5] is a fast and scalable subspace clustering algorithm. It forms clusters iteratively by assigning points to the nearest cluster. ORCLUS computes the dissimilarity between a pair of points as a set of orthonormal vectors in a subspace. However, it requires (i) the subspace dimensionality and (ii) the number of clusters as input parameters. The performance of ORCLUS depends on these parameters. It may also sometimes miss some small clusters. δ-Clusters [399] starts with an initial seed and improves the overall quality of the clusters iteratively by swapping dimensions with instances. δ-Clusters uses coherence as a similarity measure. However, dependency on two input parameters, i.e., number and size of the clusters is a major limitation of this algorithm. COSA [124] starts with an equally weighted dimension for each instance and then examines the k-nearest neighbors (KNN) of an instance. It calculates the respective dimension weights for each instance and assigns higher weighted dimensions to those instances which have less dispersion within the neighborhood. This process is repeated with new instances until the weights stabilize. The advantage of this method is that the number of dimensions in clusters need not be specified and the dimension weights are calculated automatically.

3.4.1.4 Discussion

Based on our discussion of various unsupervised learning approaches, we put forward the following observations.

- Partitioning algorithms typically represent a cluster by a prototype and use an iterative control strategy to optimize the whole clustering, such as minimizing the average or squared distances of instances to its cluster centers (prototypes). This approach is effective in determining clusters of convex shape, almost similar size and density, if the number of clusters can be reasonably estimated a priori. However, determining the appropriate number of clusters is very difficult.

- Hierarchical clustering decomposes the dataset into several levels of partitions and represents them by a tree structure which splits the dataset recursively into smaller subsets. Usually, the cost of creating the cluster hierarchy is very expensive for large datasets.

- Density-based approaches identify clusters of arbitrary shape as regions in the data space where the objects are dense and are separated by regions of low density (noise). The performance of this type of clustering is highly dependent on two parameters, *Minpts* or the minimum number of points in a neighborhood, and ϵ, or the radius of the neighborhood.

- Grid-based clustering quantizes the space into a finite number of cells (hyper-rectangles) and then considers those cells with more than a certain number of points as dense. Dense cells are united to form clusters. With increase in dimensionality, most grid-based methods suffer from exponential order complexity.

- An algorithm seeking better results could, instead of integrating all the requirements into a single algorithm, try to build a combination of base clustering algorithms. However, the selection of the base algorithms and a combination function to genetrate a consensus play a crucial role.

- Soft computing techniques can identify clusters that are not well separated or disjoint in nature. Distributed and parallel clustering approaches are useful in managing and processing massive amounts of data.

- For high dimensional clustering, subspace clustering algorithms have given quite good results. In the case of large datasets with high dimensionality, this approach with the appropriate use of sampling techniques and subspace sizes can produce significantly better results.

3.4.2   Outlier Mining

Outlier mining aims to identify patterns in data that do not conform to the rest of the data based on an appropriate proximity measure. Such patterns are often found interesting and carry useful information regarding nonconformity or abnormality of the system described by the data. These nonconforming patterns are usually referred to as outliers, noise, anomalies, exceptions, faults, defects, errors, damage, surprise, novelty or peculiarities in various application domains. Accurate identification of outliers is a well-established research problem in machine learning and pattern recognition.

An outlier detection algorithm may have to be dependent on some prior knowledge. A labeled training dataset is one such piece of information that can be used with techniques from machine learning [255] and statistical learning theory [375]. The labels associated with a data instance denote if that instance is normal or an outlier. Based on the extent to which these labels are available or utilized, outlier detection techniques can be either supervised or unsupervised. Supervised outlier detection techniques assume the availability of a training dataset which has labeled instances for the normal as well as the outlier class. In such techniques, predictive models are built for both normal and outlier classes. Any unseen data instance is compared against the two models to determine which class it belongs to. An unsupervised outlier detection technique makes no assumption about the availability of labeled training data. The techniques in this class may make other assumptions about the data. For example, parametric statistical techniques assume a parametric distribution for one or both classes of instances. Several techniques make the basic assumption that normal instances are far more frequent than outliers. Thus, a frequently occurring pattern is typically considered normal while a rare occurrence is an outlier.

Outlier detection is of interest in many practical applications. For example, an unusual flow of network packets, revealed by analyzing system logs, may be classified as an outlier, because it may be a virus attack [131] or an attempt at an intrusion. The problem of outlier detection typically arises in the context of high dimensional datasets. However, much of the recent work on finding outliers uses methods which make implicit assumptions regarding relatively low dimensionality of the data. A specific point to note in outlier detection is that the great majority of objects analyzed are not outliers. Moreover, in many cases, it is a priori difficult to characterize which objects are outliers. Which objects are identified as outliers often depends on the applied detection methods and other hidden assumptions. Outlier detection methods can be classified into three categories: (i) distance-based outlier methods, (ii) density-based outlier methods and (iii) machine learning and soft-computing outlier methods. We discuss each of these approaches below.

(i) *Distance-Based Outlier Detection*: This approach calculates distances among objects in the data to compute a so-called *outlier factor* as a function $F : x \to R$ to quantitatively characterize an outlier [294]. The function F depends on the distance between the given object x and other objects R in the dataset being analyzed.

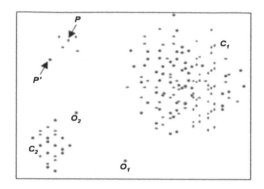

FIGURE 3.9:   A 2-D dataset

Hawkins [163] defines outliers as observations which deviate significantly from other observations so as to arouse suspicion that these are generated by a different mechanism [163]. The notion of a Hawkins outlier was further formalized by Knorr and Ng [202], who define an outlier, the so called $DB(pct, dmin)$ outlier, as an object p in a dataset D if at least pct percentage of the objects in D lies at a distance greater than $dmin$ from p, i.e., the cardinality of the set $\{q \in D | d(p, q) \leq dmin\}$ is less than or equal to $(100 - pct)\%$ of the size of D [202]. $d(p, q)$ is the distance between objects p and q.

To illustrate, consider a 2-D dataset depicted in Figure 3.9. This is a simple 2-dimensional dataset containing 602 objects. There are 500 objects in the first cluster C_1, 100 objects in the cluster C_2, and two additional objects O_1 and O_2. In this example, C_1 forms a denser cluster than C_2. According to Hawkins' definition, both O_1 and O_2 are outliers, whereas objects in C_1 and C_2 are not. In contrast, within the framework of distance-based outliers, only O_1 is a reasonable $DB(pct, dmin)$ outlier in the following sense. If for every object q^{O_i} in C_1, the distance between q^{O_i} and its nearest neighbor is greater than the distance between O_2 and C_2 (i.e., $d(O_2, C_2)$), we can show that there is no appropriate value of pct and $dmin$ such that O_2 is a $DB(pct, dmin)$ outlier but the objects in C_1 are not. The reason is as follows. If the $dmin$ value is less than the distance $d(O_2, C_2)$, all 601 objects ($pct = 100 * 601/602$) are further away from O_2 than $dmin$. But the same condition holds also for every object q in C_1. Thus, in this case, O_2 and all objects in C_1 are $DB(pct, dmin)$

outliers. Otherwise, if the $dmin$ value is greater than the distance $d(O_2, C_2)$, it is easy to see that O_2 is a $DB(pct, dmin)$ outlier, implying that there are many objects q in C_1 such that q is also a $DB(pct, dmin)$ outlier. This is because the cardinality of the set $p \in D | d(p, O_2) \leq dmin$ is always bigger than the cardinality of the set $p \in D | d(p, q) \leq dmin$.

Another definition of outlier, introduced in [308], states that for a given dataset with N points, parameters n and k can be used to denote a D_n^k outlier for a point p if there are no more than $n - 1$ other points p' such that $D^k(p') > D^k(p)$. $D^k(p)$ denotes the distance of point p from its kth nearest neighbor. The points can be ranked according to their $D^k(p)$ distances. For a given value of k and n, a point p is an outlier if no more than $n - 1$ other points in the dataset have a higher value of distance than $D^k(p)$. As seen in Figure 3.9 for $n = 6$, D_6^k is an outlier for a point p, since there is no more than $(6 - 1) = 5$ other points p', such that $D^k(p') > D^k(p)$.

This definition makes it possible to rank outliers based on $D^k(p)$ distances. Outliers with larger $D^k(p)$ distances have fewer points close to them and are thus intuitively stronger outliers. Various proximity measures can be used to measure the distance between a pair of points with numeric as well as categorical data.

Based on these definitions, we observe the following.

- Distance-based outliers are those objects located away from the majority of objects using some geometric proximity measure with reference to a fixed or changeable user-defined threshold related to the domain of interest.

- A major advantage with the distance-based outlier detection approach is its high degree of accuracy. With the use of an appropriate proximity measure, it is possible to achieve high outlier detection accuracy.

- Typically, high dimensional data are sparse in nature in some dimensions or attributes. Because of the sparsity of data, usually most distance-based approaches do not perform well in situations where the actual values of the distances are similar for many pairs of points.

- Most researchers [203] working with distance-based outlier detection methods take a nonparametric approach for handling the high dimensional sparsity problem.

- With distance-based nonparametric approaches, a major limitation is the requirement of large computation time. However, the use of an appropriate heuristic method for adaptive or conditional thresholding can improve the performace of a distance-based outlier detection method substantially.

(ii) *Density-Based Outlier Detection*: This approach [53] estimates the density distribution of the input space and then identifies outliers as those lying in regions of low density [206]. It estimates the density of the neighborhood of a given input instance. An instance that lies in a neighborhood with low density is declared to be an outlier while an instance that lies in a dense neighborhood is declared normal. Breunig et al. [53] introduce a generalized definition of a density-based outlier, called local outlier factor (LOF). The authors compute a local outlier factor for each object in the dataset, indicating its degree of outlierness. This quantifies how outlying an object is. The outlier factor is local in the sense that only a restricted neighborhood of each object is taken into account. The LOF of an object is based on a single parameter called *MinPts*, which is the number of nearest neighbors used in defining the local neighborhood of the object. The LOF of an object p can be defined as

$$LOF_{MinPts}(p) = \frac{\displaystyle\sum_{o \in N_{MinPts}(p)} \frac{lrd_{MinPts}(o)}{lrd_{MinPts}(p)}}{|N_{MinPts}(p)|}. \tag{3.3}$$

The outlier factor of object p captures the degree to which we can call p an outlier. It is the average of the ratio of the local reachability density of p and those of p's $MinPts$-nearest neighbors. The lower p's local reachability density (lrd) is, and the higher lrd of p's $MinPts$-nearest neighbors are, the higher is the LOF value of p. The local reachability density (lrd) of an object p is the inverse of the average reachability distance $(reach\text{-}dist)$ based on the $MinPts$ nearest neighbors of p. Note that the local density can be ∞ if all the reachability distances in the summation are 0. This may occur for an object p if there are at least $MinPts$ objects, different from p, but sharing the same spatial coordinates, i.e., if there are at least $MinPts$ duplicates of p in the dataset. lrd is defined as:

$$lrd_{MinPts}(p) = \left(\frac{\sum\limits_{o \in N_{MinPts}(p)} reach\text{-}dist_{MinPts}(p, o)}{|N_{MinPts}(p)|} \right)^{-1} . \quad (3.4)$$

The reachability distance of an object p with respect to object o is $reach\text{-}dist_{MinPts}(p, o)$:
$reach\text{-}dist_{MinPts}(p, o) = max\{MinPts\text{-}dist(o), dist(p, o)\}.$

For any positive integer k, the k-distance of object p, denoted as k-distance(p), is defined as the distance $d(p, o)$ between p and an object $o \in D$ where D is a dataset such that

(i) for at least k objects $o' \in D \mid \{p\}$, it holds that $d(p, o') \le d(p, o)$, and

(ii) for at most k-1 objects $o' \in D \mid \{p\}$, it holds that $d(p, o') < d(p, o)$.

The *k-distance neighborhood* of p contains every object whose distance from p is not greater than the k-distance, i.e., $N_{k\text{-}distance(p)}(p) = q \in D| \{p\} |d(p, q) \le k\text{-}distance(p)$. These objects q are called the k-nearest neighbors of p. The notation $N_k(p)$ is used as a shorthand for $N_{k\text{-}distance(p)}(p)$. k-distance(p) is well defined for any positive integer k, although the object o may not be unique. In such a case, the cardinality of $N_k(p)$ is greater than k. For example, suppose that there are (i) 1 object with distance 1 unit from p, (ii) 2 objects with distance 2 units from p and (iii) 3 objects with distance 3 units from p. Then 2-*distance*(p) is identical to 3-*distance*(p). Assume now that there are 3 objects of 4-*distance*(p) from p. Thus, the cardinality of $N_4(p)$ can be greater than 4. In this case it is 6.

Figure 3.10 illustrates the idea of reachability distance with $k = 4$. Intuitively, if object p (e.g., p_2 in the figure) is far away from o, the reachability distance between the two is simply their actual distance. However, if they are sufficiently close (e.g., p_1

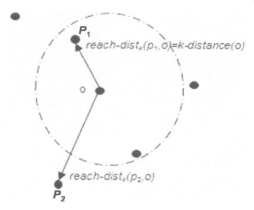

FIGURE 3.10:   Reachability distance

in the figure), the actual distance is replaced by the k-distance of o. The reason is that in so doing, the statistical fluctuations of $d(p, o)$ for all the p's close to o can be significantly reduced. The strength of this smoothing effect can be controlled by the parameter k. The higher the value of k, the more similar is the reachability distances for objects within the same neighborhood.

Based on previous discussion on density-based outlier detection, we observe the following.

- Density-based outlier detection is a parameter-based approach.

- The performance of this approach is largely dependent on the selection of parameter values. With an appropriate selection of parameter values, one can achieve excellent performance in the identification of outliers.

- In network anomaly detection, density-based outlier detection has an important role to play. Objects or instances lying in low density region(s) over a subset of relevant attributes or parameters and with respect to a given user-defined threshold can be considered as anomalous.

(iii) *Outlier Detection Based on Soft Computing*: In this section we discuss outlier estimation techniques inspired by soft computing approaches, such as rough set and fuzzy set theoretic approaches. In [287, 190], the authors define the rough membership function or RMF-based outliers. To define an RMF, assume $IS=(U, A, V, f)$ is an information system, $X \subseteq U$ and $X \neq \Phi$. U

is a nonempty finite set of objects, A a set of attributes, V the union of attribute domains and $f : U \times A \to V$ a function such that for any $X \in U$ and $a \in A$, $f(x,a) \in V_a$. Let ν be a given threshold value. For any $x \in X$, if $ROF_X(x) > \nu$, x is called a *rough membership function (RMF)-based outlier* with respect to X in IS, where $ROF_X(x)$ is the rough outlier factor of x with respect to X in IS. Thus, the *rough outlier factor* $ROF_X(x)$ is defined as

$$ROF_X(x) = 1 - \frac{\sum_{j=1}^{m}\left(\mu_X^{A_j}(x) \times |A_j|\right) + \sum_{j=1}^{m}\left(\mu_X^{\{a_j\}}(x) \times W_X^{\{a_j\}}(x)\right)}{2 \times |A|^2}$$

(3.5)

where $A=\{a_1, a_2, \ldots, a_m\}$. $\mu_X^{A_j}(x)$ and $\mu_X^{\{a_j\}}(x)$ are RMFs for every attribute subset $A_j \subseteq A$ and singleton subset $\{a_j\}$ of A, $1 \leq j \leq m$. For every singleton subset $\{a_j\}$, $W_X^{\{a_j\}} : X \to (0,1]$ is a weight function such that for any $x \in X$, $W_X^{\{a_j\}}(x) = \sqrt{(|[x]_{\{a_j\}}|)/(|U|)}$. $[x]_{\{a_j\}} = \{u \in U : f(u, a_j) = f(x, a_j)\}$ denotes the indiscernability [287] class of relation $indisc(\{a_j\})$ that contains element x. The RMF is $\mu_X^B :\to (0,1]$ such that for any $x \in X$

$$\mu_X^B(x) = \frac{|[x]_B \cap X|}{|[x]_B|}$$

(3.6)

where $[x]_B = \{u \in U : \forall a \in B(f(u,a) = f(x,a))\}$ and $B \subseteq A$ denotes the indiscernibility class of relation $indisc(B)$ that contains element x.

Rough sets have been effectively used in classification systems, where complete knowledge of the system is not available [321]. A classifer aims to form various classes where members of a class are not noticeably different. These indiscernible or indistinguishable objects are viewed as basic building blocks (concepts) used to build a knowledge base about the real world. This kind of uncertainty is referred to as rough uncertainty and rough uncertainty is formulated in terms of rough sets.

The concept of fuzzy logic, introduced by Zadeh [415] provides for a language with syntax and local semantics for translating qualitative knowledge about a problem to be solved. The mathematical

framework of fuzzy logic, called fuzzy set theory, deals with uncertainty, imprecision and approximate reasoning. In fuzzy sets,
the membership of an element in a set is not crisp. It can be
anything in between *yes* and *no*. In a fuzzy set, an element x
has a membership function $\mu P(x)$ that represents the degree to
which x belongs to the set P. Fuzzy sets and rules are useful in
representing a high level description of the patterns of behavior
found in network data meaningfully. Hence, they have a tremen-
dous application in pattern classification. Thus, fuzzy and rough
sets represent different facets of uncertainty.

Based on our discussion of soft computing based outlier detection
using rough set and fuzzy set theoretic approaches, the following
are our observations.

- Rough sets deal with coarse nonoverlapping concepts [105].

- Fuzziness deals with vagueness among overlapping sets [43].
  In fuzzy sets, each granule of knowledge can have only one
  membership value for a particular class. However, rough
  sets assert that each granule may have different membership
  values for the same class.

- Neither roughness nor fuzziness depends on the occurrence
  of an event.

- Since roughness appears due to indiscernibility in the input pattern set and since fuzziness is generated due to the
  vagueness present in the output class and the clusters, to
  model a situation where both vagueness and approximation
  are present, the concept of fuzzy-rough sets [105] can be employed.

3.4.3   Association Rule Learning

Association mining plays an essential role in many data mining tasks
that try to find interesting patterns from databases. The original motivation for searching for association rules came from the need to analyze
supermarket transactions data, that is, to examine customer behavior
in terms of the purchased products. In this chapter, we discuss basic concepts associated with association rule mining and present some
influential algorithms introduced since the 1990s.

3.4.3.1 Basic Concepts

The formal statement of the association rule mining problem is given by Agrawal et al. [7]. Let $I = I_1, I_2, \ldots, I_m$ be a set of m distinct attributes, T be a transaction that contains a set of items such that $T \subseteq I$ and D be a database of transaction records. An association rule is an implication in the form of $X \longrightarrow Y$, where $X, Y \subset I$ are sets of items called itemsets and $X \cap Y = \phi$. X and Y are, respectively, *antecedent* and *consequent* and the rule means X implies Y. There are two important measures for defining association rules: *support s* and *confidence c*. The association mining problem handles large transaction databases and analysts are concerned about only frequent patterns, such as frequently purchased items. Hence, appropriate thresholds for the support and confidence measures are provided by users to drop those rules that are not interesting or useful. These two thresholds are often referred to as *minsup*, i.e., minimum support, and *minconf*, i.e., minimum confidence, respectively.

The support s of an association rule is defined as the percentage or fraction of records that contain $X \cup Y$ to the total number of records in the database. The count for each item is incremented every time the item is encountered in different transactions T in the database D during a scanning process. For example, to handle a transaction where a customer buys three bottles of beer, one is to increase only the support count of the item *beer* by one. In other words, if a transaction contains an item, the support count of this item is increased by one. Thus, s is calculated for XY as follows.

$$s(XY) = \frac{Support\ count\ of\ (XY)}{Total\ number\ of\ transactions\ in\ D} \qquad (3.7)$$

A high support is desired for more interesting association rules. Before the mining process, an analyst is required to specify *minsup* to find only those association rules generated based on the itemsets with support count greater than *minsup*.

The confidence of an association rule is defined as the percentage or fraction of the number of transactions that contain $X \cup Y$ to the total number of records that contain X, where if the percentage exceeds the confidence threshold *minconf*, an interesting association rule $X \longrightarrow Y$ is generated.

$$Confidence(X \mid Y) = \frac{Support(XY)}{Support(X)} \qquad (3.8)$$

Confidence is a measure of strength of an association rule. Suppose the confidence of the association rule $X \longrightarrow Y$ is 80%. It means that 80% of the transactions that contain X also contain Y.

Rule Generation

Once the frequent itemsets from a transaction database are found, it is straightforward to generate frequent association rules from them. A strong association rule satisfies both *minsup* and *minconf*. Association rules are typically mined by following two basic steps.

(i) For each frequent itemset l, generate all nonempty subsets of l.

(ii) For every nonempty subset s of l, output the rule $s \longrightarrow (l - s)$ if the confidence of the rule is high (i.e., $\geq$ *minconf*).

There are many types of association rules depending on the considerations given below.

(i) *Types of values handled*: Depending on the types of values handled, association rule mining can be of two types: (i) *Boolean* association mining, where each trasaction is represented in terms of two values, i.e., 0 (for the absence of an item) and 1 (for the presence of an item) and (ii) *Quantitative* association mining, where each item has numeric values. An example of a quantitative association rule is shown below.

age(X,   30, ..., 39),   income(X,   42K, ..., 48K)$\rightarrow$ buys(X, high resolution TV)

where X is a variable representing a customer.

(ii) *Dimensions of data involved*: If the items or attributes in association mining refer to only one dimension, it is single dimensional association mining. If it deals with more than one dimension, it is multidimensional association mining.

(iii) *Levels of abstraction involved*: Some methods for association mining can find rules at different levels of abstraction. For example, in the following association rules, the items bought are specified at different levels of abstraction. Here, "computer" is a higher-level abstraction of "laptop computer". If mining refers items or attributes at different levels of abstraction, then it is called multi-level association mining. Otherwise, it is a case of single-level association mining.

(i) age(X, 30, ...39) $\longrightarrow$ buys(X, "laptop computer")

(ii) age(X, 30, ...39) $\longrightarrow$ buys(X, "computer")

(iv) *Extensibility of association mining*: Association mining can be extended to correlation analysis, where the absence or presence of correlated items can be identified. It can be extended to mining maxpatterns (i.e., maximal frequent patterns) and frequent closed itemsets. A *maxpattern* is a frequent pattern, p, such that any proper *superpattern* (q is a superpattern of p, if p is a subpattern of q, i.e., q contains p) of p is not frequent. A *frequent closed itemset* is a frequent closed itemset where an itemset c is closed if there exists no proper superset of c, say c', such that every transaction containing c also contains c'. Maxpatterns and frequent closed itemsets can be used to substantially reduce the number of frequent itemsets generated during mining.

Association mining is a well-explored research area. As stated before, the second subproblem of association mining is straightforward. Most approaches focus on the first subproblem. In this section, we discuss some basic and classic approaches for frequent pattern mining. Most algorithms of mining association rules are quite similar, the difference being the extent to which certain efficiency improvements have been made. We introduce some association rule mining algorithms next.

3.4.4 Frequent Itemset Mining Algorithms

(i) *AIS* [7]: The AIS algorithm is capable of generating single item consequent association rules. For example, it generates rules like $X \cap Y \longrightarrow Z$ but not rules like $X \longrightarrow Y \cap Z$. It scans the database several times to obtain frequent itemsets. During the first pass, AIS computes the support count of each individual item. Next, based on the frequent single itemsets, it generates candidate 2-itemsets by extending those frequent items with other items in the same transaction. To avoid unnecessary or redundant candidate generation, the items are ordered and the large items obtained in the previous pass are joined with an item that appears later in the frequent itemsets. During the second pass, the *support count* of the candidate 2-itemsets is accumulated and checked against *minsup*. Similarly, candidate $(k+1)$-itemsets are generated by extending frequent k-itemsets with items in the same transaction. This process is iterated until no additional higher itemsets can be generated. To make this algorithm more efficient, (i) an estimation method is introduced to prune itemset candidates that have no hope to be large and (ii) an efficient memory management scheme is introduced, especially when memory is not enough. The main limitation of the AIS algorithm is the generation of too many candidate itemsets. It requires a lot of space and wastes significant amounts of effort. AIS also requires several database passes, which is another major limitation.

(ii) *Apriori*: The Apriori algorithm [9] is a pioneering contribution in the history of association rule mining. Unlike AIS, Apriori is more efficient during the candidate generation process for two reasons: (a) Apriori employs a different candidate generation technique and (b) Apriori uses an effective pruning technique based on the downward closure property of the support of itemsets and the confidence of association rules [351]. The same technique was also independently developed by Agrawal [9] and Mannila [244]. To find the large itemsets from a market-basket dataset, Apriori uses two processes. First, it generates the candidate itemsets and then the database is scanned to check the actual support count of the corresponding itemsets. During the initial scanning, the support count of each item is calculated and the large 1-itemsets are generated by pruning those itemsets whose supports are below the predefined threshold. In each pass, only those candidate itemsets that include the same specified number of items are generated and checked. The candidate k-itemsets are generated after the $(k-1)$th pass over the database by joining the frequent $(k-1)$-itemsets. All the candidate k-itemsets are pruned by checking their $(k-1)$ sub-itemsets. If any of its sub $(k-1)$-itemsets is not in the list of frequent $(k-1)$-itemsets, this k-itemsets candidate is pruned out because it has no hope of becoming frequent according to the Apriori property.

The Apriori algorithm still inherits all the limitations of the AIS algorithms, such as (a) the need for several database passes, (b) the generation of too many candidate itemsets and (c) the wastage of significant amounts of effort in handling large candidate sets. Over the decades, several variants of Apriori have been proposed. Some prominent among them are Apriori-TID and Apriori-Hybrid [9], DHP [280] and SON [323]. These variant algorithms either attempt to optimize the number of database passes or they try to reduce the generation of the number of candidates.

(iii) *SETM*: The SETM algorithm [174] is motivated by the need to find large itemsets using SQL. Each member of a large itemset, L_k, is in the form $\langle TID, itemset \rangle$ where *TID* is the unique identifier of a transaction. Similarly, each member of the set of candidate itemsets, C_k, is in the form $\langle TID, itemset \rangle$. Like AIS, SETM also makes multiple passes over the database. In the first pass, it counts the support of individual items and determines which of them are large or frequent in the database. Then it generates the candidate itemsets by extending large itemsets from the previous pass. In addition, SETM remembers the TIDs of the generating transactions along with the candidate itemsets. The relational *merge-join* operation can be used to generate candidate itemsets [47]. When generating candidate sets, the SETM algorithm saves a copy of the candidate itemsets together with the TID of the generating transaction in a sequential manner. Afterwards, the candidate itemsets are sorted on itemsets and small itemsets are deleted using an aggregation function. If the database is in sorted order on the basis of TID, large itemsets contained in a transaction in the next pass are obtained by sorting L_k on TID. This way, several passes are made on the database. In addition to the requirement of multiple passes, SETM also requires a large amount of space to accommodate the TIDs.

(iv) *DIC (Dynamic Itemset Counting)* [54]: DIC identifies certain "stops" in the database, assuming that we read the records sequential as we do in other algorithms, but pauses to carry out certain computations at the "stop" points. It maintains some structures (e.g., *dashed box, dashed circle, solid box* and *solid circle*) to hold lists of itemsets for various purposes. Itemsets in the dashed category have a *counter* and *stop number* to keep track of the support value of the corresponding itemsets and to keep track of whether an itemset has completed one full pass over a database, respectively. The itemsets in the *solid* category are not subjected to any counting. Rather, the itemsets in the solid box are the confirmed set of frequent items. The itemsets in the solid circle are the confirmed set of infrequent itemsets. Though DIC drastically reduces the number of scans through the database, its performance is heavily dependent on the distribution of the data.

(v) *Partitioning Approach* [323]: This approach reduces the number of database scans to 2 by dividing the database into small partitions such that each partition can be handled in the main memory. Assume the partitions of the database are $D_1, D_2, \ldots, D_p$. The algorithm finds in its initial scan the local large itemsets for each partition D_i $(1 \leq i \leq p)$, i.e., $X|X.count \geq s \times |D_i|$. The local large itemsets, L_i, are generated by using a level-wise algorithm such as Apriori. Since each partition can fit in the main memory, there are no additional disk I/O operations for each partition after loading the partition into the main memory. In the second scan, it uses the property that a large itemset in the whole database must be locally large in at least one partition of the database. Then the union(s) of the local large itemsets found in each partition are used as the candidates and are counted through the whole database to find all large itemsets. A limitation of this approach is the overhead. With the increase in the number of partitions, the overhead increases significantly.

(vi) *FP Growth*: The FP-Tree algorithm [157] is another significant contribution in the history of frequent itemset mining algorithms. It successfully overcomes two major bottlenecks of the Apriori algorithm. The frequent itemsets are generated with only two passes over the database and without any candidate generation process. By avoiding the candidate generation process and by requiring fewer passes over the database, FP-Tree is an order of magnitude faster than the Apriori algorithm. The frequent patterns generation process includes two subprocesses: constructing the FP-Tree and generating frequent patterns from the FP-Tree.

The efficiency of the FP-Tree algorithm comes for three reasons (a) First, it is a compressed representation of the original database because only frequent items are used to construct the tree. Other irrelevant information is pruned. (b) It only scans the database twice. The frequent patterns are generated by the FP-growth procedure, constructing the conditional FP-Tree. (c) The FP-

Tree uses a divide and conquer method that considerably reduces the size of the subsequent conditional FP-Tree. Longer frequent patterns are generated by adding a suffix to the shorter frequent patterns.

A major limitation of this algorithm is that when the database is large both in terms of the number of transactions and the number of items, it is often unrealistic to construct a memory-based FP-Tree. In the case of interactive mining, users may change the threshold *minsup*. A change in the value of *minsup* may lead to repetition of the whole FP-Tree construction process.

(vii) *Inverted Matrix* [259]: This is a disk-based approach, aiming to allow interactive mining, which is difficult with FP-Trees. The three basic ideas involved in this algorithm are as follows. (a) The conversion of transactional data into a new database layout called *Inverted Matrix* that prevents multiple scanning of the database. It finds frequent patterns in less than a full scan with random access. (b) The building of a COFI-Tree (Co-Occurrence Frequent-Item-Trees) for each frequent item, summarizing the co-occurrences. (c) The use of a simple and nonrecursive mining process that reduces the memory requirements as minimum candidate generation and counting are needed. Experimental evaluation [259] shows that the Inverted Matrix approach outperforms FP-Tree and Apriori. It was evaluated by around 25 million transactions with 1,000,000 unique items.

3.4.5 Rule Generation Algorithms

In this section, we discuss some algorithms to extract rules given a set of frequent itemsets. These algorithms use a user-provided threshold called *minconf* when extracting the rules. Rules with confidence greater than *minconf* are generated.

(i) *Agrawal's Algorithm* [9]: This first rule generation algorithm uses the frequent itemsets extracted by the first phase of the rule mining process. The algorithm is straightforward and is able to generate only those rules with one item in the consequent part. For a given frequent itemset $Y = I_1 I_2 ... I_k, k \geq 2$, it generates at most k rules that use the items from the set Y. The antecedent of each of these rules is a subset X of Y such that X has $(k\text{-}1)$ items and the consequent is the item $Y - X$. It generates the rule $X \longrightarrow I_j$ with confidence equal to or greater than *minconf*. The confidence of the rule is calculated as the ratio of the support of (Y) and the support of (X), where $X \cup I_j = Y$.

A major limitation of this algorithm is that it cannot generate all the rules from the frequent itemsets. For a frequent itemset with size n, it checks a maximum of n candidate rules, though there can be 2^{n-2} number of possible rules present.

(ii) *Srikant's Simple Algorithm* [351],[352]: This is a generalization of the previous algorithm. The size of the consequent part of the rules generated is not limited to one item only. To generate the rules from a frequent itemset l, all its nonempty subsets are found first. For every such subset a, a rule of the form $a \longrightarrow (l - a)$ is generated if the ratio of *support* (l) to *support* (a) is at least *minconf*, the user-specified minimum confidence. It stores the frequent itemsets in hash tables, making it easy and simple to obtain the support count.

This simple algorithm can generate all possible rules, but it involves a lot of redundant checking, which wastes a significant amount of time.

(iii) *Srikant's Faster Algorithm* [351]: This algorithm eliminates redundant checking of rules significantly. If $\bar{a} \subset a$, the support of $\bar{a}$ cannot be smaller than that of a. Therefore, the confidence of $\bar{a} \longrightarrow (l - \bar{a})$ cannot be more than the confidence of $a \longrightarrow (l - a)$. These facts can be rewritten by saying if rule $a \longrightarrow (l - a)$ holds, all rules of the form $\bar{a} \Rightarrow (l - \bar{a})$ must also hold, $\forall \bar{a}, \bar{a} \in a$. For example, the rule $AB \longrightarrow CD$ may hold, if both the rules $ABC \longrightarrow D$ and $ABD \longrightarrow C$ hold.

The above property can also be stated as follows. For a given frequent itemset, if a rule with consequent c holds, the rules with consequents that are subsets of c also hold. This property of rules is similar to the downward closure property of frequent itemsets, which says that subsets of a frequent itemset are also frequent.

From a frequent itemset l, rules with one item in the consequent are generated first. Then the possible consequents with two items are generated using the Apriori candidate generation function. If some rules are found, it generates the 3-item consequents in the same manner and so on.

Although this algorithm is one of the best rule generation algorithms, it also has several limitations. The candidate consequents generated for rule discovery require a significant amount of memory. A considerable amount of time is wasted by generating the same consequent several times for different antecedents. For example, if $X \subset Y$, when generating the rules using X, all candidate consequents are generated. The same operation is repeated for the set Y also, although many of them have already been generated in an earlier stage since Y is a superset of X.

3.4.6 Discussion

From our discussion above, the following are our observations.

- The two-step association mining process initially generates frequent itemsets and then generates association rules based on the frequent itemsets. Most work focuses on frequent itemset generation.

- To achieve efficiency, most algorithms generate frequent itemsets in a single scan of the database.

- The performance of most algorithms suffers because they construct the tree in memory.

- The FP-Tree algorithm generates frequent itemsets without candidate generation. However, for datasets with large numbers of items and transactions, the FP-Tree approach suffers due to its memory-based tree approach.

- Most algorithms are unable to address issues in interactive mining.

- Rules generated using the support-confidence framework fail to generate rare itemset(s) and hence rare rule(s), which are often important in the network intrusion domain, especially in detecting rare attacks such as in user-to-root or remote-to-local attacks.

3.5   Probabilistic Learning

In this section, we describe four well-known probabilistic classifiers, viz., Bayesian Networks (BN), Naive Bayes (NB) models, Hidden Markov Models (HMM) and the Expectation Maximization (EM) algorithm and discuss their merits and demerits.

3.5.1   Learning Bayes Nets

A Bayesian network [188] is a model that encodes probabilistic relationships among variables of interest. It provides for knowledge representation and reasoning under conditions of uncertainty. A Bayesian network $B = (N, A, \Theta)$ is a directed acyclic graph (DAG) (N, A) where each node $n \in N$ represents a domain variable (e.g., a dataset attribute or variable) and each arc $a \in A$ between nodes represents a probabilistic dependency among the variables, quantified using a conditional probability distribution $\theta_i \in \Theta$ for each node n_i. A Bayesian network can be used to compute the conditional probability of one node, given values assigned to the other nodes. Many Bayesian network structure learning algorithms are also classified as Type 1 and Type 2 algorithms. These algorithms generally fall into two groups, search and scoring based algorithms and dependency analysis based algorithms. In the area of Bayesian network structure learning, two types of algorithms have been developed. Type 1 deals with a special case where the node ordering is given, which requires $O(N^2)$ conditional independence tests. Type 2 deals with the general case and requires $O(N^4)$ conditional independence tests.

When used in conjunction with statistical methods, Bayesian networks have several advantages for data analysis [166]. First, because Bayesian networks encode interdependencies among variables, they can handle situations where data is missing. Second, Bayesian networks have the ability to represent causal relationships. Therefore, they can be used to predict the consequences of an action. Finally, because Bayesian networks have both causal and probabilistic relationships, they can be used to model problems where there is a need to combine prior knowledge with data. Several variants of the basic technique have been proposed for network anomaly detection [34, 207, 373, 402]. The basic technique assumes independence among the attributes. Several variations of the basic technique capture conditional dependencies among different attributes using complex Bayesian networks. Within the domain of anomaly detection, Bayesian techniques have been frequently used for classification and suppression of false alarms. Kruegel et al. [207] propose a multisensor fusion approach where the outputs of different IDS sensors are aggregated to produce a single alarm. This approach is based on the assumption that any single anomaly detection technique cannot classify a set of events as an intrusion with sufficient confidence.

Bayesian networks have advantages over many other predictive models because they enable one to represent the interrelationships among the attributes of the dataset. It is easy for human experts to understand network structures. It is also easy to modify as and when needed. It is easy to extend the Bayesian network model by adding decision nodes and utility nodes for decision analysis. Furthermore, the Bayesian network model allows explicit uncertainty characterization, fast and efficient computation and quick training. High adaptiveness, ease of building and provision for explicit representation of domain specific knowledge in human reasoning frameworks make the Bayesian network model attractive from a network anomaly detection perspective. However, limitations of the method should be considered in the actual implementation. Since the accuracy of this method is dependent on certain assumptions that are typically based on the behavioral model of the target system, deviation from those assumptions will decrease its accuracy.

3.5.2 Simple Probabilistic Learning: Naive Bayes

Naive Bayes [38, 16] classifiers are simple Bayesian networks which are composed of DAGs with only one root node called the parent, representing an unobserved node and several children, corresponding to the observed nodes with a strong assumption of independence among child nodes in the context of their parents.

The naive Bayes (NB) model is a simplified Bayesian probability model [216]. This model computes the probability of an end result given several related evidence variables. The probability of an evidence variable, given that the end result occurs, is assumed to be independent of the probability of other evidence variables given that the same end results occur. When a set of classes is observed in the training data, the NB classifier assigns an observed data to a class with the highest probability. During training, the NB algorithm calculates the probabilities of a result given a particular attribute and then stores this probability. This is repeated for each attribute.

Classification is performed considering the parent node to be hidden and computing to which class an object in the test set should belong, child nodes representing different attributes specifying the object. Thus, in the presence of a training set, one should only compute conditional probabilities since the structure is unique. Once the network is computed, it is possible to classify any new object using its attribute values using Bayes' rule [38]. Since the NB model works under the assumption that these attributes are independent, their combined probability is obtained as follows:

$$P(c_i|A) = \frac{P(a_1|c_i).P(a_2|c_i). \; \dots \; .P(a_n|c_i)}{P(A)}, \tag{3.9}$$

where $P(A)$ is determined by the normalization condition.

During testing, the time taken to compute the probability of a given class for each example in the worst case is proportional to n, the number of attributes. By applying a NB classifier to an intrusion detection task, a set of training network traffic data is used to find the prior probabilities for normal or a known class of attacks. As unseen network traffic arrives, the classifier uses the Bayes' theorem to decide which class the traffic should belong to. This scheme also suffers from several limitations. (i) The classification ability of the NB model is identical to a threshold-based system that computes the sum of the outputs obtained from the child nodes [207]. (ii) Since the child nodes do not interact among themselves and their outputs only influence the probability of the root node, it is difficult to incorporate additional information.

3.5.3   Hidden Markov Models

A hidden Markov model (HMM) is a statistical model [133] where the system being modeled is assumed to be a Markov process with unknown parameters. The challenge is to determine the hidden parameters from observed parameters. Unlike a regular Markov model, where the state transition probabilities are the only parameters and the state of the system is directly observable, in a hidden Markov model, the only visible elements are the variables of the system that are influenced by the state of the system and the state of the system itself is hidden. A hidden Markov model's states represent some unobservable condition of the system being modeled. In each state, there is a certain probability of producing any of the observable system outputs and a separate probability indicating the likely next states. By having different output probability distributions in each of the states and allowing the system to change states over time, the model is capable of representing nonstationary sequences.

To estimate the parameters of a hidden Markov model for modeling normal system behavior, sequences of normal events collected from normal system operation are used as training data. An expectation maximization (EM) algorithm is used to estimate the parameters. Once a hidden Markov model has been trained, when confronted with test data, probability measures can be used as thresholds for anomaly detection. In order to use hidden Markov models for anomaly detection, three key problems need to be addressed. The first problem, also known as the *evaluation problem*, is to determine, given a sequence of observations, the probability that the observed sequence was generated by the model. The second is the *learning problem*, which involves building from the audit data a model or a set of models that correctly describes the observed behavior. Given a hidden Markov model and associated observations, the third problem, also known as the *decoding problem*, involves determining the most likely set of hidden states that have led to those observations.

An HMM correlates observations with hidden states where observation points are optimized using an acceptable set of system-wide intrusion checkpoints while hidden states are created using explicit knowledge of probabilistic relationships with these observations. These relationships, which are also called profiles, are hardened and evolved with constant usage. If observation points can be standardized, the problem of intrusion prediction can be reduced to profiling existing and new hidden states to standard observations. HMM schemes consist of observed states, hidden (intrusion) states and HMM profiles. HMM training using initial data and continuous re-estimation creates profiles that consist of transition probabilities and observation symbol probabilities. The four basic steps involved in this process are given below.

(i) Measure observed states that are analytically or logically derived from the intrusion indicators. These indicators are test points spread all over the system.

(ii) Estimate an instantaneous observation probability matrix that indicates the probability of an observation, given a hidden state $p(S_i|O_i)$. This density function is estimated using an explicit parametric model (e.g., multivariate Gaussian) or implicitly from data via nonparametric methods (e.g., multivariate kernel density emission).

(iii) Estimate hidden states by clustering the homogeneous behavior of single or multiple components together. These states are indicative of various intrusion activities that need to be identified to the administrator.

(iv) Estimate the hidden state transition probability matrix using prior knowledge or random data. The prior knowledge and long term temporal characteristics are approximate probabilities of transition of state components from one intrusion state to another.

The hidden states $S = \{S_1, S_2, \ldots, S_{N-1}, S_N\}$ are the set of states that are not visible. Each state randomly generates a mixture of the M observations or visible states O. The probability of the subsequent state depends only upon the previous state. The complete model is defined by the following components: the *transition probability matrix* $A = \{a_{ij}\}$ where $a_{ij} = p(S_i|S_j)$, the *observation probability matrix* $B = (b_i(v_m))$ where $b_i(v_m) = p(v_m|S_i)$ and an *initial probability vector* $\pi = p(S_i)$. The observation probability represents an attribute that is observed with some probability if a particular failure state is anticipated. The model is represented by $M = (A, B, \pi)$. The transition probability matrix is a square matrix of size equal to the number of states and represents the state transition probabilities. The observation probability distribution is a nonsquare matrix whose dimension equals the number of states by the number of observables and represents the probability of an observation for a given state.

3.5.4   Expectation Maximization Algorithm

Expectation maximization (EM) [94], usually called an "algorithm", is a generic method for solving MLE (*maximum likelihood estimation*) [46] problems. MLE problems are computationally intractable. This intractability results from one or more "hidden" variables that cannot be observed in the data. The fact that these variables are not observable makes the problem difficult. If these values are included in the data, solving for parameter Θ (e.g., mean and variance) becomes a mostly straightforward maximization problem. The EM algorithm is useful in such cases.

The EM algorithm can find the MLE of the parameters of a distribution from a given dataset even when the data is incomplete or has missing values. There are two main applications of the EM algorithm. In the first application, the EM algorithm is applied when the data has missing values, due to problems or limitations of the observation process. In the second application, the EM algorithm is used to optimize when optimizing the likelihood function is analytically intractable, but when the likelihood function can be simplified by assuming the existence of values for additional but missing (or hidden) parameters. The latter application of the EM algorithm is more commonly seen in pattern recognition. EM is an iterative method, whose basic outline is as follows.

1. Let Θ be the current "best guess" as to the optimal configuration of the model.

2. Let Θ̄ be the next "best guess" as to the optimal configuration of the model.

3. Expectation Step: Compute Q, the expected value of Λ with respect to Θ̄ over all possible values of the hidden parameters. The probability of observing each possible set of hidden parameter values (required to compute the expectation of Λ) is computed using Θ.

4. Maximization Step: Choose Θ̄ so as to maximize the value for Q. Θ̄ then becomes the new "best guess".

EM does not compute a globally optimal solution at each iteration. Rather, it computes a best guess as to the answer, which is guaranteed to improve at each iteration. EM has the desirable property that while it does not always converge to the globally optimal solution, it does always converge to a locally optimal solution of the various values in Θ to improve the value of Λ.

3.6   Soft Computing

Soft computing constructs computationally intelligent methods combining emerging problem solving technologies such as fuzzy logic [415], probabilistic reasoning [38], neural networks [315] and genetic algorithms [171]. Each of these technologies provides us with reasoning and searching methods to solve complex, real-world problems. In contrast to traditional hard computing, soft computing is tolerant of imprecision, uncertainty and partial truth. Typically, soft computing embraces several computational intelligence methodologies, including artificial neural networks, fuzzy logic, evolutionary computation and probabilistic computing. The various methods used in soft computing are neither independent of one another nor compete with one another. Rather, they work in a cooperative and complementary way.

Soft computing differs from conventional (hard) computing in that, unlike hard computing, it can deal with imprecision, uncertainty, partial truth and approximation [416]. Fuzzy logic, introduced by Zadeh [415], gives us a language, with syntax and local semantics, to which one can translate qualitative knowledge about the problem to be solved. Fuzzy logic's main characteristic is the robustness of its interpolative reasoning mechanism.

Probabilistic reasoning methods such as Bayesian Networks (BN) [188], based on Bayes' theorem [38] and Dempster–Shafer's theory of belief, independently developed by Dempster [95] and Shafer [334], give us the mechanism to evaluate the outcome of systems affected by randomness or other types of probabilistic uncertainty. The main characteristic of probabilistic reasoning is its ability to update previous outcome estimates by conditioning them with newly available evidence. Although we have discussed probabilistic reasoning separately in the above section, it is also a part of soft computing because of its ability to deal with imprecise and incomplete information.

Artificial Neural Networks (ANN), first explored by Rosenblatt [315] and Widrow and Hoff [384], are computational structures that can be trained to learn patterns from examples. By using a training set that samples the relation between inputs and outputs and a backpropagation type of algorithm, introduced by Werbos [383], ANNs give us a supervised learning algorithm that performs fine granule local optimization. Genetic algorithms, proposed by Holland [171], give us a way to perform a randomized global search in a solution space. In this space, a population of candidate solutions, encoded as chromosomes, is evaluated by a fitness function in terms of its performance. The best candidates evolve and pass some of their characteristics to their offspring.

3.6.1   Artificial Neural Networks

The motivation for using Artificial Neural Networks (ANN) is the recognition that methods of computation or estimation used by conventional digital computers and the human brain are entirely different [165]. The human brain has the ability to arrange its constituent structures called neurons in a way that can efficiently perform certain computations such as pattern recognition, perception or motor control. These computations are multiple times faster than similar computations on the fastest digital computer. Neural networks use massive interconnections among neurons to achieve good performance. Neural networks obtain the information to be processed from the environment as the system learns. During the learning process, systematic changes are made to the neurons interconnection strengths or synaptic weights to achieve desired objectives. The large number of neuron interconnections improves the capability for complex computation. Thus, an ANN is a complex structure of large interconnected artificial neurons which have inputs and outputs as well as other computational features. The artificial neurons are structured in a way closely related to the learning algorithms used to train the network. ANNs are frequently used for data clustering, feature extraction and similarity detection in the context of anomaly-based network intrusion detection. In Chapter 6, we discuss several applications of ANNs [59, 220, 231, 360, 408] in network anomaly detection. Most ANN-based anomaly detection systems perform well in identifying known attacks.

3.6.2   Rough Sets

Rough set theory (RST) is an approach to computing in the presence of vagueness. It is an extension of classical set theory, for use when representing vagueness or imprecision. A rough set is concerned with working on the boundary regions of a set [287]. Rough sets are used in a classification system when we do not have complete knowledge of the system [321]. In any classification task, the aim is to form various classes where each class contains objects that are not noticeably different. These indiscernible or indistinguishable objects can be viewed as basic building blocks (concepts) used to build a knowledge base about the real world. This kind of uncertainty is referred to as rough uncertainty. Rough uncertainty is formulated in terms of rough sets. RST has been widely used in pattern recognition. In [227], rough set theory is applied to intrusion detection. The authors present an effective method using rough sets for anomaly intrusion detection with low overhead and high efficiency. The method extracts a set of detection rules basd on RST with a minimal size as the normal behavior model from the system call sequences generated during the normal execution of a process. It is capable of detecting the abnormal operating status of a process and thus reporting a possible intrusion. Several other applications of RST in network anomaly detection [58, 75, 67, 139] are discussed in Chapter 6. Most RST-based anomaly detection methods have been able to achieve high detection rates in identifying known attacks.

3.6.3   Fuzzy Logic

The concept of fuzzy logic was introduced by Zadeh [415]. It provides for a language with syntax and local semantics for translating qualitative knowledge about a problem to be solved. Fuzzy logic is supported by a mathematical framework, called fuzzy set theory, which represents and deals with uncertainty, imprecision and approximate reasoning. Typically, in classical set theory the membership of an element in a set is either 100% or 0%, whereas in fuzzy set theory, an element can have a partial membership in a set. In a fuzzy set, an element x has a membership function $\mu P(x)$ that represents the degree to which x belongs to the set P. Other features further define the membership function. For a fuzzy set P, conventionally, the core membership function is the set of all elements $x \in U$ such that $\mu P(x) = 1$. The support of the set is all $x \in U$ such that $\mu P(x) > 0$. Fuzzy sets and rules have been used fruitfully in the network security domain. Fuzzy sets and rules can represent a high level description of the patterns of behavior found in network data meaningfully. Several applications of fuzzy logic [98, 388, 362, 240] in network anomaly detection are discussed in Chapter 6. Supervised fuzzy association and clustering-based methods work well in network anomaly detection.

3.6.4 Evolutionary Computation

Evolutionary computing or genetic algorithms (GA) represent a family of computational models based on principles of evolution and natural selection. These algorithms convert the problem in a specific domain into a model by using a chromosome-like data structure and evolve the chromosomes using selection, recombination and mutation operators. In computer network security applications, it is mainly used for finding solutions to problems that can be formulated as optimization. The process of evolutionary computing usually begins with a randomly selected population of chromosomes. These chromosomes are representations of solutions to the problem to be solved. According to the attributes of the problem, different positions of each chromosome are encoded as bits, characters or numbers. These positions are sometimes referred to as genes and are changed randomly within a range during evolution. The set of chromosomes during a stage of evolution is called a population. An evaluation function is used to calculate the goodness of each chromosome. During evolution, two basic operators, crossover and mutation, are used to simulate the natural reproduction and mutation of species. The selection of chromosomes for survival and combination is biased toward the fittest chromosomes. We discuss some GA-based work [30, 197] for network security applications in Chapter 6.

3.6.5 Ant Colony Optimization

Ant colony optimization (ACO) is a problem solving approach inspired by the social behavior of ants. On identification of a suitable path toward or from a source of food, an ant marks it for other followers of the colony by depositing a substance called a pheromone on the ground. The followers sense the presence of the substance and accordingly follow the path easily. Since the early 1990s, several significant optimization algorithms inspired by the behavior of ant systems have been introduced [103, 104]. ACO has been able to attract the attention of the machine learning community and provides for a general purpose framework for solving various problems, including feature selection, network anomaly detection and multisensor-based optimization. We discuss several applications of ant colony optimization [88, 170, 354, 376] in the network security domain in Chapter 6.

3.7   Reinforcement Learning

Reinforcement Learning (RL) aims to identify the best possible sequence of actions to achieve a certain goal based on experience [361]. In RL, we know the result of specific actions in specific states in terms of positive or negative rewards. Based on such knowledge, it is the responsibility of RL to discover the best possible actions to achieve the best possible total numeric reward. Generally, in most nontrivial cases, improper action(s) may not only affect the immediate reward but also can affect the next situation. As a result, all subsequent rewards may be affected. The two distinguishing characteristics of reinforcement learning are (i) it allows for trial-and-error search and (ii) it can take into account delayed reward. To understand RL, the most essential requirement is to characterize the learning problem, not to characterize the learning method. Once the problem is properly characterized, one can use any suitable approach to solve the problem. One has to capture important aspects of the real environment faced by a learning agent during its interaction when solving the problem. If the agent can visualize the work environment in terms of states, possible actions in these states with associated rewards, and an overall goal, it should be possible to find a sequence of appropriate actions that affect the environment to help achieve the target.

For better understanding, let us take a real-life RL example problem. Image that a mobile robot is to collect trash from a new room and at the same time it is to recharge its batteries. So, it is to make a decision out of two possibilities: (i) enter the room for collection of trash and (ii) find its way back to its battery recharging station. The robot perhaps will apply its past experience with recharging and cleanup and decide the option that enables the quickest recharging.

From this example, it is perhaps easily understood that RL involves an active agent to interact with its environment and to decide the best possible sequence of actions that help achieve the target or the expected reward. The agent exploits its past experience as well as explores unseen situations to learn the best possible sequence of actions. The most challenging task in RL is to maintain trade-offs between exploration and exploitation. Generally, an RL agent prefers to take actions that were found friuitful in the past in achieving rewards. Based on a variety of actions attempted, the agent ranks them according to their fitness in achieving the expected reward. An effective RL method can make an appropriate balance between exploration and exploitation. Unlike other supervised learning methods, reinforcement learning considers the problem of an active agent interacting with an environment with uncertainty, and the agent is to take action(s) in real time toward achievement of the best possible overall reward. As we have stated before, one can use any method(s) suitable for an RL solution, but before applying an existing method, e.g., a supervised classifier, it is essential (i) to visualize the whole problem into a set of distinct subproblems and (ii) to use an appropriate method for each subproblem, toward achievement of the best possible numeric reward.

3.8 Hybrid Learning Methods

A supervised NIDS (Network Intrusion Detection System) requires human intervention to create, validate and deploy signatures or rules. Often, it takes a substantial amount of time, say hours or days, even for generating a signature for an attack. Obviously, it is way too expensive, especially in handling rapidly evolving attacks, such as worm propagation. Although efforts have been made toward automatic signature generation, these are still not suitable for large scale deployment. To address this issue, anomaly-based NIDSs that use machine learning algorithms were introduced. These systems compute a "normality" model to identify anomalous patterns. Considering the use of pre-existing knowledge, these approaches can be supervised methods, which need pre-existing knowledge and unsupervised methods, which do not rely on any prior knowledge. A large number of algorithms have been introduced to support development of effective anomaly-based NIDSs. However, the common problem of high false alarms still afflicts most of these systems. Hence, an appropriate combination of machine learning methods suitable for the problem domain may lead to the development of a better NIDS. Machine learning researchers have developed hybridized NIDSs with better detection accuracy in ways such as (i) developing a multi-layer IDS where each layer incorporates an efficient classifier for detection of class-specific known attacks or unknown attacks, (ii) developing a multi-agent framework to deal with a dynamic network and to provide real-time performance and (iii) developing ensembles of multiple classifiers such as SVMs, random forests, decision trees or ANNs and by using an appropriate combination function to achieve better detection accuracy.

3.9 Discussion

Based on our discussion of various machine learning approaches in this chapter, we enumerate the following observations.

1. A supervised learning method typically builds a predictive model for normal vs. anomaly classes based on pre-existing knowledge. However, labeled or pure training data is not always available.

2. Unsupervised learning methods are useful due to two major reasons: (i) nonavailability of training data and (ii) expense of manual classification of a large volume of data.

3. Clustering performance may be influenced by three characteristics of input data, viz., (i) dimensionality, (ii) data distribution and (iii) resolution. Depending on the approach used, the type of data that can be handled, or the target application domain of the algorithm, we categorize clustering algorithms into ten distinct classes. All clustering approaches cannot identify clusters of all shapes. Many algorithms are not scalable in terms of dimensionality and the number of instances.

4. Outlier mining is useful in identifying occurrences of nonconforming instances or anomalies or abnormality or noise in a system described by the data. Outlier identification may be helped by prior knowledge.

5. Rules generated using the support-confidence framework refer to two user-defined thresholds, *minsup* and *minconf*. However, certain rare rules (which do not satisfy user thresholds) also may be interesting when detecting attacks that are themselves rare.

6. In an ensemble approach, the best features of each individual classifier are used to improve the overall performance of the system in terms of accuracy or precision.

7. Hybrid learning methods combine the advantages of both supervised and unsupervised learning to achieve better detection performance. However, inappropriate combination of these methods may lead to high computation costs.

Chapter 4

Detecting Anomalies in Network Data

In this chapter we introduce the readers to network anomaly detection approaches, their architectures, components and other important details. We also identify issues that stand out in each of these architectures and analyze their capabilities and limitations. Intrusion datasets play a very important role in the evaluation of any intrusion detection system. Therefore, in this chapter we introduce the reader to some well-known benchmark intrusion datasets and their characteristics. Furthermore, the chapter also describes the authors' hands-on experience in generating their own dataset based on the various types of packet and flow features corresponding to the transport layer protocol.

4.1 Detection of Network Anomalies

Intrusion detection has been studied for almost 20 years. The idea of intrusion detection is predicated on the belief that an intruder's behavior is noticeably different from that of a legitimate user and that many unauthorized actions are detectable [269]. Intrusion detection systems (IDSs) are deployed as a second line of defense along with other preventive security mechanisms, such as user authentication and access control. Based on its deployment, an IDS can act either as a host-based or as a network-based IDS.

4.1.1 Host-Based IDS (HIDS)

A HIDS monitors and analyzes the internals of a computing system rather than its external interfaces. It monitors all or parts of the dynamic behavior and the state of a computer system [385]. A HIDS may detect internal activity such as which program accesses what resources and attempts illegitimate access, for example, a word-processor that has suddenly and inexplicably started modifying the system password database. Similarly, a HIDS may look at the state of a system and its stored information whether it is in RAM or in the file system or in log files or elsewhere. Thus, one can think of a HIDS as an agent that monitors whether anything or anyone internal or external has circumvented the security policy that the operating system tries to enforce.

4.1.2 Network-Based IDS (NIDS)

An NIDS detects intrusions in network data. Intrusions typically occur as anomalous patterns. Most techniques model the data in a sequential fashion and detect anomalous subsequences [385]. The primary reason for these anomalies is attacks launched by outside attackers who want to gain unauthorized access to the network to steal information or to disrupt the network. In a typical setting, a network is connected to the rest of the world through the Internet. The NIDS reads all incoming packets or flows, trying to find suspicious patterns. For example, if a large number of TCP connection requests to a very large number of different ports are observed within a short time, one could assume that there is someone committing a port scan at some of the computer(s) in the network. Various kinds of port scans and tools to launch them are discussed in detail in [45]. Port scans mostly try to detect incoming shell codes in the same manner that an ordinary intrusion detection system does. In addition to inspecting the incoming traffic, an NIDS also provides valuable information about intrusion from outgoing or local traffic. Some attacks might even be staged from the inside of a monitored network or network segment, and therefore, not regarded as incoming traffic at all. The data available for intrusion detection systems can be at different levels of granularity, e.g., packet level traces or Cisco netflow data. The data is high dimensional, typically, with a mix of categorical as well as continuous numeric attributes.

Misuse-based NIDSs attempt to search for known intrusive patterns but an anomaly-based intrusion detector searches for unusual patterns. Today, the intrusion detection research is mostly concentrated on anomaly-based network intrusion detection because it can detect known as well as unknown attacks. Hence, this book emphasizes network anomaly detection fundamentals, various detection approaches, methods, tools and systems for the network security research community.

4.1.3   Anomaly-Based Network Intrusion Detection

Anomaly detection is essentially a multistep process for the mitigation of anomalies or failures when they occur. An anomaly usually attempts to compromise the defence mechanism and to degrade the performance of a network. An anomaly may arise due to various reasons, as discussed in Chapter 2. It may occur due to malicious actions (e.g., scanning or denial of service) or due to misconfigurations and failures of network hardware and software components (e.g., disruption of link or routing problems) or even legitimate but rare events such as strange large file transfers or flash crowds. The purpose of an anomaly detection mechanism is to analyze, understand and characterize network traffic behavior, as well as to identify or classify the abnormal traffic instances such as malicious attempts from normal instances. So, from a machine lerarning perspective, the anomaly detection problem is a classification problem. Our literature survey [139] shows that the existing anomaly classification methods work basically in four modes, as given below.

(i) *Supervised anomaly detection*: Techniques trained in supervised mode need a training dataset which has labeled instances for normal as well as anomaly classes. The typical approach in such cases is to build a predictive model for normal vs. anomaly classes. Any unseen data instance is compared against the model to determine which class it belongs to. There are two major issues that arise in supervised anomaly detection. First, usually anomalous instances are far fewer compared to normal instances in the training data. Issues that arise due to imbalanced class distributions have been addressed in the data mining and machine learning literature [191]. Second, obtaining accurate and representative labels, especially for the anomaly classes, is usually challenging. A number of techniques have been proposed that inject artificial anomalies in a normal dataset to obtain a labeled training dataset [366]. Other than these two issues, the supervised anomaly detection problem is similar to building predictive models.

(ii) *Semi-supervised anomaly detection*: Techniques that operate in a semi-supervised mode assume that the training data has labeled instances for only the normal class. Since they do not require labels for the anomaly class, they are more widely applicable than supervised techniques. For example, in spacecraft fault detection

[125], an anomaly scenario may signify an accident, which is not easy to model. The typical approach used in such techniques is to build a model for the class corresponding to normal behavior and use the model to identify anomalies in the test data.

(iii) *Unsupervised anomaly detection*: Techniques that operate in unsupervised mode do not require training data and thus are more difficult to use to achieve the goals at hand. Generally, the techniques in this category make the implicit assumption that normal instances are far more frequent than anomalies in the test data. If this assumption is not true, such techniques suffer from a high false alarm rate. Many semi-supervised techniques can be adapted to operate in an unsupervised mode by using a sample of the unlabeled dataset as training data. Such adaptation assumes that the test data contains very few anomalies and the model learned during training is robust in spite of these few anomalies.

(iv) *Hybrid anomaly detection*: A hybrid intrusion detection method combines supervised and unsupervised network intrusion detection methods. Supervised methods have the advantage of being able to detect known attacks with high accuracy and low false alarms. On the other hand, an unsupervised method has the ability to detect novel attacks. Thus, a hybrid intrusion detection method is capable of detecting both known as well as unknown attacks with high accuracy.

In this chapter, we discuss each of these approaches in terms of architectures and components and also highlight various pertinent issues. We also discuss several other important aspects of network anomaly detection. Our discussion in this chapter is restricted to only three major approaches, i.e., supervised, unsupervised and hybrid.

4.1.4   Supervised Anomaly Detection Approach

Supervised network anomaly detection attempts to classify network traffic into normal and various attack categories based on the characteristics or features of the traffic with reference to a set of labeled training sample instances. To provide an appropriate solution in network anomaly detection, we need the concept of *normality*. The idea of normality is usually introduced by a formal model that expresses relations among the fundamental variables involved in system dynamics. Consequently, an event or an object is detected as anomalous if its degree of deviation with respect to the profile or behavior of the system, specified by the normality model, is high enough. For better understanding, let us take a supervised anomaly detection system S. It can be defined as a pair (M, D), where M is the model of normal behavior of the system and D is a proximity measure that allows one to compute, given an activity record, the degree of deviation that such activities have with regard to the model M. So, each such system has two basic modules: (i) a modeling module and (ii) a detection module. One trains the system to generate the normality model M. The obtained model is subsequently used by the detection module to evaluate new events or objects or traffic instances as anomalous or outliers. It is the measurement of deviation that allows classification of events or objects as anomalous or outliers. In particular, the modeling module needs to be adaptive to cope with dynamic scenarios.

A Generic Architecture

The responsibilities of a supervised network intrusion detection system are (i) to monitor events occurring in a network or in a computer system and (ii) to analyze them for nonconforming patterns or intrusions. Anomaly-based intrusion detection characterizes the "normal" behavior of the system to be protected and generates alarm information when significant deviation is observed in an instance compared to predefined normal behavior [63, 297, 141]. Another way is to say that an IDS models anomalous behavior due to the occurrence of certain event(s) and generates alarms when the deviation between the observed pattern and the expected pattern(s) becomes noticeable [63, 62, 423, 141]. A generic architecture of a supervised anomaly detection system (ANIDS) is shown in Figure 4.1. The basic components of such a system are given below.

(i) *Traffic Capture*: Traffic capturing is an important module in any NIDS. The raw traffic data is captured at both packet and flow levels. Packet level traffic can be captured using a common tool, e.g., Gulp, Wireshark[1] and then preprocessed before sending to

---

[1]http://www.wireshark.org/

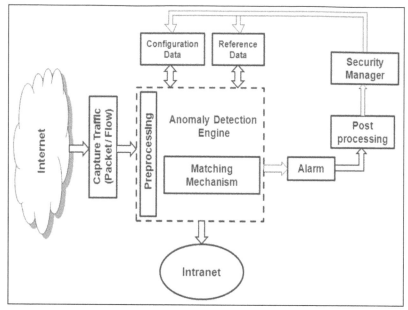

FIGURE 4.1:   A generic architecture of supervised ANIDS

the detection engine. Flow level data, in case of high speed networks, is composed of information summarized from one or more packets. Some common tools to capture the flow level network traffic include Nfdump[2], NfSen[3] and Cisco Netflow V.9[4]. A detailed discussion of a large number of tools is available in Chapter 8. The components of a network traffic capture tool are given in Figure 4.2. The raw Internet traffic captured and buffered through the network adapter is stored in a file in tcpdump format. It uses the *libpcap* library to receive and store the filtered traffic in tcpdump format.

(ii) *Anomaly Detection Engine*: This is the heart of any network anomaly detection system. It attempts to detect the occurrence of any intrusion either online or offline. In general, any network traffic data needs preprocessing before it is sent to the detection engine. If the attacks are known, they can be detected using a misuse detection approach. Unknown attacks can be detected

---

[2]http://nfdump.sourceforge.net/
[3]http://nfsen.sourceforge.net/
[4]http://www.cisco.com/en/US/docs/ios/12_3/feature/gde/nfv9expf.html

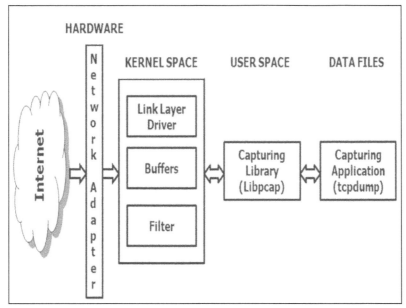

FIGURE 4.2: Network traffic capturing components

with the anomaly-based approach using an appropriate matching mechanism. The following are some important requirements that a matching mechanism must satisfy.

- Matching must be fast.
- Matching may be inexact. The membership of a test instance in a given predefined class represented by its profile depends on (a) the proximity computed between the profile and the new test instance using a relevant subspace of features and (b) a user-defined proximity threshold. Thus, the selection of an appropriate proximity measure and an appropriate threshold is crucial here.
- The profiles must be efficiently organized to facilitate improved search performance.

(iii) *Reference Data*: The reference data stores information about signatures or profiles of known intrusions or normal behavior. Reference data must be stored in an efficient manner. Possible types of reference data used in the generic architecture of a NIDS are shown in Figure 4.3. In the case of an ANIDS, it is mostly profiles.

The processing elements update the profiles as new knowledge about the observed behavior becomes available. These updates are performed in a batch-oriented fashion by resolving conflicts if they arise.

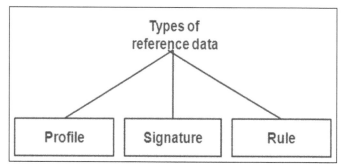

FIGURE 4.3:   Types of references used in supervised NIDS

(iv) *Configuration Data*: Intermediate results such as partially created intrusion signatures are stored as configuration data. The space needed to store such information can be quite large. The main steps for updating configuration data are given in Figure 4.4.

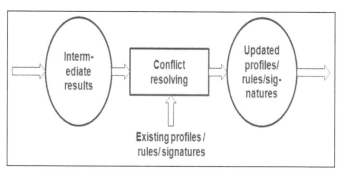

FIGURE 4.4:   Steps for updating configuration data in ANIDS

(v) *Alarm*: This component of the architecture is responsible for the generation of an alarm based on the indication received from the Detection Engine. In addition to indicating the occurrence of an attack, alarms are useful for post-diagnosis of the performance of the detection system. Alarms should indicate (a) the causes for the alarm to be raised, (b) the source IP/port address and target IP/port address associated with the attack and (c) any background information to justify why it is a putative alarm.

(vi) *Post-Processing*: This is an important module that processes the generated alarms for diagnosis of actual attacks. Appropriate post-processing activities can help reduce the false positive rate significantly.

(vii) *Security Manager*: Stored intrusion signatures are updated by the Security Manager (SM) as and when new intrusions become known. The analysis of novel intrusions is a highly complex task. The SM has a multifaceted role to play, such as (i) to analyze alarm data, (ii) to recognize novel intrusion(s) and (iii) to update the signature or profile base.

4.1.5 Issues

In supervised anomaly detection, frequently the normal behavior model is established by training the system with a labeled or purely normal dataset. These normal behavior models are used to classify new network connections. The system generates an alert if a connection is classified as abnormal. In practice, to train a supervised ANIDS, an exhaustive collection of labeled or purely normal data may not be easily available. Acquiring such a complete and pure normal dataset is a time-consuming task and requires the involvement of skilled security professionals. Moreover, the manual labeling task is error-prone.

4.1.6 Unsupervised Anomaly Detection Approach

In network-based intrusion detection, frequently new or previously unknown threats arise. A possible detection approach for novel intrusions is anomaly based. In anomaly-based supervised detection, obtaining labeled or purely normal data is an onerous problem. Unsupervised anomaly-based detection can be used for novel intrusion detection without prior knowledge or purely normal data. Unsupervised network anomaly detection works well due to two major reasons:

(i) nonavailability of labeled or purely normal data and (ii) expense of manual classification of a large volume of network traffic. When collecting normal traffic data, it is extremely difficult to guarantee that there is no anomalous instance. In the literature [224, 225, 74, 429], clustering is a widely used method for anomaly-based unsupervised detection of intrusions. From classical data mining, we know that clustering is a method of grouping of objects based on similarity among the objects. The similarity within a cluster is high whereas dissimilarity among clusters is high. Clustering is a method of unsupervised study and analysis [423]. Clustering is performed on unlabeled data. It places similar data in the same class and dissimilar data in different classes. Unsupervised anomaly detection clusters test dataset into groups of similar instances which may be either intrusion or normal data.

A generic architecture of an unsupervised ANIDS is given in Figure 4.5. The architecture includes almost all the modules found in a supervised ANIDS. However, two modules, the detection engine and the labeling technique, are different. We discuss these two modules next.

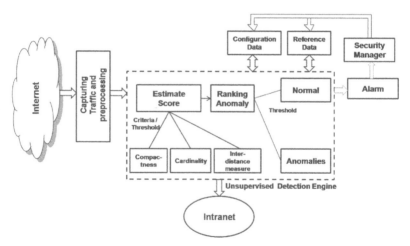

FIGURE 4.5:   A generic architecture of unsupervised ANIDS

(i) *Unsupervised Engine*: This is the actual anomaly detection component of the system. It consists of two modules, *Detection* and *Label*. Based on the approach used, the Detection module either groups similar instances or identifies exceptional instances in input data. The Label module works after completion of the Detection module to label instances either as normal or anomalous based on the characteristics of each individual group, such as size, compactness and the dominating subset of features.

(ii) *Labeling Strategy*: A clustering method merely groups the data, without any interpretation of the nature of the groups. To support appropriate interpretation of the groups, labeling techniques are used. Although clustering generates the clusters, labeling of these clusters is a difficult issue. A labeling strategy typically makes the following assumptions [297].

- The number of normal instances vastly outnumbers the number of anomalous instances.

- Anomalies themselves are qualitatively different from normal instances.

- Similarity among the instances of an anomalous group is higher than the same in a normal group of instances.

Based on the first assumption, we can surmise that larger clusters correspond to normal data and smaller clusters correspond to intrusions. However, a method based simply on this assumption may lead to a large number of false alarms, since it may not be always true in practice. For example, most DoS and DDoS (Distributed Denial of Service) attacks usually generate a large number of similar instances which may form clusters that are larger than a cluster that corresponds to normal behavior. On the other hand, clusters of anomalous instances belonging to remote to local (R2L) and user to root (U2R) anomaly categories are quite similar to clusters of normal or legitimate user request instances. Thus, anomalous groups identified by unsupervised methods may include normal instances. Consequently, these can raise the false alarm rate. However, the second and third assumptions enable us to handle this issue in an appropriate manner. Therefore, our strategy must not decide the label of a test instance based simply on the size of the group, but it must also consider characteristics such as compactness and dominating feature subset.

An example labeling strategy, available in [355], attempts to solve this problem based on such characteristics. To estimate the compactness of a group, cluster quality indices are often used to distinguish clusters from one another. Dunn's index [107], C-index [180], Davies–Bouldin's index [91], Silhouette index [316] and Xie–Beni's index [390] are some commonly used cluster indices.

4.1.7 Issues

Unsupervised anomaly detection approaches work without any training data. In other words, these models are trained on unlabeled or unclassified data and they attempt to find intrusions lurking inside the data. The biggest advantage of the anomaly detection approach is the detection of unknown intrusions without any previous knowledge. In order to label clusters, an unsupervised ANIDS models normal behavior by using certain assumptions [297]. If these assumptions hold, intrusive instances can be identified based on characteristics of the group the instances belong to. However, these assumptions are not always true, especially in the case of DDoS attacks. Therefore, accurate labeling of an instance is a significant and crucial issue in an unsupervised ANIDS.

4.1.8 Hybrid Detection Approach

A hybrid anomaly detection approach combines both supervised and unsupervised methods of network anomaly detection. Such approaches can detect known as well as unknown attacks. A hybrid approach attempts to identify known attacks based on a supervised model with reference to a set of training sample data, using an appropriate matching mechanism. The test instances that neither belong to normal nor to any of the known attack instances are handled by the unsupervised model for the identification of new normal or novel intrusions. In the recent past, several successful ANIDSs have been developed [420, 400, 343, 28].

A Generic Architecture

A generic architecture of a hybrid ANIDS is given in Figure 4.6. The modules in this architecture are the same as the ones found in the supervised and unsupervised architectures. As shown in the figure, the unsupervised method is used for only those undetected test instances forwarded by the supervised method. Once a novel intrusion

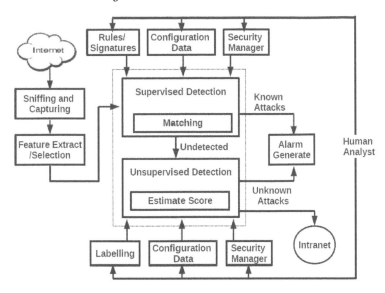

FIGURE 4.6: A generic architecture of a hybrid ANIDS

is identified and confirmed, its reference (e.g., rule or signature) is built
and inserted into the rulebase for future reference of the supervised
module.

4.1.9   Issues

The performance of an individual classifier, either supervised or unsupervised, is not equally good for classification of all categories of
attack as well as normal instances. It is possible to obtain good classification accuracy for all categories in a dataset by using an appropriate
combination of multiple well-performing classifiers. The objective of
such a combination is to provide the best performance from each of the
participating classifiers for each of the attack classes. The selection of
a supervised or unsupervised classifier at a particular level for a given
dataset is the critical issue for the hybrid ANIDS.

4.2   Aspects of Network Anomaly Detection

In this section we introduce readers to three important topics in
network anomaly detection, viz., proximity measures, relevant feature

selection and anomaly scores. The success of an ANIDS depends on each of these. The proper selection or use of a good approach in each of these can improve the performance of an ANIDS significantly.

4.2.1   Proximity Measure and Types of Data

In solving any pattern recognition problem, such as classification, clustering or information retrieval, using supervised or unsupervised learning, the choice of proximity measure plays an important role. The proximity measure can be either a dissimilarity or a similarity measure. From a mathematical point of view, distance, a synonym of dissimilarity, between a pair of objects quantifies how far apart the objects are from each other. All distance measures may not satisfy the metric properties of *nonnegativity, symmetricity* and *triangular inequality*. Distance measures which do not satisfy the metric properties are called *divergence*. Similarity measures are also referred to as similarity coefficients by some. The choice of a proximity measure for a set of objects depends on (i) the type of data used to represent the objects, (ii) the type of measurement required and (iii) the number of attributes or dimensionality of the dataset. Proximity measures differ based on the type of data used, i.e., *numeric, categorical* or *mixed-type*. To define an appropriate distance measure for a set of *numeric* data objects, which may be discrete or continuous, one can usually exploit the geometric properties of the representations of the objects. Detailed discussions on various numeric proximity measures are available in [61, 141, 139]. To handle categorical data, either a data-driven categorical proximity measure can be used or one can adopt an appropriate procedure to encode the categorical data into binary or numeric and subsequently use any proximity measure for such data. A detailed discussion on categorical proximity measures is available in [48, 139]. Handling of mixed-type data is more complex, especially when the attributes have different weights. Two straightforward ways of handling mixed type data are (i) to represent categorical values using numeric values and to use a numeric proximity measure or (ii) to convert the numeric values into categorical and to use categorical proximity measures. One can also handle mixed-type data by directly finding proximity [139] between a pair of categorical values using an exact matching approach. If the values are identical, the distance will be 0 and 1 if they are distinct. A detailed discussion on mixed-type proximity measures can be found in [139].

4.2.2 Relevant Feature Identification

Feature selection plays a significant role in anomaly detection. Feature selection methods have been used in intrusion detection to eliminate unimportant or irrelevant features. Feature selection reduces computational complexity, eliminates information redundancy, increases the accuracy of the detection algorithm, facilitates data understanding and improves generalization. Feature selection algorithms have been classified into wrapper, filter, embedded and hybrid methods [15]. While *wrapper* methods optimize some predefined criteria in respect to the feature set as part of the selection process, *filter* methods rely on the general characteristics of the training data to select features that are independent of one another and are highly dependent on the output. Feature selection methods use a search algorithm to navigate through the whole feature space and evaluate possible subsets. To evaluate these subsets, one needs a feature goodness measure that grades any subset of features. In general, a feature is good if it is relevant to the output and is not redundant with respect to other relevant features. A feature goodness measure helps evaluate the relevance, strong or weak, of a feature to a given class. A detailed discussion of this important aspect is available in Chapter 5.

4.2.3 Anomaly Score

Detection of anomalies depends on scoring techniques that assign an anomaly score to each instance in the test data. A score specifies the degree to which an instance is considered anomalous. Thus the output of such a technique is a ranked list of anomalies. An analyst may choose to either analyze the top few anomalies or use a cut-off threshold to select anomalies from the list. Several anomaly score estimation techniques have been recently developed. These techniques can be classified into three broad categories: *distance based, density based* and *machine learning or soft computing based.* Below, we discuss anomaly score estimation for each of these categories.

A **Distance-based anomaly score estimation**
  Several authors define anomaly scores and formulate effective estimation techniques using the distance based approach. We discuss a few of such efforts, in brief.

A.1 *LOADED (Link-Based Outlier and Anomaly Detection in Evolving Datasets) anomaly score estimation* [134]: This method assumes that a dataset contains both continuous and categorical attributes. It computes a measure of link strength using a similarity metric to define the degree of association or linkage between the points. Two data points p_i and p_j are assumed to be linked if they are considerably similar to each other. p_i and p_j are linked over a categorical attribute space if they have at least one pair of attribute values in common. Thus, the associated link strength between two points is simply the number of common attribute-value pairs shared between the points. The score function developed based on frequent itemset mining assigns a score to a point that is inversely proportional to the sum of the strengths of all its links. Let I be the set of all possible attribute value pairs in the dataset M. Let $D = \{d : d \in PowerSet(I) \land \forall_{i,j:i\neq j} d_i \cdot attrib \neq d_j \cdot attrib\}$ be the set of all itemsets, where an attribute occurs only once per itemset. The score function for a *categorical* attribute is defined as

$$Score_1(p_i) = \sum_{d \subseteq p_i} \left(\frac{1}{|d|} |supp(d) \leq s \right) \tag{4.1}$$

where p_i is an ordered set of categorical attributes. $supp(d)$ is the number of points p_i in the dataset where $d \subseteq p_i$, otherwise known as the *support* of itemset d. $|d|$ is the number of attribute-value pairs in d. s is a user-defined threshold of minimum support or minimum number of links.

A point is defined to be linked to another point in the mixed data space if they are linked together in the categorical data space and if their continuous attributes adhere to the joint distribution as indicated by a correlation matrix. Points that violate these conditions are defined to be outliers. The modified score function for a mixed attribute is

$$Score_2(p_i) = \sum_{d \subseteq p_i} \left(\frac{1}{|d|} |(C_1 \lor C_2) \land C_3 \text{ is true} \right) \tag{4.2}$$

where $C_1 \equiv sup(d) \leq s$, $C_2 \equiv$ at least $\delta\%$ of the correlation coefficients disagree with the distribution followed by the continuous attributes for point p_i and $C_3 \equiv C_1$ or C_2 hold true for every superset of d in p_i. Condition C_1 is the same condition used to find outliers in a categorical data space using $Score_1(p_i)$. Condition C_2 adds continuous attribute checks to $Score_1(p_i)$. Condition C_3 is a heuristic and allows for more efficient processing because if an itemset does not satisfy conditions C_1 and C_2, none of its subsets are considered.

A.2 *RELOADED (REduced memory LOADED) Anomaly Score* [275]: RELOADED score defines an anomalous data point as one that has a subset of attributes that take on unusual values, given the values of the other attributes. When all categorical attributes of a data point have been processed, the anomaly score of the data point is computed as a function of the count of incorrect predictions and the violation score as

$$Score[P_i] = \frac{\left(\frac{\sum_{j=1}^{m} i - W_j}{i}\right)}{m} + \frac{V_\tau}{mn^2} \qquad (4.3)$$

where W_j is the cumulative number of incorrect predictions of categorical attribute j for the previous i data points. There are m categorical attributes and n continuous attributes. V_τ is the cumulative violation score of point P_i.

B **Density-based anomaly score estimation**
The density based approach has been shown to be quite useful for various machine learning tasks. Here, we discuss a *density-based* anomaly score estimation technique for mixed-type attributes.

B.1 *ODMAD (Outlier Detection for Mixed Attribute Datasets) Anomaly Score* [206]: OMAD computes an anomaly score for each categorical or mixed-type test instance by considering the irregularity of the categorical values, the continuous values and the relationship between the two different types of attribute spaces. For a given instance X_i over a categorical space in dataset D, the authors define a score estimation technique as follows.

$$Score_1(X_i) = \sum_{d \subseteq X_i \wedge supp(d) < \delta \wedge |d| \leq Max} \frac{1}{supp(d) \times |d|}. \qquad (4.4)$$

Here, $|d|$ is the size of the set d. δ and Max are a user-defined support threshold and the size of the attribute set, respectively. An instance is anomalous if it contains single values that are infrequent or sets of values that are infrequent. A categorical value or a combination of values is infrequent if it appears less than δ times in the dataset.

The authors also introduce a modified score estimation technique for mixed-type data that works with categorical values as well as continuous values as

$$Score_2(X_i) = \frac{1}{|a \in X_i^c|} \times \sum_{\forall a \in X_i^c} cos\left(X_i^q, \mu_a\right) \qquad (4.5)$$

where X_i is an instance of mixed-type data containing m_c categorical values and m_q continuous values. X_i^c and X_i^q are, respectively, the categorical and continuous parts of X_i. Let a be one of the categorical values of X_i^c that occurs with support $supp(a)$. μ_a is the mean and $cos\left(X_i^q, \mu_a\right)$ represents the cosine similarity between point X_i^q and μ_a. As the minimum cosine similarity is 0 and maximum 1, instances with similarity close to 0 are more likely to be outliers.

C Soft computing and machine learning-based score estimation

We now introduce our readers to some outlier estimation efforts based on soft computing and other machine learning approaches.

C.1 *RNN (Replicator Neural Network) Outlier Detection Anomaly Score* [164]: The anomaly score δ_i of the i-th data record is a measure of its outlyingness. δ_i is defined by the average reconstruction error over all features (variables) as

$$\delta_i = \frac{1}{n} \sum_{j=1}^{n} (x_{ij} - o_{ij})^2 \qquad (4.6)$$

where x_{ij}'s are reconstruction data instances, o_{ij} is a reconstruction output instance and n is the number of features over which the data is defined. The reconstruction error is used as the anomaly score.

C.2 *GMM (Gaussian Mixture Model) Anomaly Detection* [347]: Assume each data instance d is represented as $[x, y]$. If U is the contextual data and V the behavioral data, the mapping function $p(V_j|U_i)$ indicates the probability of the indicator part of a data point y to be generated from a mixture component V_j, when the environmental part x is generated by U_i. The anomaly score for a test instance d is given as

$$\text{Anomaly Score } = \sum_{i=1}^{n_U} p(x \in U_i) \sum_{j=1}^{n_V} p(y \in V_j)\, p(V_j|U_i) \quad (4.7)$$

where n_U is the number of mixture components in U and n_V is the number of mixture components in V. $p(x \in U_i)$ indicates the probability that a sample point x is generated from the mixture component U_i while $p(y \in V_j)$ indicates the probability that a sample point y is generated from the mixture component V_j.

C.3 *Markov Chain Model Anomaly Score* [402]: This model is used to represent the temporal profile of normal behavior in a computer or network system. The Markov chain model for the normal profile is learned from historic data collected from the system's normal behavior. The observed behavior of the system is analyzed to infer the probability that the Markov chain model of a normal profile supports the observed behavior. A low probability of support indicates an anomalous behavior that may result from intrusive activities. The likelihood $P(S)$ of sequence S is given as

$$P(S) = q_{S_1} \prod_{t=2}^{|S|} p_{S_{t-1}S_t} \quad (4.8)$$

where q_{S_1} is the probability of observing the symbol S_1 in the training set and $p_{S_{t-1}S_t}$ is the probability of observing the symbol S_t after S_{t-1} in the training set. The inverse of $P(S)$ is the anomaly score for the given sequence S.

A general comparison of the anomaly or outlier scores estimation techniques discussed above is given in Table 4.1. We see in the table that most score estimation methods can handle mixed data.

In addition to the important topics in network anomaly detection discussed above, a network security researcher or professional needs to have knowledge of existing intrusion datasets available for evaluating the performance of an ANIDS. In the following section, we discuss characteristics of several intrusion datasets available in the public domain and the testbeds used for their generation.

TABLE 4.1:   Anomaly Score Estimation: A General Comparison

Author & Year	Score Formula		Approach	Data type
Ye, 2000	$P(S) = q_{S_1} \prod\limits_{t=2}^{|S|} p_{S_{t-1}S_t}$		Soft computing based using HMM [402]	Mixed
Hawkins, 2002	$\delta_i = \frac{1}{n} \sum\limits_{j=1}^{n} (x_{ij} - o_{ij})^2$		Soft computing based using RNN [164]	Categorical
Ghoting, 2004	$Score_1(p_i)$ $\sum\limits_{d \subseteq p_i} \left(\frac{1}{|d|} |sup(d) \le s \right)$	=	Distance based	Categorical
Ghoting, 2004	$Score_2(p_i) = \sum\limits_{d \subseteq p_i} \left(\frac{1}{|d|} |(C1 \vee C2) \wedge C3 \text{ is true} \right)$		Distance based	Mixed
Otey, 2005	$Anomaly\ Score[P_i] = \left(\frac{\sum_{j=1}^{m} i - W_j}{i} \right)/m + \frac{V_\tau}{mn^2}$		Distance based	Mixed
Song, 2007	$Anomaly \qquad Score$ $\sum\limits_{i=1}^{n_U} p(x \in U_i) \sum\limits_{j=1}^{n_V} p(y \in V_j)\ p(V_j|U_i)$	=	Soft computing based in GMM-CAD [347]	Mixed
Koufakou, 2010	$Score_1(X_i)$ $\sum\limits_{d \subseteq X_i \wedge supp(d) < \sigma \wedge |d| \le Max} \dfrac{1}{supp(d) \times |d|}$	=	Density-based	Categorical
Koufakou, 2010	$Score_2(X_i)$ $\frac{1}{|a \in X_i^c|} \times \sum\limits_{\forall a \in X_i^c} cos\left(X_i^q, \bar{\mu}_a \right)$	=	Density-based approach	Mixed

4.3   Datasets

Various security research groups have introduced several network intrusion datasets to support assessment of intrusion detection methods for known as well as unknown attacks. These datasets can be classified into three categories based on their sources as (i) public datasets, (ii) private datasets and (iii) network simulation datasets. Out of these three, the datasets used in the third category are not truly intrusion datasets; rather they are created by simulating normal and attack traffic by considering various attack scenarios. A large number of tools are also used in generating most public and private intrusion datasets. These tools assist (i) in identifying victims, (ii) in capturing and pre-process traffic, (iii) in launching attacks of various types and (iv) in monitoring traffic patterns. We discuss some of these datasets and how they are generated in detail below.

4.3.1 Public Datasets

In this section, we describe three commonly used datasets, their characteristics, list of attacks covered by the datasets and the distribution of the attacks in these datasets and the testbeds used for their generation. With increased sophistication of attackers' skills and due to imbalanced distribution of attack and normal traffic in these datasets, these datasets are often considered old and biased and hence insufficient to establish the effectiveness of an ANIDS in the present day network scenario. However, for a network security researcher or practitioner, it is quite essential to acquire knowledge of these datasets, how they were generated and their strengths and weaknesses. This knowledge can be of great help for researchers in creating their own testbed for capturing, pre-processing, extracting features of various types and in generating an unbiased dataset.

4.3.1.1 KDD Cup 1999 Dataset

The KDD Cup 1999 [195] is an intrusion detection benchmark dataset. In this dataset, the connection between two network hosts is represented in a record in terms of 41 attributes, where 38 are numeric continuous and numeric discrete and 3 are categorical attributes. Each record is labeled as either normal or as a specific kind of attack. The attacks belong to one of four categories: *Denial of Service* (DoS), *Remote to Local* (R2L), *User to Root* (U2R) and *Probe*. A detailed discussion of these attack types and their respective tools is available in Chapter 8. We now present statistics regarding the distribution of attack and normal instances in this dataset, followed by the testbed used for its generation.

(i) *Dataset Characteristics:* This benchmark intrusion dataset is available in two versions: (a) *Corrected KDD* dataset and (b)

10 *percent KDD* dataset. The numbers of samples of each category of attacks in these two versions are shown in Table 4.2.

TABLE 4.2: Attack Distribution in KDD Cup Datasets

Datasets	*DoS*	*U2R*	*R2L*	*Probe*	*Normal*	*Total*
Corrected KDD	229853	70	16347	4166	60593	311029
10-percent KDD	391458	52	1126	4107	97278	494021

The description of attacks of each category in the KDD Cup 1999 dataset is given in Table 4.3.

TABLE 4.3: KDD Cup Attack List

Name	DoS Attack
	Prevents valid users from using a service of a system
Smurf	A spoofed source address is flooded with echo replies. The replies are caused when many ping (ICMP echo) requests using the spoofed source address are sent to one or more broadcast or multicast addresses.
Neptune	Session establishment packets are sent against a victim machine using a forged source IP address and resources of the victim machine are used up to wait for the session to be established.
Back	An attacker requests an Apache server with a URL consisting of several backslashes.
Teardrop	It is attempted to reboot some systems by using misfragmented UDP packets.
Ping-of-death	Large sized packets are sent over a network by fragmenting and reassembling at the destination using the Ping command. On reassembly the excess packet size causes buffer overflow where the OS either crashes, aborts or hangs.
Land	Attacker attempts to modify the packet header by sending messages to a system with an IP address indicating that the message is initiated from a trusted host.
	R2L Attack
	To gain entrance to victim machine without having an account on it
FTP-write	Takes advantage of a common anonymous FTP misconfiguration. It is possible if the anonymous FTP root directory or its subdirectories are owned by the FTP account or they are in the same group as the FTP account and they are not write protected.
Guess-password	To discover passwords through telnet or a guest account.
Imap	Remote buffer overflow uses the imap port leading to root shell.

Continued on next page

TABLE 4.3 – continued from previous page

Multihop	Attempts to break into one machine in a multiday scenario.
Phf	Exploitable CGI scripts are used to enable a client to execute any command on a machine with a misconfigured web server.
Spy	In a multiday scenario, attempts to break into a system by applying several different exploiting methods to find sensitive information.
Warezclient	Attempts to download illegal software, previously posted by the warezmaster through an anonymous FTP.
Warzmaster	Anonymous FTP upload of warez (here a user attempts to log into an anonymous FTP site and execute a hidden directory to keep illegal copies of copyrighted software) onto an FTP server.

U2R Attack
Attempts to gain privilege of superuser

Buffer-overflow	Server receives data/commands from client and stores in stacks (contiguous). Attempts to infiltrate the server by sending a block of data from a client longer than the application or process is expecting.
Loadmodule	The attacker attempts to reset IFS for a legitimate user and a root shell is created.
Perl	Perl sets the user ID to root in a perl script and creates a root shell.
Rootkit	In a multiday scenario, an attacker installs one or more components of a rootkit.

Probe Attack
Attempts to gather information about target host

Ipsweep	It performs either a port sweep or ping on multiple host addresses.
Nmap	Network mapping using the nmap tool to map the network.
Portsweep	It performs a sweep across many ports to determine the services which are supported during a period on a single specific host.
SATAN	SATAN (Security Administrator Tool for Analyzing Networks) is a tool to probe the network for well-known vulnerabilities of a network.

4.3.1.2   NSL-KDD Dataset

NSL-KDD [273] is a network-based intrusion dataset. It is a filtered version of the KDD Cup 1999 intrusion detection benchmark dataset generated using the same testbed as described above. In the KDD Cup 1999 dataset, a large number of instances are redundant, potentially biasing learning mechanisms toward frequent records. To solve this problem, only one copy of duplicate records is kept in the NSL-KDD dataset. The NSL-KDD consists of two datasets: (i) $KDDTrain^+$ and (ii) $KDDTest^+$. The numbers of samples of each attack category in the NSL-KDD datasets are shown in Table 4.4.

TABLE 4.4:   Attack Distribution in NSL-KDD Datasets

Datasets	DoS	U2R	R2L	Probe	Normal	Total
$KDDTrain^+$	45927	52	995	11656	67343	125973
$KDDTest^+$	7458	67	2887	2422	9710	22544

4.3.2   Private Datasets: Collection and Preparation

4.3.2.1   TUIDS Intrusion Dataset

The TUIDS dataset was collected and prepared by the authors of this book and their students at Tezpur University [140]. The generation of the dataset involves a number of tasks to extract features from network packet and flow data using a laboratory where isolated networks were set up. We use existing attack tools to generate attacks against a local network server or host and collect the produced traffic as known attack traffic. Based on the type, characteristics and attack distribution used, TUIDS datasets are categorized: (i) packet traffic feature dataset, (ii) network flow traffic feature dataset and (iii) portscan. The dimensionalities of these datasets, which depend on the features extracted, are different. We now discuss the testbed used to generate these datasets and then describe the process of the generation of these datasets, along with some characteristics of these datasets.

(i) *Testbed Used*: The setup of the testbed for network traffic capture includes two L2 switches, one L3 switch, one router, one server, two workstations and 40 nodes. Using the L3 and the L2 switches, six VLANs are created. Nodes and workstations are connected to separate VLANs. The L3 switch is connected to an internal IP router and the router is connected to the Internet through an external IP router. To observe traffic activity to the switch, the server is connected to the L3 switch through a mirror port. Another LAN of 350 nodes is connected to other VLANs through five L3 and L2 switches and three routers. The attacks are launched within our testbed as well as from another LAN through the Internet. To launch attacks within the testbed, nodes of one VLAN are attacked from nodes of another VLAN as well as the same VLAN. Normal traffic is created within our testbed in a restricted manner after disconnecting the other LAN. Traffic activities to our testbed are observed on the computer connected to the mirror port. The diagram in Figure 4.7 shows how

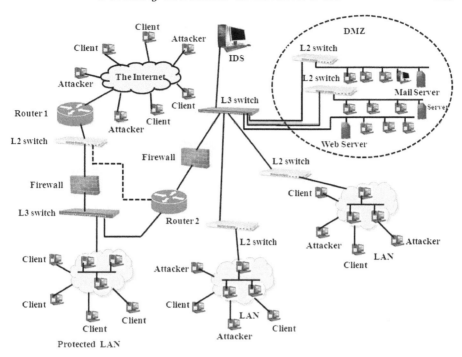

FIGURE 4.7:   Testbed for generation of the TUIDS intrusion dataset

the TUIDS intrusion detection datasets are generated using the testbed. The attacks for which we capture data and the tools [85], [14] used to generate the traffic are presented in Table 4.6. The description of the attacks is given in Table 4.5.

Table 4.5: Description of Attacks Present in the TUIDS Datasets

Name	Description
Bonk	Manipulates the fragment offset field in TCP/IP packets to cause the victim machine to reorganize packets so that they are too large to reassemble.
Jolt	Sends very large, fragmented ICMP packets to the victim machine to cause incompatibility when the victim machine tries to rebuild them for use.
Land	Sends a TCP SYN spoofed packet with the target host's IP address and an open port used as source and destination port to cause the victim machine to respond to itself.
Nestea	Launches IP fragments to a Linux machine connected to the Internet/network and exploits a bug called the *off by one IP header* bug in the refragmentation code.
Newtear	Attempts to misform UDP header information, which changes padding length and increases the UDP header length field to twice the size of the packet.
	Continued on next page

Table 4.5 – continued from previous page

Name	Description
Syndrop	Makes the size of the packet too small to create a kernel problem, which may lead to crash of the system.
Teardrop	Exploits an overlapping IP fragment bug causing the TCP/IP fragmentation reassembly code to improperly handle overlapping IP fragments.
Winnuke	Sends OOB (Out-of-Band) data to a Windows machine on the Internet/network through port 139. On receipt, the victim machine is unable to handle resulting in odd system behavior.
1234	Sends an oversized ping packet that cannot be handled by the network software, causing the victim machine to slow down until it hangs.
Saihyousen	Sends a stream of UDP packets causing firewalls to crash. It consumes resources and causes a messy reboot if it continues for 10–30 seconds after the machine freezes.
Oshare	Sends a novel packet structure to Windows 98 and NT machines to increase CPU load or cause momentary delays, depending upon configuration of the computer.
Smurf	Sends a large number of ICMP echo request (ping) packets to IP broadcast addresses, where all of them have the spoofed source IP address of the targeted victim.
Fraggle	Sends a large number of UDP echo packets to IP broadcast addresses, where all of them have a spoofed source address.
Syn Scan	This default scan acts on any compliant TCP stack. A SYN packet indicates the port is open (listening), while an RST (reset) is indicative of a nonlistener. If a SYN packet is received in response, the port is considered open.
Xmass Tree Scan	This scan sets the flags such as TCP FIN, PSH and URG. A port is considered closed if an RST packet is received and it is open when no response comes. If an ICMP unreachable error is received, the port is marked filtered.
Window Scan	It examines the returned RST packets in the TCP Window field. On some systems, closed ports use a zero window size while open ports use a nonzero window size. So instead of listing a port every time as unfiltered on receipt of RST return, this scan lists the port as open or closed depending on the window size.

(ii) *Characteristics of Packet Traffic Feature Datasets*: Packet level network traffic is captured using the open source software tool called *gulp* [322]. Gulp captures packets directly from the network and can write to disk at a high rate because of its enhanced buffering technique. The packets are analyzed using the open source packet analyzing software called *wireshark* [80]. The raw packet data is preprocessed and filtered before extraction and construction of new features. From the packet level network traffic, 50 features are extracted. To extract these features, we use the open source tool called *tcptrace* [338], *C* programs and *Perl*

TABLE 4.6: Attacks and Tools Used in TUIDS Datasets

Attack Values	Generation Tool	Attack Values	Generation Tool
bonk	*targa2.c*	1234	*targa2.c*
jolt	*targa2.c*	*saihyousen*	*targa2.c*
land	*targa2.c*	*oshare*	*targa2.c*
nestea	*targa2.c*	*window*	*targa2.c*
newtear	*targa2.c*	*syn*	*Nmap*
syndrop	*targa2.c*	*xmas*	*Nmap*
teardrop	*targa2.c*	*fraggle*	*fraggle.c*
winnuke	*targa2.c*	*smurf*	*smurf4.c*

scripts. These features are classified as (i) *basic*, (ii) *content based*, (iii) *time based* and (iv) *connection based*. The list of features is given in Tables 4.7–4.10.

(iii) *Characteristics of Network Flow Traffic Feature Datasets*: The network flow data consists of a sequence of unidirectional packets passing through a point of observation in the network between source and destination hosts during a certain time interval. The NetFlow protocol (IPFIX standard) [305, 79] supports a summarization of the traffic to a router or switch. Network flow is identified by IP addresses of source and destination machines as well as by port numbers. To identify flow uniquely, NetFlow also uses several fields, viz., the type of protocol, the type of service (ToS) from the IP header and the router or the switch for logical input interface. The router or the switch cache is used to store the flows and export to a collector under the following constraints.

- Flows which have been idle for a specified duration of time are expired. The default setting for expiry is 15 seconds. The user can configure this time duration to be between 10 and 600 seconds.

- Flows which are longer lived than 30 minutes are expired.

- If the cache storage reaches its maximum size, a large number of heuristic expiry functions are used to export the flows.

TABLE 4.7: Basic Packet Features in TUIDS Dataset

Sl.	Feature Name	Type*	Feature Description
1.	Duration	C	Time since occurrence of first frame
2.	Protocol	D	Protocol of layer 3: IP, TCP, UDP
3.	Src IP	C	Source IP address
4.	Dst IP	C	Destination IP address
5.	Src port	C	Source port of machine
6.	Dst port	C	Destination port of machine
7.	Service	D	Network service on the destination, e.g., http, telnet, etc.
8.	num-bytes-src-dst	C	Number of data bytes flowing from src to dst
9.	num-bytes-dst-src	C	Number of data bytes flowing from dst to src
10.	Fr-no.	C	Frame number
11.	Fr-length	C	Length of the frame
12.	Cap-length	C	Captured frame length
13.	Head-len	C	Header length of the packet
14.	Frag-offset	D	Fragment offset value
15.	TTL	C	Time to live
16.	Seq-no.	C	Sequence number
17.	CWR	D	Congestion Window Record
18.	ECN	D	Explicit Congestion Notification
19.	URG	D	Urgent TCP flag
20.	ACK	D	Ack flag
21.	PSH	D	Push TCP flag
22.	RST	D	Reset RST flag
23.	SYN	D	Syn TCP flag
24.	FIN	D	Fin TCP flag
25.	Land	D	1 if connection is from/to the same host/port; 0 otherwise

Note: *C-Continuous, D-Discrete

- A TCP connection is finished using either the FIN or RST flag.

A flow collector tool, viz., *nfdump* [154] receives flow records from the flow exporter and stores them in a form suitable for further monitoring or analysis. Flow records are stored in the flow exporter cache. A flow exporter protocol defines how expired flows are transferred by the exporter to the collector. The information exported to the collector is referred to as flow record. NetFlow [78] version 5 is a simple protocol that exports flow records of fixed size, 48 bytes in length.

TABLE 4.8: Content-Based Packet Features in TUIDS Dataset

Sl.	Feature Name	Type*	Feature Description
1.	Mss-src-dst-requested	C	Maximum segment size from src to dst requested
2.	Mss-dst-src-requested	C	Maximum segment size from dst to src requested
3.	Ttt-len-src-dst	C	Time to live length from src to dst
4.	Ttt-len-dst-src	C	Time to live length from dst to src
5.	Conn-status	C	Status of the connection (1-complete, 0-reset)

Note: *C-Continuous, D-Discrete

TABLE 4.9: Time-Based Packet Features in TUIDS Dataset

Sl.	Feature Name	Type*	Feature Description
1.	count-fr-dst	C	Number of frames received by unique dst in the last T sec from the same src
2.	count-fr-src	C	Number of frames received by unique src in the last T sec to the same dst
3.	count-serv-src	C	Number of frames from the src to the same dst port in the last T secs
4.	count-serv-dst	C	Number of frames from dst to the same src port in the last T secs
5.	num-pushed-src-dst	C	Number of pushed packets flowing from src to dst
6.	num-pushed-dst-src	C	Number of pushed packets flowing from dst to src
7.	num-SYN-FIN-src-dst	C	Number of SYN/FIN packets flowing from src to dst
8.	num-SYN-FIN-dst-src	C	Number of SYN/FIN packets flowing from dst to src
9.	num-FIN-src-dst	C	Number of FIN packets flowing from src to dst
10.	num-FIN-dst-src	C	Number of FIN packets flowing from dst to src

Note: *C-Continuous, D-Discrete

Before analysis, all data is stored on disk. This separates the process of storing data from analysis. The data is organized in a time-stamped manner. Nfdump has a daemon process called *nfcapd* for flow record capture that reads data from the network and stores it into files. After every n minutes, typically 5, *nfcapd* rotates and renames each output file with the time stamp *nfcapd.YYYYMMddhhmm*. For instance, *nfcapd*.201012110845 contains data from December 11, 2010, 08:45 onward. Based on a time interval of 5 minutes, this stores results in 288 files per day. The analysis of the data is performed by concatenating several files for a single run. The output is stored either in ASCII or in binary into a file and it is again ready to be processed with the same tool. We use C programs to filter and

TABLE 4.10: Connection-Based Packet Features in TUIDS Dataset

Sl.	Feature Name	Type*	Feature Description
1.	count-dst-conn	C	Number of frames to unique dst in the last N packets from the same src
2.	count-src-conn	C	Number of frames from unique src in the last N packets to the same dst
3.	count-serv-src-conn	C	Number of frames from the src to the same dst port in the last N packets
4.	count-serv-dst-conn	C	Number of frames from the dst to the same src port in the last N packets
5.	num-packets-src-dst	C	Number of packets flowing from src to dst
6.	num-packets-dst-src	C	Number of packets flowing from dst to src
7.	num-acks-src-dst	C	Number of ack packets flowing from src to dst
8.	num-acks-dst-src	C	Number of ack packets flowing from dst to src
9.	num-retransmit-src-dst	C	Number of retransmitted packets flowing from src to dst
10.	num-retransmit-dst-src	C	Number of retransmitted packets flowing from dst to src

Note: *C-Continuous, D-Discrete

extract new features from the captured data. We remove unnecessary parameters. The retained parameters are *flow-start, duration, protocol, source-IP, source-port, destination-IP, destination-port, flags, ToS, bytes, packets-per-second (pps), bits-per-second (bps)* and *bytes-per-packet (bps)*. Network traffic corresponding to attack and normal traffic are gathered using our local network within a 4 week period. The numbers of records in the datasets are given in Table 4.12. We call the two datasets *Packet Level* and *Flow Level TUIDS* datasets. A detailed discussion of this dataset is available in [140].

(iv) *Characteristics of Portscan Dataset*: The generation of the Portscan dataset extracts various types of features from the network packet data captured using the isolated network described earlier. An overview of the Portscan dataset is given in Table 4.13. The experimental testbed shown in Figure 4.7 is used for generation of the Portscan dataset as well. Using the tool called *Nmap*, we generate a number of attacks against the server in a coordinated mode in the local network testbed and collect the generated traffic as attack traffic. Network traffic corresponding to normal and attack instances was captured through a port mirroring machine in our testbed during a 3-week period. The captured data were preprocessed and filtered. The extracted features of the *Portscan* dataset are given in Table 4.14.

4.3.3 Network Simulation

NS-3 is an open source discrete event network simulator that facilitates academic and network research communities in simulating network environments with various numbers of components based on user requirements. It is completely written in C++, with an option of Python binding. It provides an extensible and user-friendly interface with options for writing simulation scripts in C++ or in Python. Inclusion of several sophisticated features, such as extensive parameterization, configurable embedded training, capturing with the *pcap* library, automatic memory management, efficient object aggregation or querying for new behaviors and states, handling of multiple interfaces on nodes, effective use of IP addressing and alignment with Internet protocols, makes this simulator very effective in network security research. The simulated network architecture appears like an IP architecture stack and the nodes created using this simulator may or may not have mobility. One can use the command

$./waf -- run$

with a user file name and the data received at each node can be stored in a *pcap* file using the *tcpdump* format. NS-3 uses the concept of independent tracing sources and tracing sinks. It also uses a uniform mechanism for connecting sources to sinks. It supports various network topologies to create a testbed for generation of attacks with multiple attack scenarios. For example, some researchers have made an effective use of this simulator to validate their method of DDoS attack detection based on the dumbell topology.

4.4 Discussion

This chapter has discussed various modes of network anomaly detection, other important aspects of network anomaly detection and available datasets for assessment of the performance of an ANIDS. Below we summarize the main points of our discussion in this chapter for the reader's convenience.

- Anomaly-based intrusion detection can be either *host based* or *network based* depending on its deployment and is used as a second line of defense along with other preventive security mechanisms.

- A misuse-based NIDS can identify only known intrusive patterns. However, intrusive patterns are always evolving. As a result, intrusion detection research is primarily focused on anomaly-based network intrusion detection.

- Depending on the availability of training data for pure normal and known attack patterns, an anomaly-based NIDS can perform in three basic modes: *supervised, unsupervised* and *hybrid*. We note that obtaining pure normal or labeled traffic data of high quality is time consuming and expensive.

- In an unsupervised ANIDS, labeling of the group of instances identified by the detection mechanism is a crucial task. Typically, labeling is based on certain assumptions that may not be true for all cases.

- A hybrid NIDS attempts to overcome the shortcomings of supervised and unsupervised NIDSs by taking advantage of the benefits of both models. Even in a hybrid NIDS updating the rule or signature base without conflict when a novel intrusion is encountered is not straightforward.

- To assess the performance of an ANIDS, it is absolutely necessary to have access to an unbiased benchmark intrusion dataset. Creating an unbiased dataset in a live network environment with a complete collection of attack instances is a very difficult task.

TABLE 4.11: Flow Features of TUIDS Intrusion Dataset

Sl. Feature Name	Type*	Feature Description
Basic features		
1. Duration	C	Length of the flow (in sec)
2. Protocol-type	D	Type of protocols– TCP, UDP, ICMP
3. src IP	C	Src node IP address
4. dst IP	C	Destination IP address
5. src port	C	Source port
6. dst port	C	Destination port
7. ToS	D	Type of service
8. URG	D	Urgent flag of TCP header
9. ACK	D	Ack flag
10. PSH	D	Push flag
11. RST	D	Reset flag
12. SYN	D	SYN flag
13. FIN	D	FIN flag
14. Source byte	C	Number of data bytes transferred from src IP addrs to dst IP addrs
15. dst byte	C	Number of data bytes transferred from dst IP addrs to src IP addrs
16. Land	D	1 if connection is from/to the same host/port; 0 otherwise
Time-window features		
17. count-dst	C	Number of flows to unique dst IP addr inside the network in the last T secs from the same src
18. count-src	C	Number of flows from unique src IP addr inside the network in the last T secs to the same dst
19. count-serv-src	C	Number of flows from the src IP to the same dst port in the last T secs
20. count-serv-dst	C	Number of flows to the dst IP using the same src port in the last T secs
Connection-based features		
21. count-dst-conn	C	Number of flows to unique dst IP addrs in the last N flows from the same src
22. count-src-conn	C	Number of flows from unique src IP addrs in the last N flows to the same dst
23. count-serv-src-conn	C	Number of flows from the src IP addrs to the same dst port in the last N flows
24. count-serv-dst-conn	C	Number of flows to the dst IP addrs to the same src port in the last N flows

Note: *C-Continuous, D-Discrete

TABLE 4.12:   TUIDS Intrusion Datasets

Connection	Dataset type			
type	Training dataset		Testing dataset	
Packet level				
Normal	71785	58.87%	47895	55.52%
DoS	42592	34.93%	30613	35.49%
Probe	7550	6.19%	7757	8.99%
Total	121927		86265	
Flow level				
Normal	23120	43.75%	16770	41.17%
DoS	21441	40.57%	14475	35.54%
Probe	8282	15.67%	9480	23.28%
Total	52843		40725	

TABLE 4.13:   TUIDS Portscan Dataset

Connection	Dataset type	
type	PortscanTrain	PortscanTest
Normal	2445	1300
SYN	9750	2500
ACK	9945	4300
FIN	9780	3500
maimon	0	5145
null	0	9770
xmas	9740	3400
Total	41660	29915

TABLE 4.14: TUIDS Portscan Feature Dataset

Sl.	Feature Name	Type*	Feature Description
1.	Duration	C	Time since occurrence of first frame (seconds)
2.	Frame length	C	Length of the frame
3.	Frame number	C	Frame number
4.	Capture length	C	Captured frame length
5.	TTL	C	Time to live
6.	Protocol	D	Protocol of layer 3–TCP
7.	Source IP	C	Source IP address
8.	Destination IP	C	Destination IP address
9.	Src port	C	Source port of machine
10.	dst port	C	Destination port of machine
11.	Length	C	Number of data bytes flowing
12.	Sequence number	C	Sequence number
13.	Header length	C	Header length of the packet
14.	CWR	D	Congestion Window Record
15.	ECN	D	Explicit Congestion Notification
16.	URG	D	Urgent TCP flag
17.	ACK	D	Ack flag
18.	PSH	D	Push TCP flag
19.	RST	D	Reset RST flag
20.	SYN	D	Syn TCP flag
21.	FIN	D	Fin TCP flag
22.	Window size	C	Window size
23.	Maximum segment size	C	Maximum segment size requested
24.	class ID		Class label

Note: *C-Continuous, D-Discrete

Chapter 5

Feature Selection

Feature selection is an integral component of knowledge discovery and machine learning. It helps build robust and cost-effective learning models for the extraction of interesting hidden patterns by selecting a subset of relevant features. Feature selection, also known as variable selection, feature reduction, attribute selection or variable subset selection, is a multistep process particularly useful in analyzing real-life high-dimensional data such as network intrusion data, biological data and criminal investigation data. In supervised classification, a feature selection method may be useful in improving performance of the learning model in several ways. It helps alleviate the effect of the high dimensionality problem. It also enhances the generalization capability as well as provides for speedier learning. Finally, feature selection also helps acquire better understanding of the data by discovering important features and how they are related to one another. Feature selection has been the focus of interest for quite some time and substantial work is available. With the creation of huge databases and the consequent requirements for good machine learning techniques, new problems have arisen and novel approaches for feature selection are in demand. This chapter is a comprehensive review of many existing approaches, methods and tools from the 1970s to the present. It identifies four steps in a typical feature selection method, categorizes existing methods in terms of generation procedures and evaluation functions and also discusses combinations of generation procedures and evaluation functions. Representative methods are chosen from each category for detailed explanation and discussion via example. Benchmark datasets with different characteristics are used for comparative study. The strengths and weaknesses of the methods are explained. Guidelines for applying feature selection methods are given based on data types and domain characteristics. This chapter identifies future research areas in feature selection, introduces newcomers to this field and paves the way for practitioners who need suitable methods for solving domain-specific real-world applications.

5.1   Feature Selection vs. Feature Extraction

There is an approach called Feature Extraction related to Feature Selection, the topic of this chapter. The goal of both approaches is to reduce the number of dimensions in a dataset. There are at least two important differences between feature selection and feature extraction. (i) A feature selection method reduces the dimensionality of a feature space by selecting a subset of original features, whereas a feature extraction method, as shown in Figure 5.1, reduces the dimensionality of a feature space by *linear or nonlinear* projection of the n-dimensional vector onto a k-dimensional vector $(k<n)$. (ii) A feature selection method chooses features from the original n-dimensional set based on a measure such as information gain, correlation or mutual information and a user-defined threshold to filter out unimportant or redundant features. For example, in embedded or wrapper methods, specialized classifiers are used in association with feature selection to achieve feature selection and classification at the same time. In contrast, feature extraction methods are transformative, i.e., a transformation is applied on the data to project instances to a new feature space with lower dimension. Principal Component Analysis (PCA) and Singular Value Decomposition (SVD) are examples of this.

5.2   Feature Relevance

A feature selection technique selects a subset of relevant features from the full set of features. The definition of relevance varies from technique to technique. Based on its notion of relevance, a feature selection technique mathematically formulates a criterion for evaluating a set of features generated by a scheme that searches over the feature space.

Kohavi and John [204] define two degrees of relevance, viz., *strong* and *weak*. A feature s is called strongly relevant if removal of s de-

$$m \ll n, p \ll n, \{f_1^E, f_2^E, f_3^E, ..., f_m^E\} \cap \{f_1, f_2, f_3, ..., f_n\} = \varnothing,$$

$$\{f_1^S, f_2^S, f_3^S, ..., f_p^S\} \subset \{f_1, f_2, f_3, ..., f_n\}$$

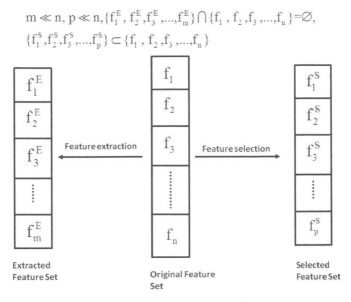

FIGURE 5.1: Feature selection vs. feature extraction

teriorates the performance of a classifier. A feature s is called weakly relevant if it is not strongly relevant and removal of a subset of features containing s deteriorates the performance of the classifier. A feature is irrelevant if it is neither strongly nor weakly relevant. Hall and Smith [155] identify a subset of features to be relevant if features in the subset have high correlation with the class and are uncorrelated with each other in terms of mutual information. Almuallim and Dietterich [13] define relevance for binary features and binary labels. According to them, a feature is relevant if it is a part of a rule set that optimizes the features involved and distinguishes all the classes. Sugumaran et al. [359] define a feature to be relevant if it is part of a decision tree prepared during the classification process. Dash and Liu [90] define a relevant feature subset as the subset of features with the lowest inconsistency rate. The inconsistency rate of a feature subset assesses how much time a unique pattern is associated with different class labels across the feature subset. Section 5.10 presents some measures devised to evaluate a feature subset.

5.3   Advantages

Feature selection offers several important advantages some of them are reported below.

- It reduces feature dimensionality and helps improve the performance of an algorithm.

- It removes redundant, irrelevant or noisy data.

- It improves data quality and hence helps improve the performance of a learning mechanism.

- It improves the accuracy of the resulting model.

- It helps in data understanding, to gain knowledge about the process that generated the data. It also helps in simply visualizing the data.

5.4   Applications of Feature Selection

Typically in most applications, objects are represented in terms of a set of feature values. The effectiveness of various techniques in such applications entirely depends on the set of features used in processing. The feature set used for a specific purpose should reflect distinctions among different entities in terms of domain knowledge. Moreover, a huge feature space may increase time requirements of a technique. So feature selection is a major preprocessing task in various applications, as shown in Figure 5.2. The figure also shows techniques, such as classification, clustering, association rule mining and pattern matching, that are frequently used in such applications. Some major applications that use feature selection are showcased here.

5.4.1   Bioinformatics

Bioinformatics is the study of methods that deal with storing, retrieving and analyzing biological data. Many modeling tasks in bioinformatics, such as sequence analysis and microarray analysis, are high

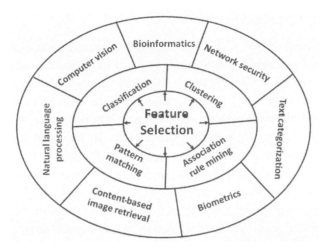

FIGURE 5.2: Feature selection in various applications

dimensional in nature. This fact has given rise to the importance of feature selection techniques in bioinformatics [318]. A major and rapidly growing area of bioinformatics is gene expression data analysis. Gene expression data is typically high dimensional and is error prone. As a result, feature selection techniques have become an integral preprocessing task in various techniques applied in gene expression data analysis, especially classification techniques. Feature selection has also been applied as a preprocessing task in clustering gene expression data [256] in search of co-expressed patterns.

5.4.2 Network Security

Network security deals with protecting computer systems in a network from unwanted intrusions. A major area of network security is designing network anomaly detection systems which attempt to identify both known as well as unknown attacks with minimum false alarms, in real time. A major problem faced by researchers in designing an effective IDS is the high computational cost incurred due to high dimensional data obtained from network activities. Along with the computational overhead, such high dimensional data makes the intrusion identification task difficult due to complex relationships among features [199]. Such issues cause consumption of significantly high computational resources and hence delay the identification of intrusions. Therefore, feature selection is an indispensable preprocessing task for an intrusion detection system.

5.4.3   Text Categorization

With the availability of billions of text documents online, efficient retrieval of desired documents has become a computationally intensive and hence a time-consuming task. Text categorization often has been found to be an effective solution. The problem of text categorization can be defined as the problem of assigning labels from a set of predefined categories to any input text document. In the past two decades, a significant number of machine learning algorithms have been discovered to provide an effective solution to the text categorization problem. However, a major problem with these algorithms is the high dimensionality of the feature space. Typically, in most medium-sized documents, the number of unique words or phrases is of the order of thousands, which is usually very large to handle for a machine learning algorithm. Hence, it is highly desirable to reduce the feature space without compromising the classification accuracy.

5.4.4   Biometrics

To verify the identity of or to authenticate a user, biometric traits such as fingerprints, hand geometry, face and voice verification are considered reliable alternatives and have been gaining high user acceptance. Depending on the type of security applications, the effectiveness of these traits may vary. However, the selection of an optimal subset of relevant features can improve the performance of an authentication system significantly. An optimal subset of relevant features helps distinguish an individual from the rest effectively and efficiently.

5.4.5   Content-Based Image Retrieval

Content-based image retrieval (CBIR) systems analyze image contents based on content-based and content-independent features such as color, texture, shape, spatial and accompanying textual description. To achieve improved performance in retrieving desired queried object(s) in terms of accuracy and speed, the selection of an optimal subset of relevant features can be of great help.

Consumption of high computing and memory resources often has been a major bottleneck in wide-scale implementation of CBIRs on devices with limited resources such as mobile devices or distributed systems. To optimize the performance of indexing and retrieval processes on content-rich image and multimedia databases, feature selection has been found to play a key role. The selection of an optimal subset of relevant features for describing and querying objects in such databases reduces the complexity of the retrieval process without compromising retrieval performance.

5.5 Prior Surveys on Feature Selection

It is not possible to include a comprehensive performance evaluation of all feature selection methods in terms of accuracy and execution time. We attempt here to compare a number of methods based on (i) approach used such as filter, wrapper, embedded or hybrid, (ii) method employed such as statistical, information theoretic, clustering, association mining, soft computing or ensemble and (iii) target domains such as 2-class, n-class and multilabeled. The statistical community has been exploring the problem of optimized feature set selection from as early as the 19th century [89],[204],[260],[234],[70],[318]. A good number of feature selection surveys and methods have been published. In addition, during the past several years, many effective tools and systems to support feature selection have been introduced. This survey organizes these methods into three basic categories, viz., 2-class, n-class and multilabeled based on the nature of the class information available with the data being handled. Methods belonging to these basic categories are discussed according to the approach used, such as filter, wrapper, embedded and hybrid. Several significant survey papers have been published to describe feature selection methods. However, our survey differs from these existing surveys in significant ways.

5.5.1 A Comparison with Prior Surveys

Feature selection is a broad research area which already boasts a number of surveys, review articles and books. An extensive survey of feature selection techniques has been provided by [89],[204],[234],[70],[318]. In [89], a comprehensive overview of several feature selection methods from the 1970s is reported. The authors categorize the methods in terms of subset generation procedures and the functions used for evaluation. A comparative study of methods based on several benchmark datasets is also given. The authors also provide guidelines for applying feature selection methods based on domain characteristics and data types used. In [204], the authors discuss strengths and weaknesses of wrapper approaches and introduce several improved methods. They highlight the relationship between optimal feature subset selection and relevance. The authors also show performance evaluation of two different families of induction algorithms, i.e., decison trees and naive Bayes based on both real and artificial datasets. The authors of [260] review several feature selection algorithms and evaluate their performance using a ranking scheme in a controlled scenario with reference to a set of known results. To evaluate the performance of the feature selection algorithms, the authors divide the experiments into three groups that take into account issues in (i) irrelevance vs. relevance, (ii) redundance vs. relevance and (iii) sample size and each group uses three families of problems, i.e., parity, disjunction and Gmonks, with four different instances for each problem with a variation of relevant features. In [234], we see a comprehensive survey of feature selection algorithms for classification and clustering. The authors include a categorizing framework based on search strategies, criteria for evaluation and data mining tasks. They also suggest guidelines for selection of feature selection algorithms and finally, an integrated system for intelligent feature selection. The authors also justify the use of feature selection in data mining based on several real-life applications. In [70], a review of feature selection techniques designed to operate on very high dimensional intrusion data is reported. The feature selection techniques in the survey are compared and grouped into filter, wrapper and hybrid approaches. Trends and challenges of feature selection are presented in the context of the intrusion detection domain. In [318], a taxonomy of feature selection techniques is presented as well as their use in a number of applications in bioinformatics such as sequence analysis and expresssion analysis.

A pie chart with percentages of various categories of methods is shown in Figure 5.3. As seen in the figure, most methods are based on the statistical filter approach. A majority of existing surveys include methods developed for specific domains only and do not include common tools and systems available to support feature selection and evaluation. However, our motivation is to present a comprehensive and structured survey of existing methods in various domains in terms of overview, a generic taxonomy, techniques, tools and systems. We also

TABLE 5.1: Comparison with Existing Survey Articles

Articles	T_1	T_2	T_3	T_4	T_5	T_6	T_7	T_8	T_9	T_{10}	T_{11}
[371]	✓	✓				✓	✓				✓
[89]	✓	✓		✓	✓	✓	✓				
[204]	✓	✓				✓	✓			✓	✓
[260]	✓	✓	✓		✓	✓	✓				
[234]	✓	✓		✓	✓	✓	✓	✓		✓	✓
[70]	✓	✓		✓	✓	✓	✓	✓			✓
[318]	✓	✓	✓		✓	✓		✓	✓	✓	✓
Chapter	✓	✓	✓	✓	✓	✓	✓	✓	✓	✓	✓

Note: *T_1: Filter methods; T_2: Wrapper methods; T_3: Embedded methods; T_4: Hybrid methods; T_5: Subset generation; T_6: Evaluation measures; T_7: Validity measures; T_8: Taxonomy suggested; T_9: Tools/Systems; T_{10}: Applications; T_{11}: Issues/Challenges

present a list of possible recommendations along with research issues and challenges on this important multidisciplinary topic. A comparison of our chapter with existing survey articles in terms of 12 essential topics is shown in Table 5.1. Our survey includes all those topics. Our chapter differs from the prior surveys in the following ways.

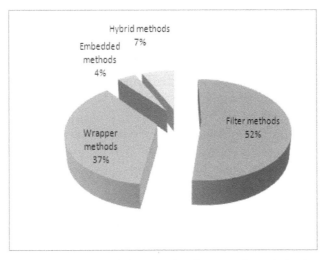

FIGURE 5.3: Statistics of the methods introduced during the years 1990 to 2012

1. We follow the classification schemes for feature selection methods suggested in [89],[204],[260],[234],[70],[318], but in a more practical way with more categories. In addition, unlike most existing surveys, we include a large number of tools, their basic features and functions, as reported in [318].

2. Unlike existing surveys [371],[89],[204],[234],[70], our survey includes a number of tools and systems supporting feature selection as well as classification and evaluation. We discuss their basic functions for the benefit of researchers.

3. Like existing surveys [89],[204],[234],[70],[318], our survey also presents several approaches for feature subset generation and several potential applications for better understanding of the methods.

4. Unlike existing surveys, our survey includes a list of recommendations for researchers interested in further development of effective feature selection methods.

5. Like [70], we also introduce a taxonomy of feature selection methods, but our focus is on practicality. We believe that the three-level classification of feature selection methods will help to gather better insight into existing methods.

6. Like some existing surveys [89],[204],[318], we also highlight important research issues and challenges from both theoretical and practical points of view.

A general comparison of various survey papers available in the literature with this chapter is shown in Table 5.1. The survey contemplated in this chapter covers most highly cited approaches and systems reported in the literature so far.

5.6   Problem Formulation

The feature selection (FS) problem can be defined as a process of identifying an optimal subset of features, say F', of the original feature set F of a given dataset, say D, which gives the best possible classification accuracy for D. Formally, the feature selection process can be defined as follows:

For a given labeled dataset D with features $f_1, f_2, f_3...f_n \in F$, feature selection is a process of finding a subset of features F' of the original feature set F, i.e., $F' \subseteq F$, where (i) $|F'|$ is optimal and (ii) the classification accuracy on D based on F' is the best possible.

5.7 Steps in Feature Selection

Feature selection is a multistep process. The four basic steps in the feature selection process, shown in Figure 5.4, are (i) generating candidate feature subsets, (ii) evaluating candidate subsets, (iii) checking goodness of candidate subsets and (iv) validating the satisfied subset. Each of these steps and their substeps are discussed next.

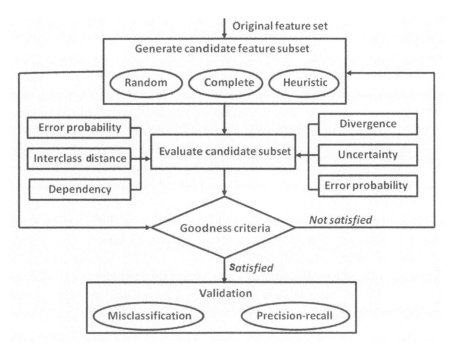

FIGURE 5.4: Basic steps of feature selection

5.7.1　Subset Generation

For an original feature set consisting of n features, there are 2^n possible candidate subsets. For high dimensional datasets such as gene microarrays, intrusion datasets or weather forecasting datasets, this number of subsets is extremely large if one intends to proceed in a brute-force manner. Based on how the feature space is explored to extract the optimal subset of features, the approach to subset generation can be classified as *random subset generation, heuristic subset generation* or *complete subset generation*. Let us discuss each of these approaches.

5.7.1.1　Random Subset Generation

In this approach, feature subsets are generated randomly and then evaluated. The number of generated random subsets is typically a lot less than 2^n. The effectiveness of this approach largely depends on the quality of the random function used to select a subset of features.

5.7.1.2　Heuristic Subset Generation

Starting from an initial state, a heuristic subset generation approach undergoes a number of transitions driven by a heuristic traversal of the solution space to reach a goal state. Such approaches are categorized into *forward, backward* and *bidirectional*. Forward heuristic subset generation techniques start with an empty set and then successively add features based on some heuristic criteria. In backward subspace generation, features are successively removed from the whole set of features. A bidirectional approach starts from both the ends, i.e., both with an empty and the whole set, and successively adds and removes features simultaneously to generate a subset of features. The appropriateness of these techniques for use with a heuristic subset generation approach mainly depends on statistical properties of the features, such as feature–feature correlation or feature–class correlation, dimensionality and heuristics used for selcting (i.e., adding) or eliminating (i.e., removing) a feature. However, based on our experience and also as stated in [155], we note that in most cases a backward or bidirectional technique works better than a forward selection technique.

5.7.1.3 Complete Subset Generation

This is an exhaustive approach where all possible subsets of the features are generated. For a dataset with n features this approach generates 2^n unique subsets.

5.7.2 Feature Subset Evaluation

Feature subsets generated in the previous step are evaluated with an evaluation criteria. Based on how the evaluation is performed, evaluation criteria can be divided into two categories: dependent criteria and independent criteria. A dependent criterion evaluates a feature subset based on results produced by the subset while an independent criterion evaluates a feature subset based on intrinsic properties of the features.

5.7.2.1 Dependent Criteria

These criteria are used to evaluate a subset of features by assessing the results produced by a technique with the selected subset of features. These criteria can be internal or external in nature. An internal criterion is not bothered about prior knowledge and uses intrinsic properties such as homogeneity and separation. An external criterion assesses the quality of results in terms of prior knowledge. This approach is computationally expensive but very effective in identifying an optimal subset of relevant features.

5.7.2.2 Independent Criteria

An independent criterion does not apply the associated technique to produce results for evaluation of a subset. Such criteria use intrinsic properties such as similarity or dissimilarity among and within the features to evaluate the effectiveness of the feature subset.

5.7.3 Goodness Criteria

A goodness criterion determines whether the generated feature subset is acceptable based on evaluation. The acceptability of a feature subset depends on whether accuracy or speed is more important. An accuracy bound technique is very strict in applying the goodness criterion whereas a technique that emphasizes speed relaxes the criterion. Examples of accuracy bound stopping criteria are successive addition of features not improving the result (applicable to forward heuristic subset generation techniques) and the feature subset generated last is sufficiently good.

5.7.4 Result Validation

In this step, subsets of features generated by the feature selection technique are validated. This validation can be performed either externally or internally. External validation uses knowledge from the domain to assess how well the results found correspond to the desired solution. Internal validation does not use such knowledge and uses some known properties of the solution to assess the feature subset.

5.7.4.1 External Validation

External validation matches obtained results with known results. In this technique, we must know the optimal feature set beforehand. The generated feature subset is compared with the known optimal feature subset. This validation is normally applicable to synthetic data and depends on the knowledge base used in validation. Some example of external validation measures are Precision-Recall, F-measure, ROC curve, Confusion matrix and purity.

5.7.4.2 Internal Validation

In internal validation, assessment is performed against some desired properties of the results without using knowledge of optimal features in the domain in question. Internal validation is usually limited and checks a few known properties of the desired optimal feature subset such as high interfeature distance. Unsupervised intracluster validity indices such as homogeneity, sum of squared error and scatter criteria determine the degree of similarity among objects in a cluster. These measures, which are commonly used in clustering, can be used in feature selection as well with reformed inputs. If we consider each feature to be an object and the entire feature set to be a cluster, these measures compute interfeature similarity. The inverse or reciprocal of such a measure may compute the degree of dissimilarity among features. Dissimilarity computation is one of the major requirements of a feature selection algorithm.

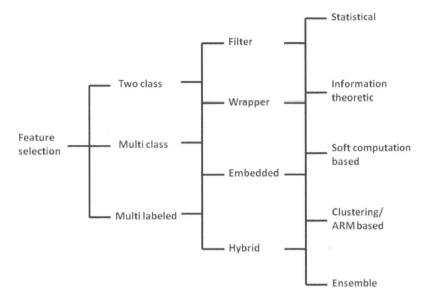

FIGURE 5.5: A taxonomy of feature selection techniques

5.8 Feature Selection Methods: A Taxonomy

Figure 5.5 presents an overall taxonomy of feature selection techniques. Feature selection techniques can be divided into three categories based on the nature of class information in the operational data used by the application being addressed: two-class, multiclass and multilabeled. Two-class feature selection techniques are applied on datasets with instances belonging to two classes while multiclass feature selection techniques are applied on datasets with more than two classes. In these datasets, objects may belong to any of the classes. Multilabeled feature selection techniques are designed to handle datasets in which an object may belong to more than one class. These techniques can be further divided into *filter, wrapper, embedded* and *hybrid* methods based on their operation. As shown in Figure 5.6, filter methods rank features based on some relevance measures and then add or remove features with high or low relevance scores successively to obtain the optimal subset of features [150]. The process terminates on satisfying the goodness criterion. A wrapper method generates feature subsets in a similar way, but the evaluation is performed and the goodness criterion is checked against results generated by a classifier, as depicted in Figure 5.7. An embedded method is integrated with the process of classifier construction [389]. As shown in Figure 5.8, in an embedded feature selection method, the inducer module of the classifier considers only the relevant features in preparing class profiles. A hybrid method, as shown in Figure 5.9, attempts to avoid the prespecification of a stopping criterion by exploiting the advantages of both filter and wrapper methods. To decide the goodness of a feature subset or to identify an optimal and relevant subset of features, a hybrid method uses an independent measure and a classifier. Based on the model used, feature selection techniques can further be categorized into *statistical, information theoretic, soft computing, clustering/association rule mining* and *ensemble* techniques.

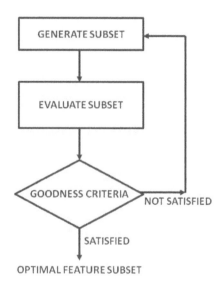

FIGURE 5.6: Operational architecture of a filter method

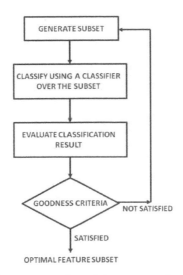

FIGURE 5.7: Operational architecture of a wrapper method

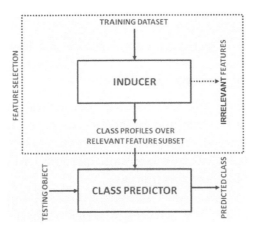

FIGURE 5.8: Operational architecture of an embedded method

5.9 Existing Methods of Feature Selection

A number of feature selection methods have been proposed in the literature for various applications. These methods vary widely across the categories shown in the taxonomy presented in Section 5.8. Here we discuss some often cited feature selection techniques. The techniques are presented in sections that correspond to their type. A general comparison among some of these methods is reported in Table 5.2.

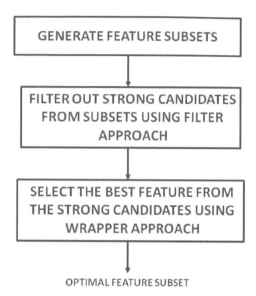

FIGURE 5.9:   Operational architecture of a hybrid method

5.9.1   Statistical Feature Selection

A statistical feature selection method uses relationships among features and class information and formalizes them in the form of equations or criteria to guide the process of feature selection. There are a number of statistical feature selection methods. In this section, we present some widely known techniques.

Dash and Liu [90] propose a measure called the *inconsistency rate*, which evaluates a subset of features in terms of the uniqueness of the labels of the patterns over the subset. The inconsistency count for a pattern across a feature subset is defined as the number of times the pattern appears in the data minus the number of objects in the class with the highest membership value associated with the pattern. The inconsistency rate of a subset is computed as the ratio of the sum of the inconsistency rates of the unique patterns to the total number of such patterns. If the inconsistency rate of a feature subset is less than a user-defined threshold, the subset is considered to be a consistent feature. The authors use exhaustive, complete, heuristic, probabilistic and hybrid feature search techniques to generate feature subsets.

Kira and Rendell [201] propose a two-class filter feature selection technique. The technique, known as *Relief*, maintains a relevance

TABLE 5.2: Comparison of Feature Selection Methods

Technique	Level 1* Category	Level 2* Category	Level 3* Category	Measure Used
Dash and Liu [90]	Multiclass	Filter	Statistical	Inconsistency rate
Kira and Rendell [201]	Two class	Filter	Statistical	Relevance
Liu et al. [233]	Multiclass	Filter	Statistical	Inconsistency rate
Kohavi and John [204]	Multiclass	Wrapper	Statistical	N/A
Liu and Setiono [232]	Multiclass	Embedded	Stastical	χ^2 score
Das [87]	Multiclass	Hybrid	Information theoretic	Information gain
Yu and Liu [411]	Multiclass	Filter	Information theoretic	Symmetric uncertainty
Hall and Smith [155]	Multiclass	Filter	Information theoretic	Heuristic goodness
Peng et al. [290]	Multiclass	Wrapper	Information theoretic	mRMR criteria
Fleuret [119]	Multiclass	Filter	Information theoretic	CMIM criteria
Zhong et al. [428]	Multiclass	Filter	Soft computing	N/A
Hu et al. [178]	Multiclass	Filter	Soft computing	Dependency
Lee et al. [218]	Multiclass	Wrapper	Soft computing	Fuzzy entropy
Setiono and Liu [332]	Multiclass	Wrapper	Soft computing	N/A
Yang and Honavar [398]	Multiclass	Wrapper	Soft computing	N/A
Zhang et al. [423]	Multilabeled	Wrapper	Soft computing	Hamming loss, ranking loss
Almuallim and Dieterich [13]	Binary	Embedded	Clustering /ARM	N/A
Mitra et al. [257]	Multilabeled	Embedded	Clustering /ARM	N/A
Sugumaran et al. [359]	Multilabeled	Embedded	Clustering /ARM	N/A

Note: * Level 1, Level 2 and Level 3 are levels in the taxonomy presented in Section 5.8.

weight vector initialized to zero, its elements corresponding to the set of features. It picks up a user-defined number of random instances and for each instance, it updates the vector weights by adding the squared distance between the value of the instance and its *nearmiss* for the feature and subtracting the squared distance between the value of the instance and its *nearhit* for the feature. A *nearhit* is the nearest neighbor of an instance belonging to the same class and a *nearmiss* of an instance is the nearest instance with a different class label. Finally, features with a relevance weight higher than a threshold are chosen.

Liu et al. [233] propose a simple probabilistic approach to find an optimal feature subset. The technique uses the Las Vegas algorithm [233] to generate a random feature subset in an iteration. If the number of features in the subset is less than the number of features in the best feature subset found so far, the current subset replaces the best feature subset. The evaluation of a feature is done using the inconsistency measure proposed by Dash and Liu [90]. The technique iterates for a user-defined number of times.

Kohavi and John [204] conduct a search through the space of subsets of features to extract an optimal subset using an induction algorithm. They initially use a forward selection scheme using hill climbing and best-first search strategy that starts with an empty set and successively adds features. They introduce a compound operator to deal with the computational overhead of the backward elimination technique where features are successively eliminated to extract an optimal set of features. If we rank the operators corresponding to the feature subsets, the ith compound operator is the combination of the best $i + 1$ operators. For evaluation, they used five-fold cross validation repeated multiple times. The number of repetitions depends on the convergence toward an optimal accuracy estimate.

Liu and Setiono [232] use χ^2 statistics to discretize values across features. Initially, the technique divides the feature values into n intervals where n is the number of distinct values. The χ^2 value is computed for each pair of consecutive intervals. The pair of adjacent intervals with the lowest χ^2 value is merged successively until all pairs have a χ^2 value more than a user-defined threshold. This merging process is repeated with a decreased value of the user-defined threshold until the inconsistency rate of a feature does not increase in two subsequent iterations. The inconsistency rate of a dataset for a feature depends on how many times two matching (excluding the class label) instances have different class labels. Finally, if a feature is merged to only one value, that feature is not relevant and is not selected for classification.

5.9.2 Information Theoretic Feature Selection

Information theoretic feature selection techniques use measures such as entropy, mutual information and information gain to evaluate the correlation between a pair of features or between a feature and a class label. Some widely known information theoretic techniques are presented next.

Das [87] proposes a hybrid feature selection method, a simple variant of which iterates a user-defined k number of times and in each iteration chooses an unselected feature with the highest information gain considering the weighted distribution of training examples. Examples that have often been misclassified are assigned higher weights. In an extended variant of the technique, a stopping criterion is incorporated to avoid the input parameter k. After choosing the feature with the highest information gain in an iteration, the learning algorithm is trained with the new subset of features. If the training accuracy does not improve the process terminates.

Yu and Liu [411] propose an information theoretic filter-based feature selection method that uses a measure called symmetric uncertainty. The *symmetric uncertainty* between two instances is defined as twice the ratio of the information gain of the instance pair to the sum of their entropies. This measure is used to determine both feature–feature and feature–class correlations. The method first selects all the features that produce a symmetric uncertainty value more than a threshold when a feature is compared with the concept (class feature). This filtered feature set is further improved by removing redundant members. Redundant members are identified by computing symmetric uncertainty among the selected features.

Hall and Smith [155] propose a filter-based feature selection method that uses greedy hill climbing search to generate feature subsets. The method uses a merit function to evaluate a feature subset. This merit takes care of both feature–feature and feature–class correlations. Feature–feature and feature–class correlations are computed using an information theoretic measure based on conditional entropy.

Peng et al. [290] introduce a mutual information-based criterion called mRMR (Max-Relevance and Min-Redundancy) that minimizes redundancy among features and maximizes dependency between a feature subset and a class label. The technique for feature selection consists of two stages. In the first stage, a candidate feature subset is generated for compaction in the second stage. In the first stage, the technique incrementally locates a range of successive feature subsets where a consistent low classification rate is obtained. The subset with the minimum error rate is used as a candidate feature subset in stage 2 to compact further using a forward selection and backward elimination based wrapper method.

Fleuret [119] proposes an information theoretic filter method for selecting a subset of features where redundancy among features is minimized and dependency among features and class labels is maximized. The method iteratively selects features which maximize their mutual information with the class labels to conditionally predict a feature that is already picked. This criterion, also known as the Conditional Mutual Information Maximization criterion (CMIM), ensures that a feature which is powerful in terms of predicting class labels, but similar to another feature, is not selected in the optimal feature subset.

5.9.3   Soft Computing Methods

A soft computing model usually compromises the accuracy of the result for reducing the time needed to solve a problem. Examples of such models include fuzzy sets, neural networks, rough sets and genetic algorithms. A feature selection technique that employs such a model is a soft computing method. Here we present some soft computing feature selection methods.

Zhong et al. [428] propose a rough set-based filter feature selection method. The method first finds a core subset from the discernibility matrix. Features are successively added to this subset to reach a reduct which corresponds to an optimal subset of features. During addition of features, it chooses a feature from the positive region of objects classified so far with the already selected features. Among these candidates, the method chooses the one with a maximal sized equivalence class. The process repeats until a reduct approximation is obtained.

Hu et al. [178] propose a feature selection method named Naive Forward Attribute Reduction based on the Neighborhood Rough Set model (NFARNRS) which can handle heterogeneous data. The method begins with an empty set of features and successively adds one new feature which leads to a maximum increment in dependency. The process terminates when the change of dependency becomes less than a user-defined threshold. The dependency is computed as the ratio of the cardinality of the positive region of a feature subset to the cardinality of the universe. Two faster variants of the technique are also proposed.

Lee et al. [218] employ a fuzzy approach to feature selection. They propose a measure named *fuzzy entropy*. The intervals of values across features are decided using fuzzy entropy and the k-means clustering algorithm. For a given dimension, the method starts with two intervals and successively increases the number of intervals by 1 until the fuzzy entropy value stops changing further. A small value of fuzzy entropy implies better relevance. k-means clustering is used to determine the ranges of the intervals. Then membership function is assigned to each interval. Finally, the backward elimination method is used to successively eliminate a feature with the highest fuzzy entropy from the feature subset until the elimination operation does not decrease the classification rate any longer.

Setiono and Liu [332] use a three-layer feedforward neural network to select an optimal subset of features. Using backward elimination, this method initially trains the network with all nodes corresponding to the features of the training set and computes the accuracy rates. Then the method uses all possible feature subsets with one feature removed. It removes the feature from the feature set to yield the best accuracy rate. The process successively removes features in a similar way until the change of accuracy rates between two successive subsets differs by more than a user-defined threshold.

Yang and Honavar [398] use a genetic algorithm to generate an optimal subset of features that fulfills a fitness criterion. The method operates on a population of size 50 and iteratively performs crossover and mutation operations on the population with probabilities 0.6 and 0.001, respectively, for 20 iterations. Each member in the population corresponds to a candidate feature subset represented by a binary vector. Fitness of an individual is computed using a neural network classifier with the number of input nodes equal to the number of features in the candidate feature subset corresponding to the individual.

Zhang et al. [423] adopt a Naive Bayes classifier to deal with multilabel instances. A PCA-based feature extraction method and a genetic algorithm-based feature selection method are used to improve the classification results. The genetic algorithm is used to find an optimal subset of features. To evaluate the fitness of an individual corresponding to a feature subset in a generation, 10-fold cross validation is performed and a final fitness score is computed using a fitness function based on two multilabel evaluation measures, viz., Hamming loss and ranking loss.

5.9.4 Clustering and Association Mining Approach

Clustering and association rule mining are two dominant approaches in data mining. Association rule mining generates rules for the target classes based on observations presented by the feature values of the objects while clustering groups objects based on the similarity of the feature values. In this section, we discuss some such feature selection methods under this category.

Almuallim and Dietterich [13] propose a method that works with binary features with binary class labels. The method builds rules for target classes. The features which do not appear in any rule are considered irrelevant. The rules are chosen by the classifier in such a way that a minimum number of features are involved.

Mitra et al. [257] propose an unsupervised method embedded within a process of discretization of the dataset. The method performs feature selection in two steps. In the first step, the original feature set is partitioned into a number of clusters. It uses a KNN based clustering method to partition the set of features. In the second step, a representative feature is selected from each cluster to form an optimal subset of features.

Sugumaran et al. [359] use decision trees to represent classification rules. Each branch from the parent node corresponds to an attribute. The presence of an attribute or feature in the tree indicates the importance of the attribute in the classification task. The importance of these attributes decreases from the root to the leaves. Features that do not appear in the decision tree are irrelevant for classification. The features with less discriminating capabilities can be consciously discarded, controlled by a user-defined threshold.

5.9.5   Ensemble Approach

In the past few years, there has been a distinct uptick in interest in ensemble methods among machine learning researchers [183, 213, 212, 337]. The basic idea behind an ensemble approach is to improve the performance of a prediction process by combining the outputs of several individual predictors. The biases of the individual predictors are eliminated or minimized by appropriate combination of the outputs of the individual predictors. To achieve high prediction accuracy, an important requirement of an ensemble approach is that individual base predictors must be diverse in nature. A substantial number of empirical studies establish that ensemble methods often outperform individual base predictors [122, 37, 99, 50, 183]. Some commonly used ensemble approaches are bagging, boosting and stack generalization. Several significant ensemble methods for feature selection have been published in the past two decades. Breiman's [51] tree-based ensemble approach called Random Forests and Friedman's [123] gradient boosting trees are introduced mainly (i) to provide improved predictive modeling and

(ii) to rank features for large datasets. Tuv et al. [372] exploit a tree-based ensemble in a more effective way for selection of an optimal subset of relevant features. They combine parallel and serial ensembles of trees to uncover masking and to detect irrelevant variables or features in the original data. The variable masking measure introduced in this work plays a key role in the redundancy elimination process. In [183], an effective ensemble method is introduced for feature selection combining an RFE (Recursive Feature Elimination) method and ANN ensembles. The ANN and RFE combination has been found very useful for optimal feature subset selection, especially for high dimensional gene expression data. In another ensemble approach introduced by Puuronen et al. [303], the authors develop diverse ensembles-based on (i) basic heuristics, (ii) advanced correlation-based heuristics and (iii) contextual merit-based heuristics [20, 155, 173].

5.10 Subset Evaluation Measures

Different feature selection techniques use different feature subset evaluation measures based on a criterion of feature relevance. In this section we present some of these measures used by feature selection techniques.

5.10.1 Inconsistency Rate

The inconsistency rate [90, 233] of a feature subset in a dataset is the ratio of the sum of inconsistency counts of all unique patterns over the feature subset to the total number of instances. The *inconsistency count* of a pattern is the difference between the total number of occurrences of the pattern in the dataset and the maximum number of occurrences that have a particular class label.

Suppose, in a dataset D of n instances, pattern *pat* appears n_{pat} number of times over the feature subset F. n_{pat}^A instances of *pat* are associated with class label A, n_{pat}^B instances of *pat* are associated with class label B, n_{pat}^C instances of *pat* are associated with class label C and n_{pat}^D instances of *pat* are associated with class label D such that $n_{pat} = n_{pat}^A + n_{pat}^B + n_{pat}^C + n_{pat}^D$. The inconsistency count of *pat* over the subset of features F can be computed as follows.

$$\text{Inconsistency count}_F(pat)=n_{pat} - max(n_{pat}^A, n_{pat}^B, n_{pat}^C, n_{pat}^D)$$

The *inconsistency rate* of the dataset D over the feature subset F is the ratio of the sum of inconsistency counts of all unique patterns over subset F to n. This can be mathematically formulated as follows.

$$\text{Inconsistency rate}_F(D)=\sum_{pat}\text{Inconsistency count}_F(pat)$$

5.10.2   Relevance

Relevance is a nondeterministic measure for a feature that presents how well the values of the feature correspond to the class information. Kira and Rendell [201] iteratively update the relevance score of a feature using its nearest hit and nearest miss for a randomly chosen instance. The nearest neighbor of an instance with the same class label is called its nearest hit and the nearest neighbor with a different class label is called a nearest miss of the instance. Relevance of the feature set is computed as follows.

- *Relevance*(f_i)=0, i=1,2,...,n where f_i is the ith feature, n is the total number of features and Relevance(f) is the relevance of feature f.

- For i=1 to m where m is a user-given parameter,
    - Randomly select an instance P
    - Find nearest hit H and nearest miss M of P
    - For j=1 to n
        * Relevance(f_j)=Relevance(f_j)-$|P(f_j) - H(f_j)|+|P(f_j) - M(f_j)|$

5.10.3   Symmetric Uncertainty

Symmetric uncertainty is an information theoretic measure that presents how much a pattern can predict the values of another pattern [411]. The symmetric uncertainty between two patterns P and Q is computed as

$$\text{Symmetric uncertainty}(P,Q)=2[\frac{IG(P|Q)}{H(P)+H(Q)}]$$

where $H(R)$ is the entropy of the pattern R and $IG(P,Q)$ is the information gain of Q with respect to P computed as

$$IG(P|Q) = H(P) - H(P|Q),$$

where $H(P|Q)$ is the conditional entropy of Q with respect to P. The value of symmetric uncertainty ranges from 0 to 1.

5.10.4 Dependency

The dependency [178] measure gives the amount of dependency of class labels on a subset of features. The measure computes the dependency of a class label or decision variable C on the subset of features S as

$$\text{Dependency}_S(C) = \frac{POS_S(C)}{|U|}$$

where $POS_S(C)$ is the subset of objects or instances in the dataset that are in the positive region over the feature subset S with respect to the decision variable or class labels C. The positive region of a dataset over feature subset S with respect to decision variable D is the set of objects which can be classified into one of the decision classes with certainty.

5.10.5 Fuzzy Entropy

Fuzzy entropy [218] is used to evaluate pattern distribution information. Fuzzy entropy of a fuzzy set A for a dataset D can be computed as

$$\text{Fuzzy\_Entropy}(A) = \sum_{i=1}^{n} \text{Fuzzy\_Entropy}_{c_i}(A)$$

where n is the number of classes and $\text{Fuzzy\_Entropy}_{c_i}(A)$ is the fuzzy entropy of class c_i in A and it can be computed as

$$\text{Fuzzy\_Entropy}_{c_i}(A) = -M_{c_j} \, log_2 M_{c_j}$$

where M_{c_j} is the match degree of class c_j which gives the amount of matching between fuzzy membership and class membership. M_{c_j} can be computed as

$$M_{c_j} = \frac{\sum\limits_{x \in S_{c_j}} \mu_A(x)}{\sum\limits_{x \in D} \mu_A(x)}$$

where $\mu_A(x)$ is the membership value of x in fuzzy set A and S_{c_j} is the set of objects which are in class c_j.

5.10.6 Hamming Loss

Hamming loss [423] is a measure applied on a multilabeled dataset to determine how much a multilabeled classifier misclassifies the objects. Let us consider a dataset $D = (o_i, l_i)|i = 1, 2, ...n$, where o_i is the ith object in D and l_i is the set of labels associated with object o_i. If $h(o_i)$ is the set of class labels returned by a classifier for object o_i, Hamming loss can be defined as

$$\text{Hamming\_loss}(h, D) = \frac{1}{n} \sum_{i=1}^{n} \frac{1}{n_c} |h(o_i) \Delta l_i|$$

where n_c is the number of classes in the dataset.

5.10.7 Ranking Loss

Like Hamming loss, ranking loss [423] measures how many pairs of labels are misordered. Using the notations used for Hamming loss, ranking loss can be computed as

$$\text{Ranking\_loss}(h, D) = \frac{1}{n} \sum_{i=1}^{n} \frac{1}{|l_i||\bar{l_i}|} |\{(p_1, p_2)|f(o_i, p_1) \leq$$
$$f(o_i, p_2), (p_1, p_2) \in l_i \times \bar{l_i}\}|$$

where $\bar{l_i}$ is the complementary set of l_i and $f(o_m, l_n)$ is a function of the classifier that returns a value based on how much object o_m is associated with l_n. A high value of f indicates strong association between the object and the class label.

5.11 Systems and Tools for Feature Selection

A number of available libraries have a number of feature selection techniques built in. A knowledge of these tools can be of great use to a researcher working in machine learning and feature selection. We present some widely used tools that implement one or more feature selection techniques.

(i) **SciLab** [145]

SciLab is a software library for numerical computation. The tool provides a user-friendly environment. SciLab is a fast growing library of packages. It is gaining popularity in the research community due to ease of scripting and its friendly interface. A number of packages in the tool support the task of feature selection. The mutual information toolbox available at *http://atoms.scilab.org/toolboxes/mi* implements feature selection methods based on Peng et al. [290] and Ding and Peng [100] along with capabilities for computing mutual information, joint and conditional probabilities, entropy, etc. SciLab is available at *http://scilab.in/DownloadScilab*.

(ii) **Python** [320]

Python is a widely used powerful programming language. Some packages built for Python support the task of feature selection. PyML [41] is a package that contains a number of machine learning modules. The package implements an SVM (Support Vector Machine)-based RFE (Recursive feature elimination) [151] technique and a filter feature selection technique. In a single iteration, the RFE technique trains an SVM. After training, it removes features with the smallest values in the vector w. The technique iterates a user-defined number of times. The filter technique applies a feature scoring function on the features and extracts a user-defined number of highly ranked features. The feature score used is called "golub" [41]. It evaluates feature–class correlation by computing the differences in the means of the classes across the feature, weighted by the standard deviation.

(iii) **R language** [306]

R is a computational tool and a programming language with a very rich repository of library functions. This is a very widely used tool for machine and statistical computing. A number of R packages support feature selection tasks. The Boruta package [214] implements a technique named Boruta that finds important attributes by iterative learning of the random forest classifier. The Caret package [209] is another flexible package that supports variants of recursive feature elimination and other techniques. FSelector [314] is a very flexible package with a number of feature selection modules. Table 5.3 presents some of the functions available in this package. *R* is available at *http://cran.r-project.org/mirrors.html*.

TABLE 5.3:   Some Feature Selection Functions in FSelector

Function	Description
best.first.search	Searches for feature subsets using the best first search
exhaustive.search	Searches for feature subsets using exhaustive search
greedy.search	Searches for feature subsets using greedy search
hill.climbing.search	Searches for feature subsets using hill climbing
cfs	Selects feature subset using correlation-based feature selection
chi.squared	Assigns weights to discrete attributes-based on a chi-squared test
consistency	Selects a feature subset for continuous and discrete data using a consistency measure
correlation	Assigns weights to continuous features-based on their correlation with continuous class attributes
cutoff	Selects a subset of ranked features
entropy.based	Assigns weights to discrete features-based on their correlation with continuous class attributes
oneR	Assigns weights to discrete features-based on association rules generated for each feature
random.forest.importance	Assigns weights to features using a random forest algorithm
relief	Assigns weight to continuous and discrete features based on distances between randomly sampled instances

(iv) **MATLAB®** [160]

MATLAB is a widely used computational tool and programming language. MATLAB has a number of packages that support feature selection. The machine learning tool box [374] available for MATLAB provides functions for exhaustive search and sequential search of features. In sequential search, it implements the forward and backward selection algorithms using ten-fold cross validation. The techniques use the k-nearest neighbor classifier. MIToolbox [3] is another toolbox for MATLAB mainly prepared for feature selection using mutual information. Along with a number of information theoretic functions, the toolbox implements CMIM [119], mRMR [290] and DISR [249]. FEAST (a Feature Selection Toolbox for C and MATLAB)[56] is another toolbox for MATLAB which implements RELIEF [201], CMIM [119], mRMR [290], DISR [249] and some other feature selection techniques.

(v) **Octave** [108]

GNU Octave is a computational tool and a programming language which is very similar to MATLAB. Scripts can be easily ported from MATLAB to Octave. A method named FSS (Feature Subset Selection and feature ranking) is implemented in the NAN package (*http://octave.sourceforge.net/nan/index.html*). The method implements a feature selection technique motivated by the *max-*

relevance-min-redundancy (mRMR) technique [290]. The package can be used in MATLAB as well. GNU Octave is available at *http://www.gnu.org/software/octave/download.html*.

(vi) **Weka** [172]

Weka is a GUI-based user-friendly data mining computational tool with implementations of data mining and associated techniques. Weka is widely used in the research community. For feature selection, Weka provides a very flexible interface, as shown in Figure 5.10, where the user needs to choose from a number of options to perform a search across features and to evaluate the quality of the subsets generated by the search scheme. To evaluate a feature subset, the user can choose either validation with the entire training set or cross validation. The suite also provides a means to visualize the reduced data in a user-friendly manner. Weka is available for download at *http://www.cs.waikato.ac.nz/ml/weka/index_downloading.html*.

FIGURE 5.10: Weka interface for feature selection

(vii) **Orange** [82]

Orange is a software suite for data mining and machine learning with a friendly graphical user interface and Python bindings and libraries for scripting. OrngFSS (*http://orange.biolab.si/doc/modules/orngFSS.htm*) is a module for Orange that supports a number of functions associated with the task of feature selection. Table 5.4 presents the functions available in the module. Orange can be downloaded from *http://orange.biolab.si/download/*.

TABLE 5.4: Some Functions Associated with *orngFSS*

Function	Description
attMeasure	Assigns scores to discrete features using a given scoring function
bestNAtts	Returns *n* highly ranked features from the scores list
attsAbove	Returns features with scores more than a threshold
selectBestNAtts	Returns a dataset with a user-defined number of best features
selectAttsAboveThresh	Returns a dataset with features with a score more than a user-defined threshold
filterRelieff	Selects features from a dataset using the backward elimination method until all the features have a score more than a user-defined threshold

(viii) **RapidMiner** [251]

RapidMiner is one of the most widely used data mining software suites with a graphical user interface and a large Java library for developers. Package com.rapidminer.operator.features.selection in RapidMiner Java library provides a set of operator classes for feature selection. Table 5.5 presents the available classes in Rapid-Miner under the package. A community edition of the suite is available at *http://rapid-i.com/content/view/26/84/*.

TABLE 5.5: Some Operator Classes Available in *RapidMiner*

Function	Description
AttributeWeightSelection	Selects a subset of attributes which have weights fulfilling a specified condition
BackwardElimination	Selects a feature subset using a backward elimination method
BestSelection	Selects the best feature subset
BruteForceSelection	Selects the best feature set by trying all possible combinations
ForwardSelection	Selects a feature subset using a forward selection technique
GeneticAlgorithm	Uses a genetic algorithm for feature selection
IterativeFeatureAdding	Iteratively adds features in order from a given feature name array

(ix) **TOOLDIAG** [310]

TOOLDIAG is a statistical pattern recognition library written in C. It provides a flexible means for feature selection by providing a number of search strategies such as best features, sequential forward selection and sequential backward selection. The library also allows users to choose among a number of selection criteria such as interclass distance and probability distance. TOOLDIAG can be downloaded from *https://sites.google.com/site/tooldiag/download.*

5.12 Discussion

During the preparation of this chapter on feature selection techniques, we have learned a number of lessons. These lessons provide an overall impression of which methods work well under what circumstances.

- A good feature selection method should be able to handle both numeric and categorical data.

- A filter method is preferred in a computation-constrained situation. However, a good statistical filter method is expected to take care of both feature–feature and feature–class correlation.

- A wrapper feature selection method is preferred over a filter technique if computational cost is ignored. However, a wrapper feature selection method may also suffer from the drawback of classifier bias.

- There are very few feature selection methods for datasets where an instance can have multiple class labels. This aspect of feature selection can still use additional research and development.

Though a number of feature selection techniques have been proposed and developed, a single solution to the feature selection technique still does not exist. Different feature selection techniques target different aspects of the demands put forward by the research community. A method that can properly handle both feature–feature and feature–class correlations in an effective manner with the ability to handle categorical, numeric and mixed attributes will still be greatly appreciated. While evaluating feature–feature and feature–class correlations, a technique must be careful about the requirements of these two cases. Wrapper techniques are always recommended in a situation where classification accuracy is of prime concern. Because they are slow, such a technique is infeasible to use in time-constrained applications. Researchers can explore ways to bring down the complexity of such a technique to make it usable in more applications. A possible way to improve such a technique is to devise an incremental classifier which reduces the time needed in successive classification attempts with a small change in training and testing data.

Chapter 6

Approaches to Network Anomaly Detection

This chapter introduces a few methods for network anomaly detection. We provide a comprehensive presentation of the methods, their strengths and weaknesses and highlight research issues and challenges. Following our discussion on the availability and use of labeled data and the technical approaches used in Chapter 4, we structure our discussion in this chapter in six distinct categories: supervised, unsupervised, probabilistic, soft computing, knowledge-based and hybrid. This chapter also introduces a taxonomy of existing network anomaly detection methods to support a consistent description of the methods.

6.1 Network Anomaly Detection Methods

A large number of methods have been introduced for identification of network anomalies by monitoring and analyzing network traffic. Most methods identify anomalies by finding deviations from an underlying normal traffic model. Generally, these models are trained with normal or attack-free traffic traces obtained over a long period of time. In practice, training is a hard problem. In particular, it is difficult to claim the training data are purely normal or 100% attack free. Furthermore, this training process must be repeated at periodic intervals. Typically, a network anomaly detection approach follows a 4-step process. The detection approach is spread over the first three steps and the fourth step is for validation. The first step aims to collect network traffic data, while an appropriate subset of relevant parameters or features is extracted or selected in the second step. The third step monitors, analyzes and classifies the captured and preprocessed traffic data into normal and anomalous classes. The fourth step is for validation of the approach.

6.1.1　Requirements

An ANIDS must analyze and report unusual behavioral patterns in a network in real time or near real time, with high detection accuracy. The following are some important requirements for an anomaly-based network intrusion detection method or system.

(i) It should be able to identify network anomalies with high detection accuracy with minimum or no prior knowledge of normal activities of the target system. In addition, it should have the ability to learn the expected behavior of the system from observations.

(ii) A method should perform consistently in identifying malicious activities for different network scenarios with minimum false alarms.

(iii) The number of input parameters should be minimal and their influence should be low.

(iv) A method or system should be capable of detecting not only isolated or bursty attacks, but should also be able to identify any rare class or carefully launched attacks.

(v) In addition to detecting all known attacks, it should also be able to identify unknown anomalous patterns.

6.2　Types of Network Anomaly Detection Methods

On the basis of the availability of prior knowledge, the detection mechanism used, the mode of performance and the ability to detect attacks, existing anomaly detection methods are categorized into six broad categories [184, 414, 380, 12] as shown in Figure 6.1. Each category is described in detail next.

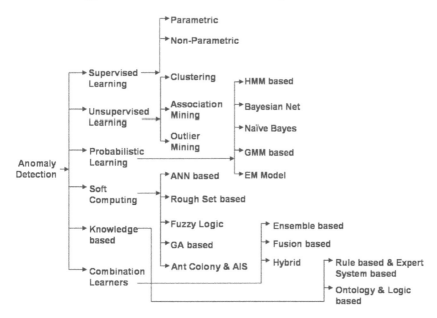

FIGURE 6.1: Classification of anomaly-based intrusion detection methods

6.3 Anomaly Detection Using Supervised Learning

In supervised learning, the availability of a training dataset is assumed. The dataset has instances labeled as normal or as belonging to known anomaly classes. The typical approach is to build a class predictive model for normal versus anomalous behavior. New data instances are tested against this model to establish their membership in a class. The following two major issues arise in anomaly detection using the supervised approach.

(i) The number of normal instances is usually greater than the number of anomalous instances in the training data.

(ii) Obtaining accurate and representative class labels, especially for anomalous instances, is very difficult.

A large number of techniques [366] have been introduced to mix artificially generated anomalous instances with normal instances to obtain labeled training datasets. Thus, based on the availability of an appropriate training dataset, the building of a predictive model is the most important task for supervised anomaly detection. In practice, obtaining purely normal data is very hard, since nothing is ever guaranteed to be purely normal during the gathering of traffic data. Supervised network anomaly detection methods are of two basic types, viz., *parametric* and *nonparametric*.

6.3.1   Parametric Methods

A parametric method assumes that normal data is produced by using a parametric distribution with parameters $\Im$ and probability density function (pdf) $f(p, \Im)$, where p is an instance of observation. The anomaly score of a test instance p is the inverse of the pdf, $f(p, \Im)$. The parameters $\Im$ are derived from the given data. Alternatively, a statistical hypothesis test [35] can also be used. The null hypothesis H_0 for such a test is that the data instance p is normal, generated using the required distribution with parameters $\Im$. p is declared to be anomalous if H_0 is rejected by the statistical test. A statistical hypothesis test is closely related to a statistical test so that it can be used to obtain a score of probabilistic anomaly for the data instance p. Several parametric anomaly detection methods are discussed in [404, 152, 153].

Network intrusion detection deals with large volumes of high dimensional network data obtained from high speed network traffic using a large number of behavioral measures. Network intrusion detection requires early detection of intrusion and generation of an alarm with a minimum delay for processing each event in a system. Therefore, for network intrusion detection, we need an anomaly-based intrusion detection method with minimum computation cost that can handle multivariate data. In [404], a distance measure is developed for obtaining a mean estimate of multivariate normal distribution using a chi-square (χ^2) test, as given in Equation (6.1)

$$\chi^2 = \sum_{i=1}^{n} \frac{(X_i - E_i)^2}{E_i} \tag{6.1}$$

Here, X_i is the ith variable's observed value, E_i is the ith variable's expected value and n is the total number of variables. If the expected and observed values of the variables are close, χ^2 is small. Using $\bar{X}_1, \bar{X}_2, \ldots, \bar{X}_n$ as expected estimation, χ^2 is obtained as shown in Equation (6.2).

$$\chi^2 = \sum_{i=1}^{n} \frac{(X_i - \bar{X}_i)^2}{\bar{X}_i} \tag{6.2}$$

Here, χ^2 is the summation of the squared differences of observed and expected values for the variables and it has an approximate normal distribution. For the χ^2 population, the mean and standard deviation can be computed by the sample mean $\bar{X}_2$ and the sample standard deviation S_X^2 from the sample data. To detect anomalies, the in-control limits [261, 33] can be set to 3 to attain 3-sigma control limits, $[\bar{X}^2 - 3S_X^2, \bar{X}^2 + 3S_X^2]$. Since it attempts to detect significantly large χ^2 values for intrusion detection, one needs to set the upper control limit to $\bar{X}^2 + 3S_X^2$. For an observation, if the computed χ^2 is greater than $\bar{X}^2 + 3S_X^2$, it is marked anomalous.

6.3.2 Nonparametric Methods

In nonparametric statistical methods of anomaly detection, usually the model is not defined a priori, but is determined from the given data. This class of methods does not assume an underlying model, but rather tailors its detection mechanism to the data. Typically, such methods make fewer assumptions about the data compared to parametric methods.

A simple statistical nonparametric technique for a maintaining normal data profile is the histogram. A histogram method is also known as a frequency- or counting-based method. Such methods have been found effective in network anomaly detection [112, 113]. Some histogram methods for multivariate data are available in [395, 396]. In Packet Header Anomaly Detection (PHAD) and Application Layer Anomaly Detection (ALAD) [241], a variant of this simple technique is applied. The basic method is to construct histograms according to attributes for multivariate data. For a test instance, it calculates an anomaly score for each attribute, i.e., its bin height. The anomaly scores for each attribute are summed for the test instance to obtain overall total anomaly score. Finally, based on this total anomaly score, it decides whether the instance is anomalous or normal with reference to a given user-defined threshold.

In [426], a nonparametric method of adaptive behavior for anomaly detection is proposed. It maps sample data to the interval $[0, 1]$. One such score function is obtained from a k-nearest neighbor graph (k-

NNG). It considers an instance anomalous if the score for the test instance falls below a predetermined error δ. Let $Q = \{q_1, q_2, \ldots, q_m\}$ be the training set of size m, belonging to the $[0, 1]^d$ unit cube. Let q_{m+1} denote a test point. The task is to identify the test point as being nominal data consistently or as deviation from nominal data. If the test point is an anomalous point, it is assumed to come from a combination of underlying nominal distribution and a different known density in the training data. The k-NNG or equivalently ϵ-neighbor graph (ϵ-NG) is constructed with the use of a distance function. k-NNG is constructed by connecting every q_i to the closest points $\{q_{i_1}, q_{i_2}, \ldots, q_{i_k}\}$ in $Q - \{q_i\}$. The k nearest distances are sorted for every q_i in ascending order $d_{i,i_1} \leq \ldots \leq d_{i,i_k}$. Let $R_Q(q_i) = d_{i,i_k}$ represent the distance between q_i and its k-th nearest neighbor. ϵ-NG is constructed such that q_i and q_j are connected if and only if $d_{ij} \leq \epsilon$. $N_Q(q_i)$ is defined as the rank of point q_i in the ϵ-NG.

In the ordinary case, if anomalous density is an arbitrary mixture of nominal and uniform densities, Equations (6.3) and (6.4) compute the associated score functions for k-NNG and ϵ-NG graphs, respectively. These score functions map γ, a test data instance, to the interval of $[0, 1]$.

$$K\text{-}LPE : \hat{p}K(\gamma) = \frac{1}{n} \sum_{i=1}^{m} \mathrm{II} \{R_Q(\gamma) \leq R_Q(q_i)\} \tag{6.3}$$

$$\epsilon\text{-}LPE : \hat{p}\epsilon(\gamma) = \frac{1}{m} \sum_{i=1}^{m} \mathrm{II} \{N_Q(\gamma) \leq N_Q(q_i)\} \tag{6.4}$$

$\mathrm{II}(.)$ defines an indicator function. The score function $k\text{-}LPE$ (or $\epsilon\text{-}LPE$) measures the relative concentration of point γ in comparison to the training set. Finally, for a given predetermined significance level β (e.g., 0.05), γ is identified as anomalous if $\hat{p}K(\gamma), \hat{p}\epsilon(\gamma) \leq \beta$. In such methods, a major difficulty is to estimate accurately the user-defined threshold β. Table 6.1 summarizes several parametric and nonparametric statistical methods for network anomaly detection.

Below, we enumerate advantages and disadvantages of parametric and nonparametric network anomaly detection methods.

(i) *Advantages*: In addition to their their inherent ability to detect network anomalies, these methods have a number of other advantages.

TABLE 6.1: Statistical Paramteric Anomaly Detection Methods

	Method	Description
Parametric approach	Mixture model [112]	(i) A mixture model for anomaly detection without training on normal data. (ii) Estimates probability distribution in the data and applies statistical tests to detect anomalies. (iii) Applied to UNIX system call traces for evaluation.
	Statistical model [243]	(i) An automatic, adaptive, pro-active and hierarchical multitier multiwindow anomaly detection method. (ii) Applied to both wired and wireless ad-hoc networks. (iii) Performance evaluated using DARPA98 datatsets and in real time.
	ScanAID technique [431]	(i) Sequences of system calls are abstracted to model the normal behavior of a privileged process; N-grams vector anomaly values are used to model the behavior. (ii) Evaluated using system calls audit trails from MIT.
	ARMA model [189]	(i) Uses 'frequency domain' traffic analysis and filtering. (ii) Traffic is separated into a baseline component that includes most low frequency traffic and presents low burstiness and the short-term traffic that includes the most dynamic part. (iii) Performance evaluated using OPNET simulator.
	CAD model [347]	(i) A general purpose conditional anomaly detection method. (ii) Presents three different expectation-maximization algorithms for learning and for conditional anomaly detection. (iii) Tested with more than 13 different datasets from the UCI repository.
	Distributed Hidden Markov model [198]	(i) Uses a control-theoretic HMM strategy for intrusion detection using distributed observations across multiple nodes. (ii) Comprises a distributed HMM engine that executes at a randomly selected monitor node and functions as a part of the feedback control engine.
	Network signal model [236]	(i) A network signal modeling technique that combines the wavelet approximation and system identification theory. (ii) Fifteen features are used as input signals for the purpose of detection. (iii) Performed a detailed analysis using DARPA99 intrusions dataset. (iv) Established to perform with a high detection rate.
	G-Hidden Markov model [342]	(i) A field selection technique using GA that generates packet-based association rules. (ii) Uses Gaussian observation HMM to exploit hidden relationships among packets-based on probabilistic estimation. (iii) Tested using MIT Lincoln Lab and real-life dataset.
	α-stable model [381]	(i) Detects anomalies in network traffic, based on a nonrestricted α-stable first-order model and statistical hypothesis testing. (ii) Tested with publicly available traffic traces and real-time datasets.

- They have the ability to learn the expected behavior of the system from observations.

- They can provide accurate notification of malicious activities occurring over long periods of time subject to setting of appropriate thresholds.

- They analyze traffic based on the theory of abrupt changes, i.e., they monitor traffic for a long time and report an alarm if any abrupt change occurs.

(ii) *Disadvantages*: Even though these methods are adequate for the

TABLE 6.2:   Statistical Nonparamteric Anomaly Detection Methods

	Method	Description
Nonparametric approach	IntruShield system [348]	(i) An adaptive statistical anomaly detection system. (ii) Applies statistical usage profiling to continuously modify the baseline, by which all activity is measured to identify anomalous behavior. (iii) Maintains two sets of usage data: (a) a long-term usage profile and (b) a short-term observed usage. (iv) Compares the short-term usage to the long-term profile during anomaly detection and reports significant deviations as potential attacks.
	Multichart CUSUM [200]	(i) A multichart CUSUM(Cumulative Sum) algorithm for detecting DoS attacks. (ii) Uses minimum amount of available information on prechange and postchange traffic models.
	Parzen-Window & KNN	(i) A hybrid feature selection method that uses optimized k-means clustering. (ii) Performance evaluated using Parzen window and k-nearest neighbors.
	Distributed SAD [73]	(i) A distributed anomaly detection method with both parametric and nonparametric variants. (ii) Detailed inspection of individual detection is not explored.
	Markov chain model [282]	(i) Uses Markov models to characterize the normal behavior of the sensor network. (ii) For each Markov chain model, an anomaly-free probability law is estimated from past traces; if any deviation is found, it is reported as an anomaly.
	Adaptive CUSUM [412]	(i) An adaptive CUSUM method for detecting network intrusions. (ii) Reports source-end-based detection against SYN flooding attacks.

intended purpose, they have some drawbacks.

- They are susceptible to being trained by an attacker in such a way that the network traffic generated during an attack is considered normal.

- Setting the values of the different parameters or metrics is a difficult task, especially because the balance between false positives and false negatives is an issue. Moreover, a statistical distribution per variable is assumed, but not all behaviors can be modeled using stochastic methods. Furthermore, most schemes rely on the assumption of a quasi-stationary process, which is not always realistic.

- It takes a long time to report an anomaly for the first time because the building of the models requires extended time.

- Several hypothesis testing statistics are applied to detect anomalies. Choosing the best statistic is often not straightforward. In particular, constructing hypothesis tests for complex distributions that are required to fit high dimensional datasets is nontrivial.

- Histogram-based techniques are relatively simple to implement, but a key shortcoming of such techniques for multivariate data is that they are not able to capture interactions among the attributes.

6.4 Anomaly Detection Using Unsupervised Learning

To obtain a set of accurately labeled data which can represent all types of behavior is often prohibitively expensive. Usually, labeling is performed manually by a skilled human expert and thus it entails substantial time and effort. Generally, a dataset containing instances labeled as normal behavior can be obtained more easily than a dataset of instances labeled anomalous covering all types of anomalies. Besides, anomalous behavior is dynamic in nature. Novel types of anomalous behavior may emerge requiring associated labeled training data. On the other hand, no training data is required for unsupervised anomaly detection [417] and hence, these methods are easier to use. An unlabeled dataset is taken as input for such an approach and the method attempts to seek intrusion instances lurking inside the data. The detected intrusion instances can then be used for training of misuse-based or supervised methods. The unsupervised method of anomaly detection is discussed in the following subsections. Often several methods are used in combination.

6.4.1 Clustering-Based Anomaly Detection Methods

Clustering methods group data into clusters-based on a similarity measure or distance computation. The most commonly used procedure [297] for clustering begins with selection of a representative point for each cluster. Each test data point is grouped as belonging to the cluster to whose representative point it is the nearest. The process is usually repeated. Clustering has the ability to learn and detect anomalies without requiring explicit explanations of classes or types of anomalies from system administrators. Consequently, anomaly detection based on clustering does not require any training data. Clustering is applied widely for network anomaly detection [331, 57, 397].

An intrusion detection approach based on clustering and classifica-

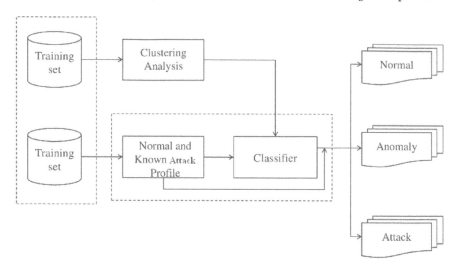

FIGURE 6.2:   Clustering-based anomaly detection

tion is presented by Yang et al [397]. It is illustrated in Figure 6.2. In this approach, clustering is performed on the training data points so that one can select some clusters as well-known attacks and others as normal on the basis of some predefined criteria. It generates profiles for these two classes. The training data points excluded from defining the profiles are used to build a classifier. During the testing stage, the method uses an influence-based classification algorithm to classify network traffic instances as normal or anomalous.

Casas et al. [60] introduce a knowledge-independent approach referred to as the Unsupervised Network Anomaly Detection Algorithm (UNADA). A clustering method using the concept of subspace density is used in UNADA to obtain clusters and outliers or nonconforming patterns. Multiple clusters are created with dimensions lower than that of the original dataset. The results are combined on the basis of the traffic structure obtained from multiple clusterings. A ranking of traffic flows is produced from the combined multiple clusterings. The conceptual framework of UNADA is given in Figure 6.3.

In UNADA, traffic is captured in fixed length consecutive time slots and is aggregated into IP flows. IP flows are additionally aggregated at multiple flow levels using different aggregation keys. Thus, the method supports coarse to fine-grained resolution. To detect anomalous time slots, time series are constructed with traffic metrics including IP flows per time slot, the number of bytes and packets. Aggregation keys are used for the purpose. A change detection method is used on the time

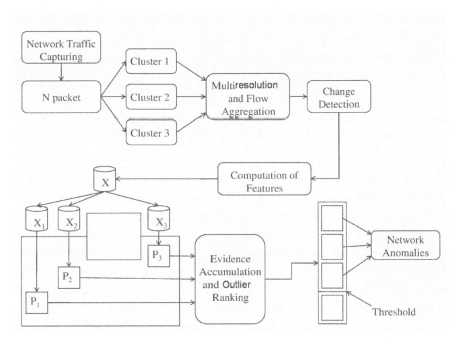

FIGURE 6.3:   Conceptual framework of UNADA

series, such that at the arrival of every new time slot, the change detection method analyzes the time series graphs using each aggregation key in order to identify any significant deviation.

IP flows in the flagged time slots are used for unsupervised attack detection. In this step, UNADA ranks the degree of abnormality for every flow using clusters and outliers. Thus, at two different resolutions, IP source or IP destination, the aggregation key IP flows are analyzed. There are two different anomalies on the basis of which traffic anomalies can be classified: 1-to-N or N-to-1 anomalies. When many IP flows are transferred from the same source to different destinations they are said to be 1-to-N anomaly patterns. Likewise, N-to-1 means IP flows from different sources to one destination. 1-to-N anomalies are highlighted by IP source, while N-to-1 anomalies are detected more easily with IP destination keys. Even when there are highly distributed anomalies, the use of both keys, i.e., IP destination key and IP source key the number of IP flows can be used to find outliers. We know that unsupervised network attack detection is usually based on clustering. Homogeneous groups with similar characteristics or clusters are formed by partitioning a set of unlabeled samples. Outliers are those samples that do not belong to any of these clusters. It is important to identify the clusters properly to determine outliers. The aim is to determine or rank how different these are. Using a simple threshold detection approach, outlying flows which are top ranked are flagged as anomalies.

6.4.2 Anomaly Detection Using the Outlier Mining

Outlier mining methods search for objects which do not match rules and expectations suited for the majority of the data. From the perspective of clustering, outlier objects in a dataset are objects outside the clusters. With reference to anomaly detection, the outliers may be considered attacks. There are many approaches to outlier detection [35, 139]. The detection of outliers often depends on the methods used, the assumptions made and the data structures employed. Outlier detection methods can be classified as [139] distance-based, density-based and soft computing approaches. The distances among the objects in a dataset are computed with geometric measures in distance-based outlier detection. In density-based outlier detection, the density of neighborhood objects for each data instance estimated. An object lying in a low density neighborhood is considered an outlier. On the other hand, an object lying in a high density neighborhood is considered normal. Recently, significant progress has been made in the domain of outlier detection with the objective of network anomaly detection [110, 134, 206].

In LOADED [134], Ghoting et al. introduce a distance-based outlier detection method for mixed attribute data. Data points are considered linked if they are similar to each other for each attribute pair. Breunig et al. [53] compute a local outlier factor (LOF) for objects in the dataset. The outlier factor quantifies the amount of outlyingness of an object. In ODMAD [206], an anomaly score is estimated for a data point considering the anomalies of the continuous values, the categorical values and the mapping between the two spaces in the dataset. Data points which have similarity near "0" are more likely outliers.

The Minnesota Intrusion Detection System (MINDS) [110] uses outlier mining techniques for detecting unknown network anomalies. The architecture of MINDS is shown in Figure 6.4. In the first step, MINDS extracts relevant important features which are used in the detection method. Then, it summarizes the features based on a time window. After feature identification, the module for known attack detection is

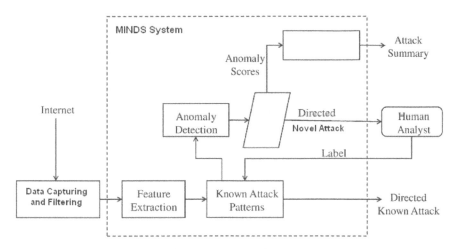

FIGURE 6.4: Architecture of the MINDS system

used for detection of network connections for which attack signatures are available. These connections are removed from further analysis. Thereafter, the data is transferred to the anomaly detection module for the identification of unknown types of anomalies, if they exist. A quantitative measure of outlyingness (LOF) [53] is computed for each object by the anomaly detection module. The LOF computation considers the density of the neighborhood objects around the point for determining its outlierness. Objects with high LOF values represent more nonconformity and hence are considered outliers. The work of a human analyst is to determine in case of the most anomalous connections whether they are truly attack instances or interesting behavior. After analyzing the created summaries, the analyst provides feedback to decide whether the summaries created should be used for known attack detection in the future.

6.4.3 Anomaly Detection Using Association Mining

Association rule mining (ARM) [8, 9, 168] is another important data mining technique. This technique identifies events that occur together. An association rule is defined as follows: Given a transaction database D such that each transaction $P \in D$ represents a set of items in the database, an association rule is an implication of the form of $A \rightarrow B$ where $A \in D$ and $B \in D$ are sets of attribute values, with $A \cap B = \emptyset$ and $\|B\| = 1$. The set A is the antecedent of the rule, whereas item B is the consequent. Two parameters are associated with the rule mining process: *support* and *confidence*. A rule $A \rightarrow B$ has support m in the transaction set P if $m\%$ of transactions in P contain $A \bigcup B$. The rule $A \rightarrow B$ has confidence t if $t\%$ of transactions in P that contain A also contain B. Association rule mining approaches have been used by several researchers to find normal patterns for anomaly detection [221, 222, 83, 242]. These methods are important in anomaly detection because association rules can be used to construct summaries of anomalous connections detected by a system.

Daniel et al. propose an ARM-based anomaly detection method, ADAM (Audit Data Analysis and Mining) [83]. A combination of ARM and classification is used in ADAM for identifying attacks in TCPdump audit data. Initially, ADAM builds a repository of "normal" frequent itemsets which are logged during attack-free periods. Next, a sliding-window algorithm finds frequent itemsets from the connections and comparisons are performed with the stored repository of normal itemsets. It discards itemsets which are most likely to be normal. A previously trained classifier is used by ADAM for classifying suspicious new connections to be either as known attack or unknown type or false alarm.

ADAM consists of modules: preprocessing engine, mining engine and classification engine. The work of the preprocessing engine is to sniff TCP/IP traffic data and to extract header information from each connection using a predefined schema. The mining engine mines association rules from the connection records. It performs in two distinct modes: training (as shown in Figure 6.5) and detection (as shown in Figure 6.6). In training, a profile of the users and the system's normal behaviors is built and labeled association rules are generated, which are used to train the classification engine. In the detection mode, unexpected association rules which are different from the profiles are mined. These unexpected association rules are classified by the classification engine into normal events or abnormal events. Abnormal events are classified further for their attack names. Table 6.3 summarizes several classifiers for network anomaly detection.

Below, we present some advantages and disadvantages of unsupervised anomaly detection methods.

(i) *Advantages*: Advantages of these methods include the following.

- For partitioning-based clustering, if k can be estimated accurately, the task becomes easy.

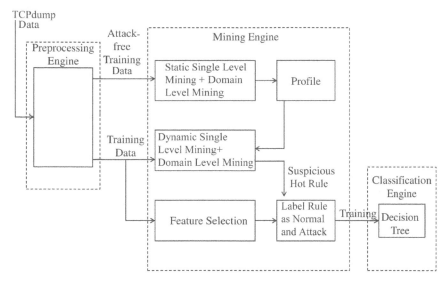

FIGURE 6.5: Training phase of ADAM

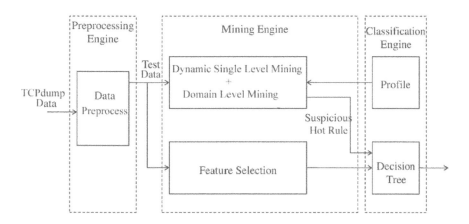

FIGURE 6.6: Detecting mode of ADAM

- Anomaly detection using density-based clustering or outlier mining is effective because it seems to naturally fit the problem of intrusion detection.

- It is helpful to group large datasets into a number of classes for detecting network anomalies, because it reduces the computational complexity during intrusion detection.

- Once profiles of the users, and the system's normal behaviors are properly built and labeled association rules are gen-

TABLE 6.3:   Unsupervised Anomaly Detection Methods

Method	Description
[331]	(i) A user profile dependent anomaly detection method. (ii) Exploits a temporal sequence clustering technique to enable real-time intrusion detection with host-based data collection and processing. (iii) In the training phase, creates user-profiles and in the testing phase, verifies user command stream data against corresponding profile(s).
[242]	(i) Learns rules for finding rare events in nominal time-series data with long range dependencies. (ii) Finds anomalies in network packets and novel intrusion TCP sessions.
[378]	(i) Presents a payload-based anomaly detector. (ii) Models the normal application payload of network traffic in a fully automatic, unsupervised and very efficient fashion. (iii) Computes profile byte frequency distribution and the standard deviation of the application payload flowing to a single host and port during the training phase.
[424]	(i) Reports a clustering-based intrusion detection technique without relying on labeled training data. (ii) For effective identification of attacks, clustering is employed twice: first, to choose candidate anomalies at Agent IDS and second, to identify true attacks at the central IDS.
[274]	(i) Introduces a distance measure for mixed-type intrusion data. (ii) Defines links between two instances by adding distance for categorical and continuous attributes separately.
[226]	(i) The method is based on Transductive Confidence Machines for k-nearest neighbors. (ii) Uses a GA-based instance selection method to limit the scale of the training set and selects the most qualified instances to ensure the quality of the dataset for training. (iii) Uses a filter-based feature selection method to extract the most necessary and relevant features to form the training set for TCM-KNN.
[362]	(i) Introduces a framework for network intrusion detection based on data mining techniques. (ii) Uses fuzzy association rules for building classifiers. (iii) Uses the rule sets as descriptive models of different classes. (iv) Introduces a method to speed up the rule induction algorithm by reducing items from extracted rules.
[419]	(i) Introduces an IDS model for mixed type data. (ii) Uses an improved version of k-means clustering.
[250]	(i) Proposes a clustering-based classifier. (ii) Selects multiple clusters for a test sample. (iii) The average performance of each classifier on selected clusters is calculated and the classifier with the best average performance is chosen to classify the test sample.
[263]	(i) Presents a k-means clustering and Naive Bayes classifier (KMNB) model. (ii) Uses clustering to group the samples into malicious and nonmalicious classes. (iii) The NB classifier is used to classify the data in the final stage into accurate classes.

erated, it is trivial to train the classification engine and subsequently detect known types of attacks.

(ii) *Disadvantages*: The following are some common limitations.

- Most techniques are able to handle continuous attributes only.

- In clustering-based intrusion detection, an assumption is that the larger clusters are normal and smaller clusters are attack or intrusion [297]. Without this assumption, it is difficult to use the technique.

- Use of an inappropriate proximity measure may negatively affect the detection rate.

- Dynamic updating of profiles is time-consuming.

- Single objective association mining using a support-confidence framework is often misleading when identifying rare class attacks.

6.5 Anomaly Detection Using Probabilistic Learning

Probabilistic learning such as Bayesian Belief Networks, based on the original work of Bayes [38] and the Dempster–Shafer theory of belief, independently developed by Dempster [95] and Shafer [334], gives us a mechanism to evaluate the outcome of systems affected by randomness or other types of probabilistic uncertainty. The main characteristic of probabilistic learning is its ability to update previous outcome estimates by conditioning them with newly available evidence. In this section, we introduce five different types of network anomaly detection methods developed using probabilistic learning.

6.5.1 Methods Using the Hidden Markov Model

A hidden Markov model (HMM) is a statistical model [133] where the system being modeled is assumed to be a Markov process with unknown parameters. An example HMM is shown in Figure 6.7. Here, the challenge is to estimate the hidden parameters-based on the observed parameters. Unlike a regular Markov model, where the state transition probabilities are the only parameters and the state of the system is directly observable, in a hidden Markov model, the only visible elements are the variables of the system that are influenced by the state of the system and the state of the system itself is hidden. A hidden Markov model's states represent unobservable conditions of the system being modeled. In each state, a certain probability is associated with producing any of the observable system outputs and correspondingly a separate probability exists indicating the likely next states. By having different output probability distributions in each of the states and allowing the system to change states over time, the model is capable of representing nonstationary sequences.

To estimate the parameters of a hidden Markov model for normal system behavior of a network, sequences of events collected from normal system operations are used as training data. Next, an expectation-maximization (EM) algorithm is used to estimate the parameters. Once a hidden Markov model is trained and is used to confront test data, probability measures are used as thresholds for identification of network anomalies. In order to use hidden Markov models for anomaly detection, the following three key problems need to be solved.

(i) *Evaluation problem*: Given a sequence of observations, determine the probability that the observed sequence was generated by the model.

(ii) *Learning problem*: To build, from the audit data, a model or a set of models that correctly describes the observed behavior.

(iii) *Decoding problem*: For a given HMM and associated observations, determine the most likely set of hidden states that have led to these observations.

In network anomaly detection, the inspection of packets provides the data that can be used to train HMM models [365]. A model derived using the information acquired through inspection of the target system is an appropriate representation for the traffic profile.

Ye [402] uses an HMM model to detect intrusions into a network system. The HMM model of the normal temporal profile is learned from historic data of the system's normal behavior. The observed behavior of the system is analyzed to infer the probability that the HMM model of the normal profile supports the observed behavior. A low probability

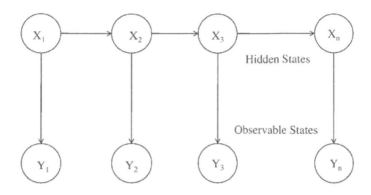

FIGURE 6.7: Example of a hidden Markov model

of support indicates anomalous behavior that may result from intrusive activities.

Yeung [405] describes the use of HMM for anomaly detection by profiling sequences of system calls and shell commands. On training, his model computes the sample likelihood of an observed sequence using forward or backward logics. A threshold on the probability, based on the minimum likelihood among all training sequences, is used to discriminate between normal and anomalous behaviors. One major limitation of this approach is that it lacks generalization and that it may not support those users not uniquely identified by the system under consideration.

6.5.2 Methods Using Bayesian Networks

A Bayesian network (BN) is a model that encodes probabilistic relationships among variables of interest. When used in conjunction with statistical methods, Bayesian networks have several advantages for data analysis [166], as given below.

(i) They are capable of handling situations with missing data since they encode interdependencies among variables.

(ii) They can represent causal relationships and hence are useful in predicting the consequences of an action.

(iii) Since they can represent both causal and probabilistic relationships, they can be used to solve modeling problems like network anomaly identification, where there is the need to combine prior knowledge with data.

The basic technique assumes independence among the attributes. Several variants of the basic technique have been proposed for network anomaly detection [34]. These techniques capture conditional dependencies among the attributes using complex Bayesian networks [207, 373, 402]. Bayesian techniques have been frequently used in the classification and suppression of false alarms. Kruegel et al. [207] propose a multisensor fusion approach where the outputs of IDS sensors are aggregated to produce a single alarm. This approach is based on the assumption that no single anomaly detection technique can classify a set of events as an intrusion with sufficient confidence. Although using Bayesian networks for intrusion detection or intruder behavior prediction can be effective in certain applications, one should be aware of their limitations. For example, the accuracy of this method is dependent on certain assumptions that are typically based on the behavioral model of the target system. So any significant deviation from the assumptions will lead to degradation of detection accuracy.

6.5.3 Naive Bayes Methods

The naive Bayes (NB) model is a simplified Bayesian probability model [216]. This model computes the probability of an end result while several related evidence variables are given. The probability of an evidence variable is assumed to be independent of the probabilities of other evidence variables, given that the same end results occur. In the training phase, the NB algorithm calculates the probabilities of a given result for a particular attribute and then stores this probability. This process is continued for each attribute. In the testing phase, the amount of time taken to calculate the probability of the given class for each example in the worst case is proportional to n, the number of attributes.

Ahirwar et al. [11] propose a method composed of an NB classifier and a weighted Radial Basis Function (RBF) Network [279], a type of artificial neural network. RBFs are embedded in a two-layer neural network, where each hidden unit implements a radially activated function. These neural networks are trained to estimate posterior probabilities of class membership using mixtures of Gaussian basis functions separated by hyperplanes.

Valdes and Skinner [373] develop an anomaly detection system that employs the NB approach to perform intrusion detection on traffic bursts. Their model, which is a part of the EMERALD [296] system, has the ability to potentially detect distributed attacks in which each individual attack session alone is not suspicious enough to generate an alert.

The NB method suffers from the following limitations.

(i) As pointed out in [207], the classification capability of the NB model is identical to a threshold-based system that computes the sum of the outputs obtained from the child nodes.

(ii) Since the child nodes do not interact among themselves and their outputs influence the probability of the root node, it becomes difficult to incorporate additional information as there is no direct interaction between the variables that contain information and the child nodes.

6.5.4 Gaussian Mixture Model

The Gaussian Mixture Model (GMM) [311] is a probabilistic learning model. It is a type of density model that is composed of a number of component functions, usually Gaussian. A Gaussian mixture density is a weighted sum of M component densities and is given by the equation

$$p(\bar{x}|\lambda) = \sum_{i=1}^{M} p_i b_i(\bar{x}) \tag{6.5}$$

where $\bar{x}$ is a D-dimensional random vector, $b_i \bar{x}$, $i = 1, 2, \ldots, M$, are component densities and p_i , $i = 1, 2, \ldots, M$, are mixture weights. Each component density is a D-dimensional variable Gaussian function of the form

$$b_i \bar{x} = \frac{1}{(2\pi)^{D/2} |\Sigma_i|^{1/2}} exp \left\{ -\frac{1}{2} (\bar{x} - \bar{\mu}_i)' \Sigma_i^{-1} (\bar{x} - \bar{\mu}_i) \right\} \tag{6.6}$$

where $\bar{\mu}_i$ is the mean and Σ_i is the covariance. The mixture weights satisfy the following constraint:

$$\sum_{i=1}^{M} p_i = 1. \tag{6.7}$$

The complete Gaussian mixture density is parameterized by the mean vectors, covariance matrices and mixture weights from all component densities. These parameters are collectively represented by the notation

$$\lambda = \{p_i, \bar{m}u_i, \Sigma_i\} \qquad i = 1, 2, \ldots, M. \tag{6.8}$$

For network anomaly detection, each classification of anomalies is represented by a GMM and is referred to by model λ. The GMM can have several forms depending on the choice of covariance matrices, such as (i) one covariance matrix per Gaussian component (nodal covariance), (ii) one covariance matrix for all Gaussian components in a model (grand covariance) or (iii) a single covariance matrix shared by all models (global covariance). The covariance matrix can also be full or diagonal. Full covariance matrices are usually deemed unnecessary by the assumption of statistical independence for the mixture components. This allows simplification by using only the diagonals of the covariance matrix.

Bahrololum and Khaleghi [27] present an anomaly detection method using GMMs. The method identifies abnormal packets in network traffic. The method learns statistics of the parameters from traffic packets. Each input set is framed by itself without any comparison to other groups. For each group, it builds the best possible probability distribution by a set of Gaussian probability distribution functions. The means and variances of the mixtures in each model have different effects on performance. In this work, nodal and diagonal covariance matrices are used for the GMM model. There are two steps in the process: training and detection. The training phase, shown in Figure 6.8, generates reference templates for normal as well as various attack types, such as DoS, U2R, R2L or Probe (a detailed discussion on these attack types is given in Chapter 8). Thus, for each attack type, the system is trained. A compact specification in terms of relevant features is derived for each attack type in order to support the detection of that attack. The features are extracted from the sample traffic data for statistical modeling. In the detection phase, the method attempts to identify any significant deviation for each test instance from the stored reference models. Accordingly, the recognition decision determines whether the test instance belongs to normal or any of the four attack categories, as shown in Figure 6.9.

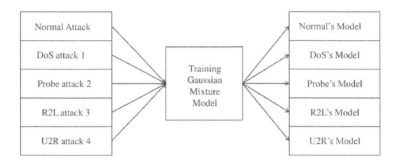

FIGURE 6.8:   Training phase of the GMM model

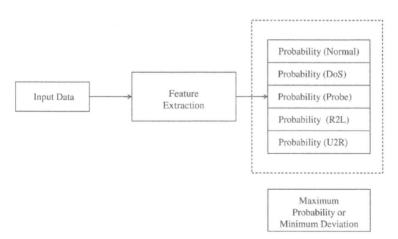

FIGURE 6.9:   Detection phase of the GMM model

6.5.5 Methods Using the EM Algorithm

The expectation-maximization (EM) algorithm [94] is a general method for finding the *maximum likelihood estimation* (MLE) [46] of the parameters of a distribution from a given dataset, even if the data is incomplete or has missing values. Two major advantages of the EM algorithm are that (i) the datasets may have several missing values due to limited observation and (ii) during optimization, when the likelihood function is analytically intractable, it can be simplified by assuming the existence of values for additional but missing (or hidden) parameters. The second application of the EM algorithm is more commonly seen in pattern recognition. EM does not compute a globally optimal solution at each iteration. Rather, it computes a best guess to the answer, which is guaranteed to improve after each iteration.

Patcha and Park [283] use the EM algorithm to cluster incoming audit network data and compute missing values. The EM algorithm starts with an initial guess for the parameters of the mixture model for each cluster and then iteratively applies the Expectation Step (E) and the Maximization Step (M), in order to converge to the maximum likelihood fit. In the E-step, the EM algorithm first finds the expected value of the complete-data log-likelihood, given the observed data and the parameter estimates. In the M-step, the EM algorithm maximizes the expectation computed in the E-step. The two steps of the EM algorithm are repeated until an increase in the log-likelihood of the data, given the current model, is less than the accuracy threshold. Typically, the EM algorithm is executed multiple times with different initial settings for parameter values. Then a given data point is assigned to the cluster with the largest log-likelihood score.

Table 6.4 summarizes several network anomaly detection methods based on probabilistic learning. We enumerate some general advantages and disadvantages of anomaly detection methods using probabilistic learning.

(i) *Advantages*: It is a popular method for detecting network anomalies. The following are some advantages.

- Training and testing with these methods are flexible. It is easy to update the execution strategies with these methods.

- They are capable of detecting known attacks accurately and on time, if appropriate training for those attacks is provided.

TABLE 6.4: Anomaly Detection Using Probabilistic Learning

Method	Description
k-means+ID3 [126]	(i) Presents a method to classify anomalous activities combining k-means and ID3 algorithms. (ii) To obtain a final decision, combines the decisions of k-means and ID3 methods using two rules: (a) the nearest-neighbor rule and (b) the nearest-consensus rule. (iii) The detection accuracy of the k-means+ID3 method is high.
APD algorithm [86]	(i) Introduces a method to detect anomalies in categorical datasets. (ii) The method consists of two steps: (a) Uses a local anomaly detector to identify individual records with anomalous attribute values and (b) Detects patterns where the number of anomalous records is higher than expected. (iii) Detects anomalous patterns in real-world, container shipping and network intrusion data.
DGSOT + SVM algorithm [196]	(i) Uses SVM and hierarchical clustering for classification of anomalies. (ii) Finds the boundary points between two classes to train SVMs to reduce training time. (iii) Combines dynamically growing self-organizing tree (DGSOT) and SVMs to find relevant boundary points to train the 2-class SVM.
CUSUM-EM algorithm [237]	(i) Uses a hybrid framework to achieve optimal performance for detecting network anomalies. (ii) Applies SNORT as the signature-based intrusion detector and two other anomaly detection methods, namely, nonparametric CUSUM and EM-based clustering.
LERAD model [62]	(i) Introduces two methods to construct anomaly detection models from past behavior. (ii) A rule-based learning algorithm is the first method to characterize normal behavior in the absence of labeled attack data. (iii) A clustering algorithm acts as the second method to identify outliers.
KPCC model [369]	(i) Presents a kernel principal component classifier (KPCC) scheme for network anomaly detection. (ii) Captures two kinds of anomalous traffic, viz., (a) extremely large values on some original features and (b) traffic patterns not conforming to the correlation structure of normal traffic.
Oday anomaly detection [276]	(i) Introduces a cognitive algorithm and a mechanism for detecting 0-day attacks. (ii) Able to instantaneously deploy new defense strategies when a new 0-day attack is encountered.
Profile-based approach [345]	(i) Monitors a network's activity for anomalies. (ii) If any deviations are found from profiles of normality previously learned from benign traffic, it reports it as anomalous.
Kernel OCSVM [381]	(i) Uses SVMs for analyzing large volumes of netflow records. (ii) Uses a special kernel function and works with both contextual and qualitative information obtained from network flows to report anomalies.

(ii) *Disadvantages*: These methods have several limitations also.

- They are highly dependent on a number of assumptions made by the systems.

- Often these methods are sensitive to input parameter(s). A slight change in the value(s) of the parameter(s) may substantially affect detection performance.

- Most probabilistic learning methods consume more resources than other methods.

- These methods are not capable of detecting or predicting unknown attack(s) or event(s) until relevant training information is fed.

6.6   Anomaly Detection Using Soft Computing

Soft computing is called soft in order to contrast it from hard computing, which entails exact communication and response. Some characteristics of soft computing are the use of probability, such as (i) randomness in Bayes reasoning and (ii) inexactness in fuzzy sets. Soft computing techniques are suitable for network anomaly detection because often one cannot find exact solutions. Soft computing is usually thought of as encompassing methods such as genetic algorithms, artificial neural networks, fuzzy sets, rough sets, ant colony algorithms and artificial immune systems. We describe several soft computing methods for network anomaly detection below.

6.6.1   Genetic Algorithm Approaches

Genetic algorithms (GAs) represent a computational model-based on principles of evolution and natural selection. In this approach, a problem is converted into a framework that uses a chromosome-like data structure. The chromosomes are evolved through many generations using operations such as selection, recombination and mutation. In computer network security applications, evolutionary computing is used mainly for finding solutions to optimization problems. In the network anomaly detection problem, a chromosome for an individual contains genes corresponding to attributes such as services, flags, logged in or not and the number of superuser attempts. Based on an experimental study, Khan's observation [197] is that attacks that are more common can be detected more accurately compared to uncommon attacks. In another effort, Balajinath and Raghavan [30] present a genetic algorithm-based intrusion detector (GBID) that learns individual user behavior. User behavior is described as a 3-tuple *<matching index, entropy index, newness index>* and is learned using a genetic algorithm. This behavior profile is used to detect network anomalies based on past behavior.

6.6.2 Artificial Neural Network Approaches

Work on ANNs (Artificial Neural Networks) has been motivated from its inception by the recognition that the human brain computes in an entirely different way from the conventional digital computer [165]. ANNs are established tools for various applications such as data clustering, feature extraction and anomalous pattern identification in a network. Cannady's approach [59] autonomously learns new attacks rapidly using modified reinforcement learning. His approach uses feedback for signature update when a new attack is encountered. Lee and Heinbuch [220] use a hierarchy of neural networks to detect anomalies. The neural networks are trained using data that spans the entire normal space and are able to recognize unknown attacks. Liu et al. [231] report a real-time solution to detect known and new attacks in network traffic using unsupervised neural nets. It uses a hierarchical intrusion detection model using Principal Components Analysis (PCA) neural networks to overcome shortcomings of single-level structures. Sun et al. [360] present a Wavelet Neural Network (WNN)-based intrusion detection method. It reduces the number of wavelet basic functions by analyzing the sparseness property of the sample data to optimize the wavelet network. The learning algorithm trains the network using gradient descent. Yong and Feng [408] use recurrent multilayered perceptrons (RMLP) [281], a dynamic extension of well-known feedforward layered networks, to classify network data into anomalous and normal. An RMLP network has the ability to encode temporal information. The authors develop an incremental kernel principal components algorithm to preprocess the data that goes into the neural network.

6.6.3   Fuzzy Set Theoretic Approach

Fuzzy network intrusion detection systems use fuzzy rules to determine the likelihood of specific or general network attacks [98]. A fuzzy input set can be defined to describe traffic in a specific network. Tajbakhsh et al. [362] describe a novel method for building classifiers using fuzzy association rules and use it for network intrusion detection. The fuzzy association rule sets are used to describe normal and anomalous classes. Such fuzzy association rules are *class association rules* where the consequents are classes. Whether a training instance belongs to a specific class is determined using matching metrics. The fuzzy association rules are induced using normal training samples. A test sample is classified as normal if the compatibility of the ruleset generated is above a certain threshold. Those with lower compatibility are considered anomalous. The authors also propose a method to speed up rule induction by reducing items from extracted rules.

Mabu et al. [240] present a novel fuzzy class association rule mining method based on Genetic Network Programming (GNP) for detecting network intrusions. GNP is an evolutionary optimization technique which uses directed graph structures instead of strings in standard genetic algorithms, leading to enhanced representation ability with compact descriptions derived from possible node reusability in a graph. Xian et al. [388] propose a novel unsupervised fuzzy clustering method based on clonal selection for anomaly detection. The method is capable of obtaining global optimal clusters more quickly than competing algorithms.

6.6.4   Rough Set Approaches

A rough set is an approximation of a crisp set (i.e., a regular set) in terms of a pair of sets that are its lower and upper approximations. In the standard and original versions of rough set theory [285, 286], the two approximations are crisp sets, but in other variations the approximating sets may be fuzzy sets. The mathematical framework of rough set theory enables modeling of relationships with a minimum number of rules [139]. Rough sets have two useful features [58]: (i) enabling learning with small training datasets and (ii) overall simplicity. They can be applied to anomaly detection by modeling normal behavior of network traffic. For example, in [75], the authors present a Fuzzy Rough C-means clustering technique for network intrusion detection by integrating fuzzy set theory and rough set theory to achieve a high detection rate. Chen et al. [67] use a two-step classifier for network intrusion detection. Initially, it uses rough set theory for feature reduction and then a support vector machine classifier for final classification.

6.6.5 Ant Colony and AIS Approaches

Ant colony optimization [104] and related algorithms are probabilistic techniques for solving computational problems that can be reformulated to find optimal paths through graphs. The algorithms are based on the behavior of ants seeking a path between their colony and a source of food. Gao et al. [129] use ant colony optimization for feature selection for an SVM classifier for network intrusion detection. The features are represented as graph nodes with the edges between them denoting the addition of the next feature. Ants traverse the graph to add nodes until a stopping criterion is encountered.

Artificial Immune Systems (AISs) represent a computational method inspired by the principles of the human immune system. The human immune system is adept at performing anomaly detection. The anomaly detection in the human immune system classifies certain external objects that enter the body as undesirable antigens, i.e., objects that may cause illness. In real life, the immune system reacts by creating what are called antibodies to fight antigens. The classification of an external object that has entered the body as an antigen requires classifying the external object as nonself, i.e., that the object is not part of our self or body. This process is called *negative selection*. Negative selection has motivated computer scientists to develop immune system inspired algorithms which work in a similar way [88, 170]. Stibor et al. [354] implement a real-valued negative selection algorithm that employs variable size detectors. They experiment with this algorithm in the domain of anomaly detection in network data. The authors conclude that the time required to generate enough detectors for high confidence negative selection is very high and impractical for high dimensional intrusion data. Visconti and Tahayori [376] present a performance-based AIS for detecting individual anomalous behavior. It monitors the system by analyzing the set of parameters to provide general information on its state. An interval type-2 fuzzy set paradigm is used to dynamically generate system status.

Tables 6.5 and 6.6 summarize several soft computing-based anomaly detection methods. We enumerate advantages and limitations of soft computing anomaly detection methods below.

TABLE 6.5:   Soft Computing-Based Anomaly Detection Methods

Method	Description
GA-based approach	
Behavior model [30]	(i) A GA-based intrusion detector (GBID) that learns individual user behavior. (ii) User behavior is described as 3-tuple <matching index, entropy index, newness index> and learned using a genetic algorithm. (iii) Detects intrusion based on past behavior.
ANN-based approach	
NSOM model [215]	(i) Preprocesses data using a sampling method to select attributes. (ii) Applies the EM algorithm for intrusion detection.
Adaptive NN [59]	(i) Applies adaptive NN to anomaly detection, capable of autonomously learning new attacks rapidly by a modified reinforcement learning method. (ii) Uses feedback for signature update.
Hierarchical NN [220]	(i) Composed of a hierarchy of NNs, it works well as an anomaly detector. (ii) NNs are trained using data that spans the entire normal space and able to recognize unknown attacks.
HNNIDS Model [418]	(i) Two hierarchical IDS frameworks using RBF. (ii) Initially a serial hierarchical IDS (SHIDS) identifies a misuse attack accurately and anomaly attacks adaptively. (iii) Then a parallel hierarchical IDS (PHIDS) enhances the SHIDSs functionalities and performance.
RT-UNNID system [14]	(i) Detects intelligently in real time using unsupervised NN. (ii) Handles new instances effectively without retraining. (iii) Uses Adaptive Resonance Theory and Self-Organizing Map NN using offline data.
Unsupervised NN [231]	(i) Detects both known and unknown attacks in real time. (ii) Uses a hierarchical intrusion model using PCA NNs to overcome the shortcomings of single level structure.
WNN model [360]	(i) A wavelet NN (WNN)-based IDS. (ii) Reduces the number of wavelet basic functions by analyzing the sparseness property of sample data which can optimize the wavelet network to a large extent. The learning algorithm trains the network using gradient descent. (iii) Performance is satisfactory.
NN-based IDS [210]	(i) Presents an experimental analysis for attack detection by using NN-based IDS. (ii) Adaptibility makes it easy to test and retrain the neural classifier.

TABLE 6.6: Soft Computing-Based Anomaly Detection Methods

Method	Description
Fuzzy set theoretic approach	
Unsupervised fuzzy clustering [388]	(i) A novel unsupervised fuzzy clustering method based on clonal selection for anomaly detection. (ii) Obtains global optimal clusters faster than other competing algorithms.
Fuzzy rule mining [240]	(i) Based on genetic network programming (GNP) for detecting network intrusions. (ii) Uses directed graph structures instead of strings in GA to enhance the representation ability with compact programs derived from node reusability from a graph structure.
Rough set-based approach	
Fuzzy rough C-means [75]	A fuzzy rough C-means clustering technique by integrating fuzzy set theory and rough set theory to achieve a high detection rate in intrusion detection.
RST-SVM method [67]	Uses rough set theory (RST) and SVM for detecting anomalies. RST helps reduce features and sends data to the SVM classifier for final classification.
Ant colony and AIS-based approach	
Ant colony and SVM [129]	(i) Uses ant colony optimization for feature selection and SVM for network intrusion detection. (ii) Represents the features as graph nodes with the edges between them denoting the adding of the next feature. Ants traverse the graph to add nodes until the stopping criteria is encountered.
AIS system [376]	(i) A performance-based AIS for detecting individual anomalous behavior. (ii) Monitors the system by analyzing the set of parameters to provide general information on its state. (iii) Uses an interval type-2 fuzzy set paradigm to dynamically enable the system status.

(i) *Advantages*: Advantages include the following.

- They are not brittle. In other words, they can solve problems that do not have exact answers.

- The nature inspired methods such as genetic algorithms, genetic programming, ant colony systems and artificial immune systems have already been established to be effective in solving very complex optimization problems efficiently.

- The learning system detects or categorizes persistent features without any feedback from the environment.

- Due to the adaptive nature of ANNs, it is possible to train and test instances incrementally using certain algorithms.

- Unsupervised learning is very effective in fuzzy clustering and rough set-based feature extraction or selection.

- Multilevel neural network-based techniques are more efficient than single level neural networks.

- To resolve inconsistency in the dataset and to generate a minimal, nonredundant rule set, the rough set approach is useful.

(ii) *Disadvantages*: Some disadvantages of soft computing methods are given below.

- Over-fitting, which may happen during neural network training, is a problem.

- If a credible amount of normal traffic data is not available, the training of the techniques becomes very difficult.

- Most methods have scalability problems.

- Lack of completeness that guarantees the generation of all possible rules is a major shortcoming of the rough set approach.

- In the fuzzy association rule-based technique, dynamic rule updating is a difficult task.

6.7   Knowledge in Anomaly Detection

In knowledge-based methods, network or host events are checked against predefined rules or patterns of attack. Examples of knowledge-based methods are expert systems, rule-based, ontology-based, logic-based and state-transition analysis [270, 328, 392]-based systems. An example of knowledge-based misuse detection system that uses degrees of attack guilt is reported in [299]. Such techniques search for instances of known attacks by matching against predetermined attack representations. The search begins as all intrusion detection techniques begin, with a complete lack of knowledge of any attack. Subsequent matching of an activity against a known attack helps the acquisition of knowledge. This gained knowledge corresponds to moving lower on the known-guilt scale. In practice, new attacks or even sufficiently different variations of known attacks may be missed. A few prominent knowledge-based methods for network anomaly detection are given below.

6.7.1 Expert System and Rule-Based Approaches

The expert system approach is one of the most widely used knowledge-based methods [96, 17]. An expert system, in the traditional sense, is a rule-based system, with or without an associated knowledge base. An expert system has a rule engine that matches rules against the current state of the system and depending on the results of matching, fires one or more rules. An expert system separates the specification of the rules from the processing of the rules.

Snort [312, 146] is a quintessentially popular rule-based IDS. This open-source system matches each packet it observes against a set of rules. The antecedent of a Snort rule is a boolean formula composed of predicates that look for specific values of fields present in IP headers, transport headers and in the payload. Thus, Snort rules identify attack packets based on IP addresses, TCP or UDP port numbers, ICMP codes or types and contents of strings in the packet payload. Snort's rules are arranged into priority classes based on the potential impact of alerts that match the rules. Snort's rules have evolved over its history of 15 years. Each Snort rule has associated documentation with the potential for false positives and negatives, together with corrective actions to be taken when the rule raises an alert. Snort rules are simple and easily understandable. Users can contribute rules when they observe new types of anomalous or malicious traffic. Currently, Snort has over 20,000 rules, inclusive of those submitted by users.

An intrusion detection system like Snort can run on a general purpose computer and can try to inspect all packets that go through the network. However, monitoring packets comprehensively in a large network is obviously an expensive task since it requires fast inspection on a large number of network interfaces. Many hundreds of rules may have to be matched concurrently, making scaling almost impossible. To scale large networks that collect flow statistics, Duffield et al.[106] use a machine learning algorithm called Adaboost [324] to translate packet level signatures to work with flow level statistics. The algorithm is used to correlate packet and flow information. In particular, Duffield et al. associate packet level network alarms with a feature vector they create from flow records on the same traffic. They create a set of rules using flow information with features similar to those used in Snort rules. They also add numerical features such as the number of packets of a specific kind flowing within a certain time period. Duffield et al. train Adaboost on concurrent flow and packet traces. Adaboost is a meta-learning algorithm that can be used with other learning algorithms to improve classification performance. It starts with a simple classifier and creates subsequent classifiers that improve performance by focusing on misclassified instances and making sure that the misclassification rate goes down incrementally. Duffield et al. are able to obtain performance comparable to Snort's with flow data.

Prayote [299] presents an approach to anomaly detection that attempts to address the brittleness problem in which an expert system makes a decision that human common sense would recognize as impossible. He uses a technique called *prudence* [81], in which for every rule, the upper and lower bounds of each numerical variable in the data seen by the rule are recorded, as well as a list of values seen for enumerated variables. The expert system raises a warning when a new value or a value outside the range is seen in a data instance. Prayote improves this approach by using a simple probabilistic technique to decide if a value is an outlier. He also allows the expected range for a variable to decrease or increase in size over time depending on values seen in data instances. Prayote builds the expert system based on cases seen and classified by an expert. Every time the expert system produces a result different from the actual expert, the rule base is changed appropriately. He also records whether a warning was generated correctly or falsely and uses it to adapt the rules. When working with network anomaly data, the author partitions the problem space into smaller subspaces of homogeneous traffic, each of which is represented by a separate model, described in terms of rules. The author finds that this approach works reasonably well for new subspaces when little data has been observed.

Scheirer and Chuah [325] develop an intrusion detection scheme that uses both syntax and semantics present in a string that represents a worm program. The syntactic part of their approach divides the worm code into variable-length partitions until break marks are detected. They create Rabin fingerprints [307],[55] and compare these rolling fingerprints to detect polymorphic worms. The semantic part of their approach uses a template-based method that extends the program profiling approach presented in Christodorescu et al. [77] to capture more syntactic variants of the worm. Thus, for this method to be successful, it requires one to be able to write templates that describe the expected behavior of the worms it wants to catch. The authors claim that with high quality templates they are able to detect wide syntactic variations in worms that exhibit the same behavior.

6.7.2 Ontology- and Logic-Based Approaches

It is possible to model attack signatures using expressive logic structures in real time by incorporating constraints and even statistical properties. For example, Naldurg et al. [266] present a framework for intrusion detection based on temporal logic specification. Intrusion patterns are specified as formulas in an expressively rich and efficiently monitorable logic called EAGLE that supports data values and parameterized recursive equations. They develop a monitoring algorithm that matches specification of the absence of an attack with system execution traces and raises an alarm when the specification is violated.

Shabtai et al. [333] describe an approach for detecting previously unencountered malware targeting mobile devices. Time-stamped security data is continuously monitored within the target mobile devices like smart phones and PDAs. Then it is processed by what is called the knowledge-based temporal abstraction (KBTA) methodology. The authors evaluate the KBTA model using a lightweight host-based intrusion detection system, combined with central management capabilities for Android-based mobile phones.

Hung and Liu [181] use an ontology as a way of describing the knowledge of a domain. This enables them to express the intrusion detection system in terms of the end user's domain. Ontologies are also used as a conceptual modeling tool allowing a nonexpert person to model intrusion detection applications using concepts of intrusion detection more intuitively. Of course, individuals with domain expertise are also used.

Table 6.7 summarizes some prominent knowledge-based anomaly detection methods. Below we enumerate some advantages and limitations of these knowledge-based anomaly detection methods.

(i) *Advantages*: The main advantages of knowledge-based anomaly methods include the following.

- They are usually flexible and robust in performance.
- They can obtain a high detection rate if appropriate knowledge about the attack as well as normal instances is acquired, represented and referred to during anomaly identification.

(ii) *Disadvantages*: These methods also suffer from the following limitations.

- Acquiring and developing high-quality knowledge is often difficult and time consuming.

- Due to lack of unbiased and complete knowledge about the normal and possible attack instances, these methods often generate a large number of false alarms.

- They are generally incapable of handling unknown attacks.

- Dynamic updating of rule or knowledge base is a costly affair.

6.8   Anomaly Detection Using Combination Learners

This section describes methods which apply combinations of multiple learning techniques. The major objective of these methods is to achieve high detection accuracy or low false alarm rates. The methods are divided into three major categories: *ensemble, fusion* and *hybrid*.

6.8.1   Ensemble Methods

The idea behind the ensemble methodology is to weigh several individual classifiers and combine them to obtain an overall classifier that outperforms every one of them [295],[135],[313]. In fact, human beings tend to seek several opinions before making any important decision. These techniques weigh the individual opinions and combine them to reach the final decision. Three main approaches to developing ensemble methods are (i) bagging (ii) boosting and (iii) stack generalization. Table 6.8 summarizes several ensemble methods for network anomaly detection.

Below we present advantages and limitations of ensemble network anomaly detection methods.

(i) *Advantages*: An ensemble method obtains higher accuracy than the individual techniques. The following are the major advantages.

- Even if the individual classifiers are weak, the ensemble methods perform well by combining multiple classifiers.

- Ensemble methods can scale for large datasets.

- Ensemble classifiers need a set of control parameters to obtain the best possible accuracy based on individual performances of the base classifiers. However, these parameters are comprehensive and can be easily tuned.

- The user is usually able to understand easily the ensemble's result.

- Stack generalization is another effective ensemble approach because of its ability to exploit the diversity in the predictions of multiple base level classifiers.

(ii) *Disadvantages*: Here are some disadvantages.

- Selecting a subset of classifiers from a pool of classifiers for obtaining better performance is difficult.

- The greedy approach for selecting a sample classifier is slow for large datasets.

- Retraining of all the new instances for multiple base classifiers is time-consuming.

- It is difficult to provide real-time performance.

6.8.2 Fusion Methods

Several fusion techniques have been applied to network anomaly detection [136, 340, 278, 427]. These techniques can be classified as (i) data level, (ii) feature level and (iii) decision level. Some methods work in high dimensional feature spaces to extract and concatenate different semantic meanings. Others attempt to combine classifiers trained on different features divided on the basis of hierarchical abstraction levels or the types of information contained. A pattern recognition approach to network intrusion detection based on the fusion of multiple classifiers is proposed by [136]. Shifflet [340] provides a platform that enables a multitude of techniques to work together toward creating a more realistic model of the state of a network, able to detect malicious activity effectively.

Table 6.9 summarizes several fusion methods for network anomaly detection. Below we enumerate advantages and limitations of existing fusion-based network anomaly detection methods.

Some advantages of fusion methods include: (i) typically such methods take less training time and hence are more cost effective, (ii) fusion methods produce reduced false alarm rates and (iii) with appropriate training data, decision level fusion usually yields high detection rate. Drawbacks include: (i) the computational cost becomes high for rigorous training on the samples, (ii) feature level fusion is a time-consuming task and (iii) building hypotheses for different classifiers at the same time is difficult.

6.8.3   Hybrid Methods

Most current network intrusion detection systems employ either misuse detection or anomaly detection. However, misuse detection cannot detect unknown intrusions and anomaly detection usually has high false positive rate [23]. To overcome the limitations of the techniques, hybrid methods exploit features from several network anomaly detection approaches. A hybrid learning method aims to handle both known as well as unknown instances with high accuracy. Researchers [2] have hybridized ANN and CBR (case-based reasoning) within a Multi-Agent System (MAS) to identify anomalies in dynamic networks. The authors propose a dynamic real-time multiagent architecture for anomaly detection which allows the inclusion of both reactive and deliberative prediction agents. Here, time-bounded CBR is incorporated in two of the deliberative agents. A major advantage of this hybrid system is that it allows us to adapt the paradigm to real-time requirements. The FLIP [235] is another hybridization effort to host security that prevents binary code injection attacks. The FLIP model includes three basic components: viz. (i) an anomaly-based classifier, (ii) a signature-based filter and (iii) a supervision framework. FLIP captures the injected code and attempts to construct signatures for zero-day exploits. In another attempt [289], the authors introduce an ensemble of decision trees (DT) and SVMs for network anomaly detection, referred to as a hierarchical hybrid intelligent system model. The approach derives benefits of both proven classifiers in terms of minimum false alarm rates. It also minimizes computational complexity.

A systematic framework is introduced in [420] to exploit the random forests algorithm [51] for misuse-, anomaly- and hybrid-network-based intrusion detection. The system is able to improve the detection performance of known attacks significantly. In another effort, a hybrid RBF/Elman neural network model is introduced [370] for both anomaly detection as well as misuse detection. It uses its memory of past events for effective identification of temporally dispersed and collaborative attacks. Another effective and flexible ANN-based intelligent hybrid NIDS is introduced in [413]. The model can be extended to meet different network scenarios with improved detection performance. Selim et al. [330] recently report a hybrid intelligent detection system consisting of multiple levels containing hybrid neural networks and decision trees. The performance of the system is better than competing approaches in terms of known and unknown attacks.

Table 6.10 summarizes a few hybrid methods for network anomaly detection. Advantages of hybrid network anomaly detection include the following: (i) Generally such methods perform better than individual signature-based methods and anomaly-based NIDSs in terms of attack detection rate and (ii) appropriate hybridization enables us to detect both known and unknown attacks. Drawbacks include the following: (i) Inappropriate hybridization may lead to high overhead and low execution performance and (ii) the updating of rules or signatures without conflict with the existing rules and without human intervention is still difficult.

6.9 Discussion

In this chapter, we have discussed a large number of methods for network anomaly detection under different categories. We make the following summary observations.

(i) All anomaly-based network intrusion detection techniques and systems discussed in previous sections have unique strengths and weaknesses. The suitability of an anomaly detection technique depends on the nature of the problem one needs to address.

(ii) For complex datasets, the techniques face various challenges. Nearest neighbor and clustering techniques do not perform well when the number of dimensions is high because distance measures are not able to differentiate well between normal and anomalous instances in high dimensions. Subspace clustering techniques explicitly address the high dimension problem by mapping data to lower dimensional subspaces. But identification of appropriate subspaces is again a time-consuming task. Classification techniques often perform better in such scenarios. However, they require labeled training data for both normal and attack classes. Improper distribution of classes in the training data often makes the task of learning challenging. Semi-supervised nearest neighbor and clustering techniques that only use normal labels are often more practical than classification techniques. The success of the statistical techniques is largely influenced by the validity of the statistical assumptions in real-life scenarios.

(iii) Nearest neighbor and clustering techniques require proximity computation between pairs of data instances. Such techniques assume that a proximity measure can help distinguish anomalous instances from normal instances. In situations where identifying a good distance measure is difficult, classification or statistical techniques may be a better choice. For real-time intrusion detection, the time complexity of the anomaly detection process is important. For classification, clustering and statistical methods, although training is expensive, they are still acceptable because testing is faster and training is offline.

(iv) Anomaly detection techniques typically assume that anomalies in data are rare, compared to normal instances. Generally, such assumptions are valid, but not always. Often unsupervised techniques suffer from high false alarm rates, when the anomalies occur in bulk. Techniques operating in supervised or semi-supervised modes [349] perform better in detecting bulk anomalies.

TABLE 6.7: Knowledge-Based Anomaly Detection Methods

Method	Description
Rule-based approach	
Adaptive intrusion detection [223]	(i) Computes activity patterns from system audit data and extracts predictive features from patterns. (iii) Generates rules to detect intrusions by applying machine learning algorithm on audit records according to feature definitions.
Rule-GA [197]	(i) A rule-based method that uses GA. (ii) Evaluated based on the DoS and probe attacks.
IP flow-based anomaly detection [106]	Introduces a network wide system architecture for flow-based anomaly detection. (ii) Evaluated using machine learning techniques.
Expert system approach	
DCEIPCA algorithm [408]	(i) Introduces an incremental kernel PCA algorithm to handle large datasets. (ii) Uses an expert system to identify network anomalies. (ii) Evaluated using KDDcup99 intrusion datasets.
Syntax vs. Semantic-based approach [325]	(i) Introduces a syntax-based scheme that uses variable-length partition with multiple break marks to detect polymorphic worms. (ii) Provides semantics-aware capability. (iii) Can capture polymorphic shell codes with additional stack sequences and mathematical operations.
Ontology- and logic-based approach	
Markov chain model [116]	(i) Describes a finite state machine methodology, where a sequence of states and transitions among them seem appropriate for modeling network protocols. (ii) Can detect illegitimate behavioral patterns effectively.
EAGLE logic model [266]	(i) Introduces a framework based on temporal logic specification to detect intrusions. (ii) Specifies the intrusion patterns as formulas in an expressively rich and efficiently monitorable logic called EAGLE. (iii) Evaluated using DARPA log files.
Ontology-based algorithm [181]	(i) Uses ontologies as a way of describing the knowledge of a domain. (ii) Expresses the intrusion detection mechanism in terms of end users domain. (iii) Uses ontologies as a conceptual modeling tool allowing a nonexpert to model intrusion detection application using only the concepts of intrusion detection more intuitively.
Logic-based model [262]	(i) Introduces a federated data model for security systems to query and assert knowledge about security incidents and the context in which they occur. (ii) Includes a consistent and formal ground to represent information that is required to reason about complementary evidence, in order to confirm or invalidate alerts raised by intrusion detection systems.
KBTA model [333]	(i) Detects unknown malware targeting mobile devices. (ii) Monitors continuously time-stamped security data within the target mobile devices like smart phones and PDAs. (ii) Processed by knowledge-based temporal abstraction (KBTA) methodology. (iii) Evaluated using a lightweight HIDS combined with central management capabilities for Android-based mobile phones.

TABLE 6.8: Ensemble Methods for Anomaly Detection

Method	Description
Class specific ensemble IDS model [65]	(i) Introduces an ensemble approach by combining two classifiers, Bayesian networks (BN) and Classification and Regression Trees (CART). (ii) A hybrid architecture for combining different feature selection algorithms for real-world intrusion detection is incorporated to get better results.
Cluster ensemble [264]	(i) A cluster ensemble approach to find more natural clusterings by combining multiple clusterings, hypothesizing that multiple views of the data will improve the detection of attacks. (ii) Each clustering rates how anomalous a point is. Ratings are combined by averaging or taking the minimum, the maximum or median scores.
One-class SVM classifier model [293]	An approach to construct a high speed payload-based anomaly IDS using an ensemble of one-class SVM classifiers intended to be accurate and hard to evade.
Heterogeneous classifiers ensemble [49]	Outputs of four base classifiers ANN, SVM, kNN and decision trees are fused using three combination strategies: (i) majority voting, (ii) Bayesian averaging and (iii) based on a belief measure.
McPAD model [292]	(i) McPAD (Multiple classifier Payload-based Anomaly Detector) is a payload-based anomaly detection system that consists of an ensemble of one-class classifiers. (ii) The anomaly detector is very accurate in detecting network attacks that bear some form of shell code in the malicious payload.
GEdIDS model [120]	(i) A distributed data mining algorithm to improve detection accuracy when classifying malicious or unauthorized network activity. (ii) Developed using genetic programming (GP) extended with the ensemble paradigm. (iii) Data is distributed across multiple autonomous sites and the learner component acquires useful knowledge from data in a cooperative way. (iv) Network profile is used to predict abnormal behavior.
FRaC model [272]	(i) An approach to semi-supervised anomaly detection built on an ensemble of predictors from a single-class examples training set. (ii) A novel, information-theoretic anomaly measure that experimental results show works in the presence of noisy and irrelevant features.
Cluster-based ensemble [268]	(i) Individual classifiers are built using both the input feature space and an additional subset of features given by k-means clustering. (ii) The ensemble combination is calculated based on the classification ability of classifiers on different local data segments given by k-means clustering.

TABLE 6.9: Anomaly Detection Using Fusion Methods

Method	Description
MCS model [136]	(i) Introduces a network intrusion detection method based on fusion of multiple classifiers. (ii) Evaluates five decision fusion methods and compares their performance.
SVO model [118]	(i) Introduces an event-driven intrusion detection architecture that integrates Subject-Verb-Object (SVO) multipoint monitors and an impact analysis engine. (ii) Implements alert fusion and verification models to provide more reasonable intrusion information from incomplete, inconsistent or imprecise alerts acquired by SVO monitors.
D-S and PCA algorithm [64]	(i) Introduces heterogeneous data level fusion for network anomaly detection. (ii) Uses the Dempster–Shafer theory of evidence and PCA to develop the technique. (iii) Evaluated in emulation and simulation scenarios.
dLEARNIN system [278]	(i) Introduces an ensemble approach to intelligently combine information from multiple sources. (ii) Explicitly tuned toward minimization of cost of errors as opposed to the error rate itself. (iii) Achieves better performance.
NAS model [132]	(i) Merges two methods with multisource information fusion technology. (ii) Ensures a more accurate decision for suspicious behaviors with more information gathered from different levels of the system. (iii) Can update the profiles automatically.
IDEA model [147]	Introduces an ANN-based method to perform data fusion and intrusion analysis and to prune unwanted information from multisensors. (ii) Achieves high detection accuracy.
HMMPayl model [22]	(i) Represents the payload as a sequence of bytes. (ii) Performs analysis using HMM. (ii) Extracts features and uses HMM to guarantee the same expressive power as that of n-gram analysis, while reducing computational complexity. (iii) Follows the Multiple Classifiers System paradigm to provide better classification accuracy to increase the difficulty of evading the IDS. (iv) Mitigates weaknesses due to a nonoptimal choice of HMM parameters.

TABLE 6.10: Hybrid Anomaly Detection

Method	Description
DH-ABIDERS model [193]	(i) Introduces a method to detect active attacks causing DoS attacks as well as the usage of access point discovery tools in a wireless network. (ii) Performs in real time by sending out alerts to the network administrator.
FLIPS model [235]	(i) Presents a method to prevent binary code injection attacks by using FLIPS (Feedback Learning Intrusion Prevention System). (ii) Incorporates three major components: an anomaly-based classifier, a signature-based filtering scheme and a supervision framework that employs Instruction Set Randomization (ISR). (iii) Captures the injected code and allows FLIPS to construct signatures for zero-day exploits.
Random forests hybrid method [418]	Reports a method that combines misuse detection and anomaly-based intrusion detection using the random forests algorithm. (ii) Obtains a better detection rate.
DT-SVM hybrid model [289]	(i) Presents a method to combine decision trees and support vector machines as a hierarchical hybrid intelligent system model for intrusion detection. (ii) Maximizes detection accuracy and minimizes computational complexity.
E-FSM model [36]	(i) Introduces a HIDS architecture for converged VoIP applications. (ii) Uses communicating extended finite state machines formal model to provide both stateful and cross-protocol detection. (iii) Combines signature-based and specification-based detection techniques along with combining protocol syntax and semantics.
RFIDS model [421]	(i) Introduces a systematic framework that applies the random forests algorithm in misuse-, anomaly- and hybrid-network-based IDS. (ii) Shows better performance on several datasets.
Hybrid ANN-based model [44]	(i) Presents a hybrid method to assess impacts of undetected attacks using ANN. (ii) Also uses GA-based approach. (iii) Implements a stochastic model which enables a cost/benefit analysis for systems security and enables the making of informative decisions regarding intrusion detection and system protection.
Hybrid IDS model [277]	(i) Introduces an automated system to detect DoS attacks. (ii) Designed as a two-stage architecture incorporating the change-point detection methodology used for early attack identification and further spectral profiling used for confirmation of the attack presence.
Hybrid RBF/Elman neural network model [370]	(i) Employs a hybrid RBF/Elman neural network model for both anomaly detection and misuse detection. (ii) Detects temporally dispersed and collaborative attacks effectively because of its memory of past events.
Hybrid IDS [146]	Uses an anomaly preprocessor that extends the functionality of SNORT IDS.
Hybrid classifier [76]	(i) Introduces an ensemble of a feature-selecting classifier and a data mining classifier to identify network anomalies. (ii) Fuses both classifiers to make the final decision.
Intelligent hybrid IDS [413]	(i) Introduces an ANN-based intelligent hybrid IDS model. (ii) Model is flexible and can be extended to meet different network environments improve detection performance and accuracy.
Hybrid multilevel IDS model [330]	(i) Introduces a hybrid intelligent IDS to improve the detection rate for known and unknown attacks. (ii) Consists of multiple levels: hybrid neural networks and decision trees.

Chapter 7

Evaluation Methods

It is common knowledge that nothing is absolutely secure, without any fear of compromise ever. An evaluation or assessment of quality or accuracy of a system, mechanism or method is usually a snapshot in time. With the passage of time after a system is initially built, the environment changes, new vulnerabilities arise and accordingly the evaluation must be performed again after parameter tuning. However, it is worth mentioning that the information obtained during one evaluation process plays a significant role in subsequent evaluations as well as in the final end product that results. In this chapter, we discuss 16 different evaluation measures under three broad categories: *correctness*, *data* and *efficiency*. Figure 7.1 shows these measures in a three-dimensional axis diagram.

7.1 Accuracy

Accuracy is used to evaluate the performance of a NIDS in terms of correctness. It measures detection and failure rates as well as the number of false alarms that the system produces [24], [25], [230]. A NIDS with an accuracy of 95% implies that it correctly classifies 95 instances out of 100 to their actual class. Usually attacks are very diverse in manner and the number of attack traffic instances is generally much smaller than normal instances [297], [191], [101]. As a result, most currently available NIDSes generate a large amount of false alarms. In other words, the current state-of-the-art systems are not as efficient and accurate as ideally desired. The accuracy metric helps evaluate a NIDS to determine how correctly it can detect an attack. The accuracy of a NIDS can be assessed in terms of five measures: (i) sensitivity and specificity, (ii) misclassification rate, (iii) confusion matrix entries, (iv) precision-recall and F measures and (v) receiver operating character-

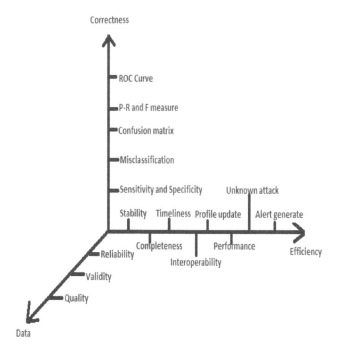

FIGURE 7.1:   3-D perspective of evaluation measures

istics (ROC) curve. Let us now discuss each of these measures in more detail.

7.1.1   Sensitivity and Specificity

To make effective use of these two measures, a NIDS developer models the network traffic classification problem as a 2-class (viz., *normal* and *anomalous*) classification problem. It labels the attack or anomalous data positive, while the normal data is labeled negative. Since during the classification of the traffic, outcomes can be correct as well as incorrect, it uses a *True* label for decisions it thinks correct and *False* for decisions it thinks incorrect. As a result, as shown in Figure 7.2, there can be four possibilities out of these two variables: True Positive (*TP*), True Negative (*TP*), False Positive (*FP*) and False Negative (*FN*).

When a NIDS correctly classifies an anomalous instance, we call it a *TP*, whereas an *FP* is said to occur when a legitimate action is misclassified as anomalous. Similarly, a *TN* occurs when a normal instance is correctly classified as a legitimate action, while an *FN* oc-

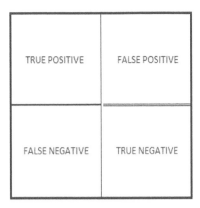

FIGURE 7.2: Decision possibilities for 2-class problem

curs when an anomalous instance is not detected by the NIDS [382], [12],[191],[101],[380]. An illustration of these four possibilities out of two variables is shown in Figure 7.3. The decision threshold should be picked to minimize false alarms.

Sensitivity is the ratio between *TP* and (*TP+FN*). In other words, it is defined as (*TP/(TP+FN)*). *Specificity* is the ratio between *TN* and (*FP+TN*). In other words, it is defined as (*TN/(FP+TN)*). Sensitivity is also called *hit rate* in Computer Science. Between these two measures, sensitivity is given high priority when the system is to be protected at all costs and specificity gets more priority when efficiency is the primary concern.

7.1.2 Misclassification Rate

Misclassification is the situation where a NIDS predicts a class (either normal or anomalous) for a traffic instance and the predicted class is different from the actual. This measure is useful in estimating the probability of disagreement between the true and predicted classification rates of a NIDS and is obtained by dividing the sum (*FN+FP*) by the total number of paired observations, i.e., (*TP+FP+FN+TN*). In other words, the misclassification rate of a classifier is defined as (*FN+FP*)/(*TP+FP+FN+TN*).

7.1.3 Confusion Matrix

A confusion matrix can be used to show how a NIDS performs in a general manner. The confusion matrix can be used in the case of *n*-

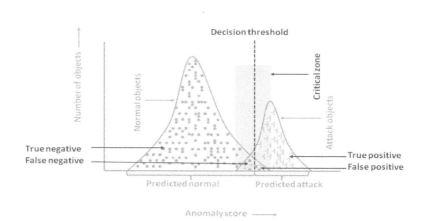

FIGURE 7.3:   An illustration of TP, TN, FP and FN

class problems, whereas the matrix discussed earlier is used for 2-class problems. The size of the matrix depends on the number of distinct classes in the dataset to be detected. It compares the class labels predicted by the classifier against the actual class labels. For better understanding, let us look at the following example.

Example 1: Consider an intrusion dataset with 100 instances, out of which 45 are normal, 35 are DoS, 15 are probe and 5 are U2R attack instances. Assume also that out of 45 normals, the NIDS predicts 38 correctly and 4 as U2R, 2 as probe and 1 as DoS; out of 35 DoS, the NIDS predicts 31 correctly and 4 as normal; out of 15 probe, the system predicts 11 correctly and 4 as normal; and finally, out of 5 U2R, the system predicts 3 correctly and 1 as normal and 1 as probe. The confusion matrix for this situation is shown in Figure 7.4.

As we see in a confusion matrix, the diagonal from top left to bottom right represents the instances the NIDS classifies correctly and so, from the nondiagonal elements we can find the incorrect predictions and what kinds of misclassifications occur.

7.1.4   Precision, Recall and F-measure

Precision and recall are two well-known evaluation measures in the field of information retrieval. *Precision* is defined as the fraction of retrieved objects (e.g., documents) that are relevant to a given query

Actual class \ Predicted class	Normal	DoS	Probe	U2R
Normal	38	1	2	4
DoS	4	31	0	0
Probe	4	0	11	0
U2R	1	0	1	3

FIGURE 7.4: Confusion matrix for a 4-class problem

or search request. Mathematically, it is the fraction obtained by dividing |*retrieved objects* ∩ *relevant objects*| by total retrieved objects, i.e., |*retrieved objects*|. *Recall* is the fraction of the objects that are relevant to a given query or search request and are correctly retrieved. Mathematically, it is the fraction obtained by dividing |*retrieved objects* ∩ *relevant objects*| by the total number of relevant objects. In the case of a 2-class problem, recall is the same as sensitivity. In other words, recall is the probability that a relevant document is retrieved by a search request or a query. It is possible to return all the relevant objects (mixed with a lot of irrelevant ones) with respect to a given query to achieve 100% recall. Thus recall alone is not sufficient to judge the effectiveness of a retrieval method. We need to take into account the number of irrelevant objects retrieved along with the retrieved ones. Thus it is necessary to compute precision along with recall.

In the context of network anomaly detection, precision measures the effectiveness of a NIDS in identifying anomalous as well as normal instances. A flagging is considered to be correct and referred to as TP if the identified instance is actually from a malicious user. Precision and recall are often inversely proportional to each other and there is normally a trade-off between these two ratios. An algorithm that produces low precision and low recall is most likely ill-designed with conceptual errors in the underlying theory. The types of attacks that are not identified can indicate which areas of the algorithm need more attention. Exposing these flaws and establishing the causes assist future improvement.

F-measure or *Balanced F-score* is calculated by combining precision and recall into a simple metric. The traditional *F*-measure (also known as the *F1* measure) is the harmonic mean of precision and recall [382]. Mathematically, it can be defined as $2 \times (precision \times recall)(precision + recall)$. For an n-class intrusion classification problem, it is the most preferred accuracy metric. *F1* is maximum when precision and recall both reach 100%, i.e., 1 signifying that the classifier has 0% false alarms and also detects 100% of the attacks. Thus, a good classifier must strive to achieve an *F1* measure as high as possible.

7.1.5   Receiver Operating Characteristics Curves

ROC curves are a popular evaluation measure for visualization of the relationship between True Positive (*TP*) and False Positive (*FP*) rates of an intrusion detection system. It can also be effectively used to compare the accuracy of two or more classifiers. However, the use of this measure is not restricted to network traffic classification for anomaly identification. Its origin is in signal processing theory and it is used in a large number of application domains such as medical diagnosis, radiology, bioinformatics as well as artificial intelligence. It uses the orthogonal coordinate system [302],[248] to visualize the detection performance of a classifier. In ROC curves, the x-axis represents *FP*, while the y-axis represents *TP*. The following conventions are used by a ROC curve to represent the accuracy of a classifier in the xy-plane [302],[24], [25],[248],[12].

1. The bottom-left point (0,0) is used to represent an IDS that performs with 100% normal identification accuracy, with a zero false alarm rate. Such an IDS will identify all data as normal all the time. However, at the same time it does not detect anything.

2. The top-right point (1,1) represents an IDS that generates an alarm for each new traffic instance it encounters. So, such an IDS will show a 100% detection rate, but with a 100% false alarm rate.

3. A line connecting the two points mentioned above represents all IDSs that anyone can ever build, since this line is a linear combination of the extreme two points. The detection engine of such an IDS uses a randomized engine for detecting intrusions and so,

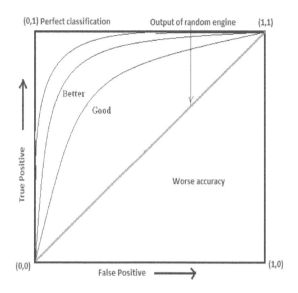

FIGURE 7.5: Receiver operating characteristics

in the case of a real IDS, the ROC curves will always reside above this diagonal.

4. The top-left point $(0,1)$ represents the performance of an ideal IDS with a 100% detection rate with a 0% false alarm rate. As a result, the accuracy of a real IDS is considered to be better if it starts near $(0,0)$ and moves to $(1,1)$ but remains close to the $x = 0$ and $y = 1$ in the process. In Figure 7.5, we show ROC curves corresponding to several IDSs and compare them.

7.2   Performance

Comprehensive performance evaluation of a NIDS is an important task. It involves many issues that go beyond the NIDS itself. Such issues include the hardware platform, the operating system or even the deployment of the NIDS. The most important evaluation criterion for a NIDS's performance is the system's ability to process traffic on a high speed network with minimum packet loss when working in real time. In real network traffic, the packets can be of various sizes. Thus, the effectiveness of a NIDS depends on its ability to handle packets of any size. In addition to processing speed, the CPU and memory usage can also serve as measurements of NIDS performance [327]. These are usually used as indirect measures that take into account the time and space complexities of an intrusion detection mechanism. Finally, the performance of any NIDS is highly dependent upon (i) its individual configuration, (ii) the network it is monitoring and (iii) its position in that network.

7.3   Completeness

This evaluation measure attempts to judge a NIDS against a complete set of known attacks. It considers the total space of all vulnerabilities and attacks and checks whether a given NIDS covers them all or not. However, for an effective use of this measure, one has to possess complete knowledge of attacks or abuses of privileges, which may not be practically feasible. The ability of a NIDS is complete if one can establish its ability to successfully handle all the known vulnerabilities or attacks. Obviously, such a complete solution needs to employ some mechanisms to address unknown attacks.

7.4   Timeliness

A network anomaly detection system should perform its analysis, detection and alert generation as quickly as possible, so that it can alert the system administrator or security manager who can then take necessary action promptly before the system is significantly damaged. It may prevent the attacker from subverting the audit source or the IDS itself.

In a network anomaly detection system, there will be an obvious delay between the occurrence of the attack (T_A) and the generation of the response (T_R) by the detection system. This delay, δ obtained by subtracting T_A from T_R, i.e., $(T_A - T_R)$, plays a crucial role in the evaluation of a NIDS. The smaller the value of δ, the better is the timeliness performance of the NIDS.

7.5 Stability

A robust network anomaly detection system is expected to behave consistently in different network scenarios and circumstances. In addition, the system should consistently generate similar alert messages for identical events, so that the security manager can take necessary action without ambiguity. Allowing users to configure different alerts to provide different messages in different network environments may lead to an unstable state of the system.

7.6 Interoperability

Even if multiple IDSs (may be anomaly-based NIDS, signature-based NIDS or HIDS) are deployed on the same network, there will be a time lag between the starting time of an attack and its detection. An effective intrusion detection mechanism should be able to correlate information from any of these sources or from a system log or a firewall log. This can help maintain interoperability when an organization deploys a range of HIDSs or NIDSs from various vendors. Also, we have already stated, the effectiveness of an anomaly detection system is judged based on its correctness and timeliness. The system should strive to generate responses while an attack occurs. It is of no use to have good detection accuracy if the detection time is hours or days!

7.7 Data Quality, Validity and Reliability

The usefulness of training data for the purpose of intrusion detection depends on several factors, such as source(s), correctness, timeliness, validity, reliability and consistency of data. A NIDS can be evaluated based on data quality in terms of three important parameters: quality, validity and reliability.

Quality of data is influenced by several factors, such as (i) the source of data, which should be reliable and appropriate, (ii) the selection of sample, which should be unbiased, (iii) the sample size, with neither over nor under-sampling, (iv) the time of data collection, which should be recently updated and (v) the complexity of data, which should be simple enough to be handled easily. Data validity implies whether the data used actually represent what we think is being analyzed. Though there are several types of validity, two types are most commonly accepted by most researchers, viz., *internal validity* and *external validity*. Internal validity attempts to measure the degree of certainty that observed effects in a detection experiment are actually the result of the experimental treatment or condition (the cause), rather than intervening, extraneous or confounding variables. With appropriate selection and use of parameters or variables, the internal validity of data can be enhanced. External validity is more concerned with external research findings and the applicability of a method in the real world. In other words, external validity attempts to measure the generic characteristics of a method or a classifier. However, attempting to increase the internal validity may result in reduction of the degree of applicability in external research findings, i.e., the external validity. To identify the major factors influencing data validity, such as missing values, overestimation, underestimation or outliers, various techniques or statistical tests can be conducted. These include careful examination of the distribution patterns and frequencies of occurrence values of the attributes. Several outlier estimation methods have already been discussed in the previous chapters. Reliability implies that for any intrusion dataset used, the performance is complete (i.e., it includes all the variables and observations relevant to a given task), consistent (data should be unambiguous and clear enough, so that similar analysis will always give similar results), accurate (data should originate at the actual or correct source(s) and also should have been captured and preprocessed correctly) and purposeful (should serve the purpose meant for it). To ensure the reliability of data, necessary intra- and interobserver reliability analysis should be carried out during capture and collection of data. A common statistical reliability test is kappa-analysis, which quantifies the agreement or match score between two unique observers and multiple ratings. Generally, it is scaled between 0 and 1. A perfect match or agreement implies 1 and it is 0 when the match score is what would be expected when observed by chance.

7.8 Alert Information

Alerts generated by a NIDS should be meaningful enough to clearly identify (i) the reason causing the event to be raised, (ii) the reason the event is of interest and (iii) the source and target of an attack. It should assist the system administrator or analyst in determining the relevant and appropriate reaction to a particular alert. The appropriate source and the target information can help the analyst significantly in minimizing the damage to systems or networks.

7.9 Unknown Attacks Detection

A vulnerability or attack outside the scope of definition of the existing signatures or profiles is considered an unknown attack. New vulnerabilities or exploits are created almost every day. In addition to known attack detection, an anomaly-based intrusion detection system should be capable of identifying unknown or modified intrusions. A NIDS should be equipped with both supervised as well as unsupervised mechanisms to enable identification of both known and unknown or modified intrusions consistently.

7.10 Updating References

A NIDS should have provisions to adapt to new vulnerabilities or attacks. Once new vulnerabilities or exploits are discovered, it should update the references or profiles to enable identification of such vulnerabilities as known attacks in the future. However, in the current high-speed network scenario, writing or modifying references or profiles in real time without causing conflicts with the existing rules or profiles is a challenging task.

7.11   Discussion

We have discussed several measures to evaluate an anomaly detection method, system or mechanism under three broad categories, as shown in Figure 7.1. The relevance or effectiveness of these measures to a particular method or system depends on the approach adopted to develop the method or the system. However, as reported in the previous discussion, an assessment made based on these measures for a system or a method is usually a snapshot in time. With the passage of time and with changes in the environment and in the context of new vulnerabilities, such an assessment may not be true and hence reassessment with new parameter settings may be necessary.

Chapter 8

Tools and Systems

8.1 Introduction

To protect digital assets and systems, the three major objectives of a network security system are to provide confidentiality, integrity and availability [92] to them. Intruders usually attempt to breach these measures mostly with malicious intentions. These days, people with such intentions can download many tools from the Internet and use them for such purposes. Due to the increased availability of sophisticated attack tools such as HOIC and LOIC [298], people can disrupt a network fairly easily. On the other hand, network administrators need other tools to defend their networks or to monitor and analyze the activities in the network. Without a good understanding of the attack behavior, it is very difficult to predict or detect an attack. Network security tools are used for purposes such as information gathering, victim identification, attack generation, packet capture, network traffic analysis and visualization of traffic behavior. With the increased sophistication and complexity of attacks, vigilant approaches to defend networks have become absolutely necessary. In this chapter, we provide a comprehensive survey and analysis of network security tools and their purposes, uses and effectiveness.

8.1.1 Attacker's Motivation

Different classes of attackers attack a network with different intentions. Suppose an individual comes to know that there are tools available on the Web to generate attacks. Such an individual may become curious and may experiment with and execute such tools, causing attacks without premeditated malice. Another class of individual may be quite knowledgeable about systems as well as attacks and their intention may be simply to create nuisance in the network to annoy or

vex other people. But there are many dangerous hackers who attack
a network intentionally for profit. They attack networks to capture
or sniff important and useful information. Finally, there is a class of
individuals who attack a network to degrade network performance or
to challenge the security system to express political views. Others may
simply be terrorists intent on causing maximum harm.

8.1.2   Steps in Attack Launching

As we have seen in Chapter 2, an attacker generally executes four
basic steps [45] to launch an attack. The steps are given below once
again.

(i) *Prepare* or gather relevant information. The attacker attempts to
gather vulnerability information from the network with the hope
that some of the information can be used to aid in the ensuing
attack.

(ii) *Exploit* or identify victim and launch attack. Based on the vulnerabilities learned in the previous step, the attacker attempts to
exploit them to launch an attack or multiple attacks.

(iii) *Leave behind* or leave scope for future access. After successful
attack launching, the attacker leaves or installs additional tools
or software in the victim's machine(s) to access the network later
either as a sniffer or for other back door network services.

(iv) *Clean up* or remove attack evidence(s). The attacker attempts to
eliminate the attack history by cleaning the registry or log files.

An illustration of these steps is given in Figure 8.1

8.1.3   Launching and Detecting Attacks

To launch an attack, the attacker must know weaknesses or vulnerabilities in the network. Actual attacks exploit these vulnerabilities.
The vulnerabilities can be obtained by scanning the network in an information gathering step. After gathering vulnerability information,
the attacker tries to exploit the weakness(es) of the security system
to launch an attack. Scanning or information gathering may be coordinated with an attack and performed simultaneously. There are
different methods for launching an attack. For example, one may use

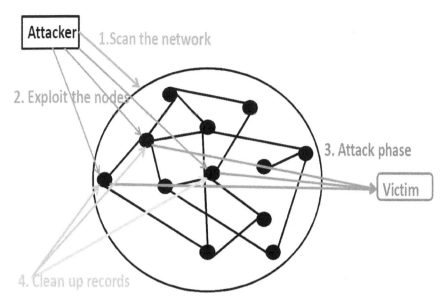

FIGURE 8.1: Steps of attack launching

Trojans or worms to generate an attack in a system or a network. One can also use attack launching tools to generate attacks in a network. The main purpose of the attacker is to disrupt services provided by the network either by consuming resources or by consuming bandwidth. These types of attacks can be launched using flooding of legitimate requests such as TCP SYN Flooding, ICMP flooding and UDP flooding. To detect an attack one must know the characteristics of an attack and its behavior in a network. The network administrator needs a visualization or monitoring system to observe differences between abnormal and normal traffic characteristics. An attack can be detected from the traffic volume based on the packet header or network flow information. However, such detection usually requires processing huge volumes of data in near real time. Obviously, designing a real-time defense mechanism that can identify all possible attacks is a challenging and quite likely an impossible task. Most detection methods need some prior information about attack characteristics to use during the detection process. The evaluation of these intrusion detection mechanisms or systems is performed using the misclassification rate or false alarm rate. To obtain satisfactory results, an IDS designer needs to be careful in choosing an approach, matching mechanism or any heuristic or in making assumptions. Approaches that have been able to obtain acceptable results include statistical [403], soft computing [68], probabilistic [187], knowledge-based [93] and hybrid [295], [135], [313]. A detailed discussion of these approaches is available in [63], [117], [139], [142].

8.1.3.1   Attack Launching Tools and Systems

At the current time, there are many attack launching tools and systems to generate network attacks in the public domain. These tools can be used on any one of the network layers in the TCP/IP network model, but most are used in the network and transport layers. Common application layer attacks include HTTP, FTP, SMTP and DNS related attacks. Most application layer attacks are generated by malware, e.g., Trojans, viruses, worms and back doors. HTTP related attacks such as DDoS using an HTTP GET request, Cross Site Scripting (XSS) and SQL Injection are very common attacks on this layer. Modern tools such as slowhttptest and AppDDoS are available to generate such attacks. In addition to these, some popularly used data link layer tools such as Dsniff [84], IRPAS [406], Ettercap [271], Libnet [326] and Gobbler are used to generate MAC attacks, ARP attacks and VLAN attacks.

8.1.3.2   Attack Detecting Tools and Systems

Identification of known as well as unknown anomalies with high detection accuracy and with minimum false alarms is the major concern in today's security environment. Hackers have a number of offensive tools to launch attacks on a network. Similarly, there are modern security tools and systems to detect intrusions occurring in a network. To detect an attack, most systems capture network traffic, preprocess and extract features, select relevant features and then analyze the traffic information, with or without the knowledge of previous references. Snort [312] is a well-known lightweight packet sniffer as well as a detection system. It can watch for activities such as Queso TCP/IP fingerprinting scans, Nmap scans or various types of probes. With the help of these sniffing or attack tools, it is very easy for hackers to steal network information. So, it is the responsibility of the network defenders to build protection mechanisms incorporating attack launching and detection software tools that are available. Usually, anti-virus software tools and spam detectors are recommended for network security, at a minimum.

A network intrusion detection system is deployed to protect a network from attackers or intruders. The detection system is designed to protect the network from different types of vulnerabilities, which may crash the network or may capture secure information. Deployment of an accurate and efficient anomaly detection system demands appropriate design as per standard security requirements and risk analysis. The detection system can be either host based or network based. A typical network structure with a protected LAN, a demilitarized zone and a deployed IDS console is shown in the Figure 8.2. In computer security, a demilitarized zone (sometimes referred to as a perimeter networking) is a physical or logical subnetwork that contains and exposes an organization's external-facing services to a larger untrusted network, usually the Internet. Here, as shown in the figure, an attacker may launch an attack from various machines connected to the network via either wired or wireless media.

The increasing number of highly sophisticated attacks of a complex and evolving nature has made the task of defending networks challenging. The appropriate use of tools and systems can simplify the task significantly. This necessitates an awareness of the characteristics and relevance of these tools and systems and their usage. This chapter intends to provide a comprehensive survey of these tools and systems. The lack of a consistent description of attack related tools often has made it difficult to understand network security literature. This chapter also introduces a taxonomy of existing attack related tools.

8.2 Attack Related Tools

People with malicious intention use various attack tools to disrupt a network for various purposes. As mentioned earlier, attackers generally target Web sites or databases as well as organizational networks by gathering information on their weaknesses. In general, attackers use relevant tools for the class of attack they desire to launch. A large number of defense tools have also been made available by various network security research groups as well as private security professionals. These tools have different purposes, capabilities and interfaces.

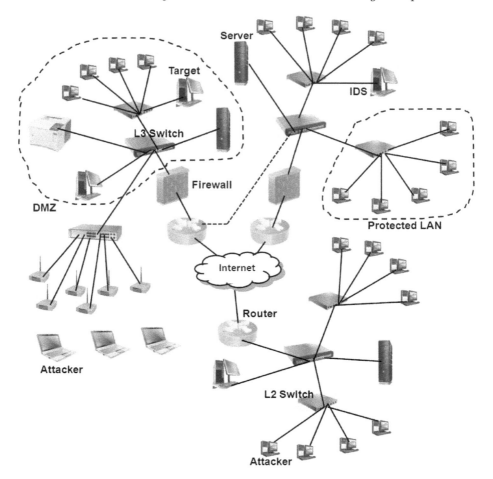

FIGURE 8.2: A typical network with protected LAN, DMZ and
IDS deployment

8.2.1 Taxonomy

We categorize existing attack related tools into three major categories: *information gathering, attack launching* and *network monitoring*. A taxonomy of the tools used in network security is shown in Figure 8.3. For each basic category, we show subcategories considering their general characteristics.

8.2.2 Information Gathering Tools

Before launching an attack, attackers need to understand the environment where the attack is to be launched. To do so, attackers first

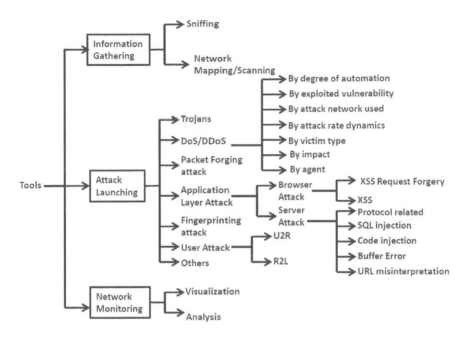

FIGURE 8.3: Taxonomy of attack-related tools

gather information about the network such as the number of machines, types of machines, operating systems and so forth. After gathering information, attackers find weaknesses in the network using various tools. Information gathering tools are of two basic types, i.e., sniffing tools and network mapping and scanning tools.

8.2.2.1 Sniffing Tools

A sniffing tool aims to capture, examine, analyze and visualize packets or frames traversing the network. To support extraction of additional packet features and for subsequent analysis, it also understands the protocols and accordingly includes protocol parameters during visualization. Some packet sniffing tools are discussed below.

(i) *Tcpdump*: Tcpdump is a premier packet analyzer for information security professionals. It enables one to capture, save and view packet data. This tool works on most flavors of the Unix operating system. One can also use third party open source software, e.g., *wireshark*, to open and visualize tcpdump captured traffic.

(ii) *Ethereal*: Ethereal is a sniffing and traffic analyzing software tool for Windows, Unix and Unix-like OSs, released under the GNU licensing scheme. It includes two primary library utilities: (i) *GTK+*, a GUI based library and (ii) *libpcap*, a packet capture and filtering library. Ethereal is also capable of reading the output of tcpdump and can apply tcpdump filters to select and display records satisfying certain parameters. Ethereal offers a large number (≥ 400) of decoding options for protocols and in network forensics and is useful in identifying and inspecting an attack in the network.

(iii) *Gulp*: This Linux-based lossless gigabit remote packet capture tool is very effective due to two basic reasons, i.e., (i) it drops far fewer packets than other competing tools and (ii) it has higher packet capture rates due to an enhanced buffering technique. To improve interactive response at low packet rates, Gulp flushes its ring buffer if nothing has been written in the last one second. With an increased data rate, Gulp adopts an effective writing policy for optimum writing efficiency. On receipt of an interrupt, Gulp does not stop filling its ring buffer until it has completed writing the data.

(iv) *Net2pcap*: This is a simple tool to read packet traffic from an interface and transform it into a pcap file. Net2pcap is a Linux tool which does not use any library during the transformation. However, it is partially dependent on *libc*, a Linux library utility. The command *%tcpdump -w capfile* almost performs the same task as Net2pcap. However, Net2pcap is usually used to capture and represent network traffic in a hostile environment to support subsequent analysis.

(v) *CDPsniffer*: CDPsniffer is a simple Cisco tool written in Perl, to sniff network traffic, to pick out CDP packets and to print out decoded protocol contents.

(vi) *Snoop*: This is a Linux tool which functions almost like tcpdump. However, the format of a Snoop file is different from pcap format and is defined in RFC 1761. An important feature of this tool is that when writing to an intermediate file, it reduces the possibility of packet loss under busy trace conditions. Snoop allows one to filter, read as well as to interpret packet data. To observe the traffic between two systems, say X and Y, we can use the command % *snoop* X, Y.

(vii) *Snort* [312]: Snort is a lightweight, yet powerful misuse detection system that runs on multiple platforms. In addition to intrusion detection, it also provides support for capturing data.

(viii) *Angst*: Angst runs on Linux and OpenBSD and is an active packet sniffer that can capture data on switched networks by injecting data into the network. Angst is capable of flooding a network using random MAC addresses and by causing switches to transmit packets toward all ports.

(ix) *Ngrep*: Ngrep provides a filtering facility on payloads of packets. It also has the sniffing functionality of tcpdump. It is dependent on the libpcap library.

(x) *Ettercap*: Ettercap is a very good sniffer that runs on almost all platforms. More of an active hacking tool, Ettercap uses an ncurses interface and is able to decode several protocols. Ettercap operates in multi-purpose mode: sniffer and interceptor or logger mode for switched LANs. Ettercap can collect passwords for multiple applications, kill connections, inject packets, inject commands into active connections and has additional plugins.

(xi) *Dsniff*: Dsniff is a collection of tools that enable active sniffing on a network. It can perform man-in-the-middle attacks against SSHv1 and HTTPS sessions. It can also sniff switched networks by actively injecting data into the network and redirecting traffic.

(xii) *Cain & Able*: This is a multipurpose sniffer that runs on Windows NT, Windows 2000 and XP systems and allows for password recovery for a number of protocols, including MSN messenger and RADIUS shared keys. It can also launch man-in-the-middle attacks for SSHv1 traffic.

(xiii) *Aimsniff*: This is a simple tool to capture the IP address of an AOL Instant Messenger user when a direct connection is established. Once the connection is established, one is able to simply click on the sniff button to capture the IP address.

(xiv) *Tcptrace*: This is a powerful tool to analyze tcpdump files and to generate various types of outputs including connection specific information, such as the number of bytes and segments sent and received, elapsed time, retransmissions, round trip times, window advertisements and throughput. It is capable of accepting a wide range of input files generated by several capture tools such as tcpdump, snoop, etherpeek, HP Net Matrix and WinDump. It also provides a graphical presentation of traffic characteristics for further analysis.

(xv) *Tcptrack*: This can sniff and display TCP connection information, as seen on a network interface. It has the following functions: (i) to watch passively for connections on the network interface, (ii) to keep track of their state and (iii) to display a list of connections. It displays source IP, destination IP, source port, destination port, connection state, idle time and bandwidth usage.

(xvi) *Nstreams*: This is a tool to display and analyze network streams generated by users between several networks and between networks and the outside. Nstreams also can output optionally the *ipchains* or *ipfw rules* matching these streams. It parses outputs generated by tcpdump or files generated using tcpdump with the -*w* option.

(xvii) *Argus*: Argus runs on several operating systems, such as Linux, Solaris, Mac OS X, FreeBSD, OpenBSD, NetBSD, AIX, IRIX, Windows and OpenWrt. It can process either live packet data or captured traffic files and can output status reports on flows detected in the stream of packets. Its reports reflect flow semantics. This tool provides information on almost all packet parameters, such as reachability, availability, connectivity, duration, rate, load, loss, jitter, retransmission and delay metrics for all network flows.

(xviii) *Karpski*: This is a user-friendly tool, with limited sniffing and scanning capabilities. It provides flexibility to include protocol definitions dynamically and also can serve as an attack launching tool against addresses on a local network.

(xix) *IPgrab*: This packet sniffing tool provides the facility for network debugging at multiple layers, such as data link, network and transport layers. It outputs detailed header field information for all network layers.

(xx) *Nast*: Nast uses libnet and libpcap to sniff packets in normal mode or in promiscuous mode and to analyze them. It captures packet header parameters and payload information and saves them in a file in ASCII or ASCII-hex format.

(xxi) *Aldebaran*: This is an advanced libpcap-based sniffing and filtering tool for the TCP protocol. It provides basic information about the source and destination addresses and ports, but no information regarding flags. One can use it to monitor data sent by connections as well as to sniff passwords. Based on libpcap rules, one can use it to sniff packet headers as well as payload contents and can transmit captured data to another host via UDP. Aldebaran also allows one (i) to encrypt the content saved in dump files, (ii) to analyze interface traffic and (iii) to report packet statistics, viz., =packet count, size and average speed in HTML or as a plain text file.

(xxii) *ScoopLM*: This is a Windows 2000-based sniffing tool for capturing LM/NTLM authentication information on the network. Such information can later be used by a tool such as BeatLM to crack authentication data.

(xxiii) *Nfdump*: This supports visualization and analysis of network flow traffic. All versions of this tool support Netflow v5, v7 and v9. It uses a capture daemon *nfcapd* to read the netflow data and stores the data in a file. It also allows one to visualize the statistics of top N flows. The tool can be optimized by using the efficient filtering option and the processed flows can either be printed in ASCII to stdout or written to a file. The binary file can be read again by Nfdump for further processing. This tool has four fixed output formats: raw, line, long and extended. However, it also provides an option for a user-customized output format.

(xxiv) *Nfsen*: This is a graphical Web-based front end for the Nfdump netflow tool. NfSen allows one (a) to display netflow data such as flows, packets and bytes using RRD (Round Robin Database) 100, (b) to navigate through the netflow data, (c) to process the netflow data within a specified time span, (d) to create history as well as continuous profiles and (e) to write one's own plugins to process netflow data on a regular interval. NfSen also allows one to have all the advantages of the command line using Nfdump

TABLE 8.1: Sniffing Tools

Tool name	Platform used	Sources
Ethereal	Linux, Unix, Windows	http:// www.ethereal.com.
Tcpdump	Linux, Unix	http://www.tcpdump.org
Net2pcap	Linux	http://www.secdev.org
Cdpsniffer		
Snoop	Solaris	http://www.softpanorama.org
Snort	Linux, Windows	http://www.snort.org
Angst	Linux, BSD	http://www.angst.sourceforge.net
Ngrep	Linux, Windows	http://www.ngrep.sourceforge.net
Ettercap	Linux, Windows	http://www.ettercap.sourceforge.net
Dsniff	Unix	http://www.naughty.monkey.org
Cain & Able	Windows NT/XP	http://www.oxid.it
Aimsniff	Linux	http://www.sourceforge.net
Tcptrace	Linux, Windows	http://www.tcptrace.org/
Tcptrack	Linux	http://www.rhythm.cx
Nstream	Linux, Windows	http://www.hsc.fr/cvs.nessus.org
Argus	Linux, Windows	http://www.qosient.com/argus/
Karpski	Linux	http://www.softlist.net
IPgrab	Linux, BSD	http://www.ipgrab.sourceforge.net/
Nast	Linux, BSD	http://www.nast.berlios.de
ScoopLM	Windows	http://www.securityfriday.com
GULP	Linux	http://staff.washington.edu/corey
Libpcap	Linux, Windows	http://www.tcpdump.org
Nfsen	Linux	http://www.nfsen.sourceforge.net
Nfdump	Linux	http://www.nfdump.sourceforge.net

directly and gives a graphical overview netflow traffic. NfSen has two different user interfaces: (a) Web interface and (b) command line interface.

Based on our experience, we have observed that Gulp is a versatile tool to capture packet traffic with minimum data loss because of its large buffer capacity. It uses the libpcap packet capture and filtering library and stores the captured packet data in the tcpdump format. However, as mentioned above, several other tools such as Ngrep, Ethereal and Snoop also follow the tcpdump format while storing the raw packet data. Among the GUI-based packet sniffing utilities, Wireshirk is popular due to its supporting functions, such as (i) IP analysis, (ii) visualizing protocol graph, (iii) reading an extended form of packet data and (iv) source and destination IP identification. In the case of network flow capture and visualization, Nfdump and Nfsen are very useful and user friendly. In addition to flow capture, Nfsen allows one to visualize a protocol specific graph and a packet intensity graph. Nfsen also allows one to present top N flows based on user priority.

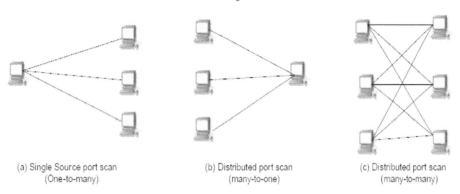

(a) Single Source port scan
(One-to-many)

(b) Distributed port scan
(many-to-one)

(c) Distributed port scan
(many-to-many)

FIGURE 8.4: Different types of port scans

8.2.2.2 Network Mapping or Scanning Tools

A network scanning tool aims to identify active hosts on a network, either (i) to attack them or (ii) to assess vulnerabilities in the network. It provides an overall status report regarding network hosts, ports, IPs, etc. The four possible types of port scans are (i) one-to-one, (ii) one-to-many, (iii) many-to-one and (iv) many-to-many. Figure 8.4 illustrates these scan types.

Below we present a few network scanning tools.

(i) *Nmap*: This network mapping tool facilitates network exploration and security auditing. It can scan large networks fast, especially against single hosts. It is effective in using raw IP packets to identify a large number of useful parameters such as available hosts, services offered by the hosts, OSs running and use of packet filters or firewalls. In addition to its use in security audits, network administrators can use it for routine tasks such as maintaining network inventory, managing service upgrade schedules and monitoring host or service uptime.

(ii) *Amap*: Amap detects an application protocol, without the TCP/UDP ports it is bound to. It identifies applications running on a specific port by sending trigger packets, which are typically an application protocol handshake. Most network daemons only respond to the correct handshake, e.g., SSL. Amap considers the responses and looks for matches. This tool supports TCP and UDP protocols, regular and SSL-enabled ASCII and binary protocols and has a wide list of options to control its behavior. It accepts an nmap machine readable output file and logs to a file and screen.

(iii) *Vmap*: This mapper tool allows one to identify the version of a daemon by fingerprinting its characteristics, based on its responses to bogus commands.

(iv) *Unicornscan*: This is an asynchronous scanner as well as a payload sender. This scalable and flexible tool gathers and correlates information quickly. For fast response, it uses a distributed TCP/IP stack and provides a user-friendly interface to introduce a stimulus into a TCP/IP-enabled device or network and measure the response. The main features of this tool include asynchronous protocol specific UDP scanning, asynchronous stateless TCP scanning with wide variations in TCP flags and asynchronous stateless TCP banner grabbing.

(v) *Ttlscan*: This tool uses libnet and libpcap utilities to identify a host by sending TCP SYN packets to each port of the host. It sniffs the response from the host and uses it to identify hosts with services by forwarding packets to another host behind a firewall. It can detect the OS and its version running on a host behind the firewall by reading specific header parameters such as TTL, window size and IPID.

(vi) *Ike-scan*: This tool assists in discovery, fingerprinting and testing of IPSec VPN servers based on the IKE protocol. Ike-scan works on Linux, Unix, Mac OS and Windows environments under the GPL license.

(vii) *Paketto*: This is a set of tools to assist in manipulating TCP/IP networks based on nontraditional strategies. These tools provide tapping functionality within the existing infrastructure and also extend protocols beyond their original intention. Example tools include (i) *Scanrand*, which facilitates fast discovery of network services and topologies, (ii) *Minewt*, which serves as a user space NAT/MAT router, (iii) *Linkcat*, which offers an ethernet link to stdio, (iv)*Paratrace*, which helps trace network paths without spawning new connections and (v) *Phentropy*, which uses *Open-QVIS* to render arbitrary amounts of entropy from data sources in 3-D phase space.

Table 8.2 shows the platforms on which these tools work and the sources from which they can be obtained. Almost all these tools are Linux based. Among these network mapping or scaning tools, Nmap

TABLE 8.2: Mapping/Scanning Tools

Tool	Platform used	Source
Nmap	Linux, Windows	http://www.insecure.org
Amap	Linux, Unix	http://www.freeworld.thc.org
Vmap	Unix	http://www.tools.l0t3k.net
Unicornscan	Linux, Unix	http://www.unicornscan.org
Ttlscan	Linux	http://www.freebsd.org
Ike-scap	Linux, Unix	http://www.stearns.org
Paketto	Linux	http://www.packages.com

has been found very effective and robust so that it can be used to explore the network in various modes such as one-to-one, one-to-many, many-to-one and many-to-many. It provides a large number of options for scanning activities. A variant of *Nmap*, viz., *rNmap*, allows scanning of remote machine(s) in a coordinated mode (i.e., many-to-one and many-to-many mode) with various flag setting options. The Portscan dataset as reported in Chapter 4 is generated mostly by using this tool. It provides several crucial pieces of information on a remote machine or a group of machines in a useful format. Such information, especially about the filter or firewall in use, availability of a host and its services, OS(s) running on the host, etc., make the victim identification task of an attacker simple and easy.

8.2.3 Attack Launching Tools

A large number of network security tools used to launch attacks are available on the Web. People can freely download these tools and use them for malicious activities such as Trojan propagation, network mapping, probe attacks, buffer overflow attacks, DoS/DDoS attacks and application layer attacks. A large number of security tools have been used for launching layer specific and protocol specific attacks such as HTTP, SMTP, FTP or SNMP related attacks. Other tools can be used to launch DoS/DDoS attacks, which can disrupt the services of a network or a Website very quickly. Some tools are used in wired networks to capture and exploit valuable information while others are

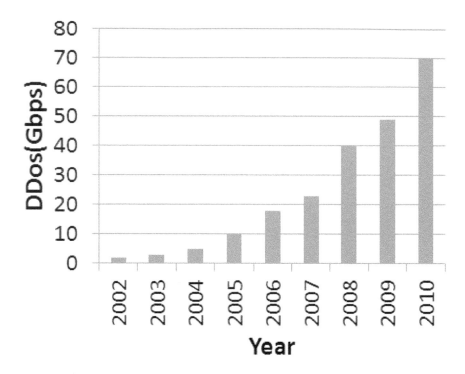

FIGURE 8.5:   DDoS attack graph

used in wireless networks.

8.2.3.1   Trojans

Trojans are malicious executable programs developed to break the security system of a computer or a network. A Trojan resides in a system as a benign program. Once the user attempts to open the file, the Trojan is executed and some dangerous action is performed. Victims generally unknowingly download the Trojan from multiple sources such as (i) the Internet, (ii) an FTP archive, (iii) via peer-to-peer file exchange using IRC and (iv) Internet messaging. Typically, Trojans are of seven distinct types.

(i) *Remote Access Trojans*: These are malware programs that use back doors to control the target machine with administrative privilege. Remote Access Trojans are downloaded invisibly with a user request for a program such as a game or an e-mail attachment. Once the attacker compromises a machine, the Trojan uses this machine to compromise more machines to construct a botnet for launching a DoS or DDoS attack. An example of a remote access trojan is *Danger*.

(ii) *Sending Trojans*: This Trojan type aims to capture and provide sensitive information such as passwords, credit card information, log files, e-mail addresses and IM contact lists to the attacker. In order to collect such information, such Trojans attempt to install a keylogger to capture and transmit all recorded keystrokes to the attacker.

(iii) *Destructive Trojans*: This Trojan type is very destructive for a computer and is often programmed to delete automatically some essential executable programs, configuration and DLL (dynamic link library) files to infect a computer. Such a Trojan acts either (a) as per the instructions of a back-end server or (b) based on preinstalled or programmed instructions to strike on a specific day, at a specific time. Two common examples of this type are *Bugbear virus* and *Goner worm*.

(iv) *Proxy Trojans*: This Trojan type attempts to use a victim's computer as a proxy server. A Trojan of this kind compromises a computer and attempts to perform malicious activities such as fraudulent credit card transactions and launching of malicious attacks against other networks.

(v) *FTP Trojans*: This type of Trojan attempts to open port 21 and establish a connection from the victim computer to the attacker using the File Transfer Protocol (FTP).

(vi) *Security Software Disable Trojans*: Such Trojans attempt to destroy or thwart defense mechanisms or protection programs such as antivirus programs or firewalls. Often such a Trojan is combined with another type of Trojan as a payload.

(vii) *DoS Trojans*: Such Trojans attempt to flood a network instantly with useless traffic, so that it cannot provide any service. Some of the examples of this category of Trojan are *ping-of-death* and *Teardrop*.

8.2.3.2   Denial of Service Attacks

Denial of Service (DoS) is a commonly occurring yet serious class of attack caused by an explicit attempt of an attacker to prevent or block legitimate users of a service from using desired resources. Such an attack occurs in both distributed as well as in a centralized setting. Some common examples of this class of attacks are *SYN Flooding, smurf, fraggle, jolt, land* and *ping-of-death.*

A Distributed Denial of Service (DDoS) attack is a coordinated attempt on the availability of services of a victim system or a group of systems or on network resources, launched indirectly from a large number of compromised machines on the Internet. Typically, a DDoS attacker adopts an $m : 1$ approach, i.e., many compromised machines attack a single victim machine or an $m : n$ approach that makes it very difficult to detect or prevent. A DDoS attacker normally initiates such a coordinated attack using either an architecture based on agent handlers or Internet Relay Chat (IRC). The attacking hosts are usually personal computers with broadband connections to the Internet and these computers are compromised by viruses or Trojan programs called *bots*. These compromised computers are usually referred to as *zombies*. The actions of these zombies are controlled by remote perpetrators often through (i) *botnet* commands and (ii) a control channel such as IRC. Some statistics on DDoS attacks are shown in Figure 8.5. Some DoS/DDoS attack generation tools are discussed below.

(i) *Jolt*: This DoS attack tool sends a large number of fragmented ICMP packets to a target machine running Windows 95 or NT in such a manner that the target machine fails to reassemble them for use and as a result, it freezes up and cannot accept any input from the keyboard or mouse. However, this attack does not cause any significant damage to the victim system and the machine can be recovered with a simple reboot.

(ii) *Burbonic*: This DoS exploit attempts to victimize a Windows 2000 machine by sending a randomly large number of TCP packets with random settings with the purpose of increasing the load on the machine so that it leads to a crash.

(iii) *Targa*: Targa is a collection of 16 different DoS attack programs. One can launch these attacks individually as well as in a group and can damage a network instantly.

(iv) *Blast20*: This TCP service stress tool is able to identify potential weaknesses in the network servers quickly. An example use of this tool is % *blast* 119.119.72.12 80 25 30 /b *"GET/some"* /e "url/HTTP/1.0"/nr/dr/v

(v) *Crazy Pinger*: This attempts to launch an attack by sending a large number of ICMP packets to a victim machine or to a large remote network.

(vi) *UDPFlood*: This tool can flood a specific IP at a specific port instantly with UDP packets. The flooding rate, maximum duration and maximum number of packets can be specified in this tool. It can also be used for testing the performance of a server.

(vii) *FSMax*: This is a server stress testing tool. To test a server for buffer overflows that may be exploited during an attack, it accepts a text file as input and executes a server through a sequence of tests based on the input.

(viii) *Nemsey*: The presence of this tool implies that a computer is insecure and infected with malicious software. It attempts to launch an attack with an attacker specified number of packets and sizes including information such as protocol and port.

(ix) *Panther*: This UDP-based DoS attack tool can flood at a specified IP at a specified port instantly.

(x) *Slowloris*: This creates a large number of connections to a target victim Web server by sending partial requests and attempts to hold them open for a long duration. As a consequence, the victim servers maintain these connections as open, consuming their maximum concurrent connection pool, which eventually compels them to deny additional legitimate connection attempts from clients.

(xi) *BlackEnergy*: This Web-based DDoS attack tool, an HTTP-based botnet, uses an IRC-based command and control method.

(xii) *HOIC*: This is an HTTP DDoS tool that focuses on creating high speed multithreaded HTTP flooding. It is able to flood simultaneously up to 256 Web sites. The built-in scripting system in this tool allows the attacker to deploy boosters, which are scripts designed to thwart DDoS countermeasures.

(xiii) *TRINOO*: This is an effective DDoS attack tool that uses a master host and several broadcast hosts. It issues commands using a TCP connection to the master host and the master instructs the broadcast hosts via UDP, to flood at a specific target host IP at random ports with UDP packets. To launch an attack using this tool, an attacker should possess prior access to the host to install a Trinoo master or broadcast, either bypassing or compromising the existing security system.

(xiv) *Shaft*: This is a variant of TRINOO, which provides statistics on TCP, UDP and ICMP flood attacks. This helps the attackers identify the victim machine's status (completely down or alive) or to decide addition or termination of zombies in the attack process.

(xv) *Knight*: This IRC-based tool can launch multiple DDoS attacks for SYN attacks, UDP flood and urgent pointer flood on Windows machines.

(xvi) *Kaiten*: This is an IRC-based attack tool, capable of launching multiple attacks, such as UDP and TCP flood, SYN attacks and PUSH+SYN attacks. It uses randomized source addresses.

(xvii) *RefRef*: RefRef is used to exploit existing SQL injection vulnerabilities using features included in MySql SELECT permissions to create a denial of service on the associated SQL server. It sends malformed SQL queries carrying payloads which force servers to exhaust their own resources. It works with a Perl compiler to launch an attack.

(xviii) *LOIC*: This is an anonymous attacking tool via IRC. It operates in three modes of attack: TCP, UPD and HTTP. It exists in two versions: binary and Web-based. It uses multiple threads to launch an attack.

(xix) *Hgod*: This is a Windows XP based tool that can spoof the source IPs and specify protocol and port numbers during an attack. By default, it is used for TCP SYN flooding. An example SYN flooding attack against 192.168.10.10 on port 80 with a spoofed address of 192.168.10.9, is shown below.

% *hgod* 192.168.10.10 80 -s 192.168.10

(xx) *TFN*: Like Trinoo, this tool, composing of a client host and several daemon hosts, is very effective in launching DDoS attacks. It is capable of launching ICMP flood, UDP flood, SYN flood and Smurf attacks. TFN2K, a variant of TFN, also includes some special features, such as encryption and decryption, stealth attacks and DoS attacks to crash a specified target host and to communicate shell commands to the daemons.

(xxi) *Stacheldrath*: This DDoS attacking tool is a hybridization of TFN and Trinoo, with some additional features, such as encrypted transmission between the components and automatic updating of the daemons.

We have presented a number of attack launching tools commonly used in practice. With increased sophistication in the attackers' skills, this list is growing every day. Among the launching tools, Targa and the individual attack source codes available with Targa have been commonly used in launching DoS attacks. However, to generate Distributed DoS (DDoS) attacks, LOIC, HOIC and individual attack source codes for TCP, ICMP and UDP flooding attacks are commonly used. From the GUI interface supported by LOIC and HOIC, an attacker can also vary the intensity of packet traffic to generate from low-rate to high-rate. Stacheldrath is another effective tool to generate DDoS attack traffic. The hybridized features of TFN and Trinoo make these tools more attractive and useful to launch DDoS attacks with multiple attack scenarios such as pulsing attack, constant rate attack, subgroup attack and increasing rate attack.

8.2.3.3 Packet Forging Attack Tools

Packet forging tools are useful in forging or manipulating packet information. An attacker can generate traffic with manipulated IP addresses based on this category of tools. Below we list some packet forging tools.

(i) *Packeth*: Packeth is a Linux-based tool with a graphical interface. It can send any packet or sequence of packets using raw sockets on the ethernet. It provides for a large number of options, correct as well as incorrect parameters such as incorrect checksum and wrong header length.

(ii) *Packit*: This network auditing tool allows one to customize, inject, monitor and manipulate IP traffic. It has been found useful in various ways such as to test a NIDS, to evaluate the performance of a firewall, to scan the network, to simulate network traffic and in TCP/IP auditing.

(iii) *Packet excalibur*: This forging tool allows an attacker to sniff packets, to build and receive custom packets and to spoof packets. It has a graphical interface to build scripts as a text file and to define additional protocols.

(iv) *Nemesis*: This Unix- and Windows-based network packet crafting and injection tool is useful for testing any NIDS, firewall, IP stack and a variety of other tasks. This command-line driven tool also provides an option for scripting. Nemesis allows an attacker to craft and inject a large variety of packets. Especially in IP and the ethernet injection modes, it allows one to craft and inject almost any custom packets.

(v) *Tcpinject*: This forging tool allows one to transmit a wide variety of TCP/IP packets by specifying multiple parameters, such as source and destination IPs and ports, packet size, payload, TCP control flags and TCP window size.

(vi) *Libnet*: This high-level API (toolkit) provides facilities to the application programmer to construct and inject network packets through a portable and simplified interface. To support underlying packet creation and injection functionality, it uses the *libnet* utility.

(vii) *SendIP*: This command line forging tool allows one to send arbitrary IP packets with a large number of options to specify the content of every header of the packets. Any data can also be added with the packet during sending.

(viii) *IPsorcery*: This TCP/IP packet generating tool has the ability to send TCP, UDP and ICMP packets with a GTK+ interface.

(ix) *Pacgen*: This Linux-based ethernet IP TCP/UDP packet generating tool allows an attacker to generate custom packets with configurable ethernet, IP, TCP and UDP layers as well as custom payloads. It also includes additional features such as packet count and programmable time interval between packets sent.

TABLE 8.3: Packet Forging Attack Tools

Tool	Platform used	Source
Packeth	Linax, Mac, Windows	http://www.sourceforge.net
Packit	Linux, Mac	http://www.packetfactory.openwall.ne
Packet Excalibur	Linux, Windows	http://www.freecode.com
Nemesis	Unix-like, Windows	http://www.sourceforge.net
Tcpinject	Linux	http://www.packetstormsecurity.org
Libnet	Linux	http://www.packetfactory.net/libnet
SendIP	Linux, Windows	http://www.softpedia.com
IPsocery	Liux	http://www.tools.l0t3k.net
Pacgen	Linux	http://www.sourceforge.net
Arp-sk	Linux	http://www.arp-sk.org
ARP-SPOOF	Linux, Windows	http://www.sourceforge.net
Libpal	Linux	http://www.sourceforge.net
Aicmspend	Linux, Unix	http://www.packetstormsecurity.nl

(x) *Arp-sk*: Arp-sk (ARP Swiss Knife) allows one to create totally arbitrary ARP requests and to manipulate ARP packets and to test network security and connectivity.

(xi) *Arpspoof*: This tool is also known as ARP Cache Poisoning. It allows one to spoof the contents of an ARP table on a remote computer on the LAN. Two addresses are used to establish a connection between two computers on an IP/ethernet network: MAC address, which is used on a local area network before packets go out of the gateway and IP address, which is used to surf the Internet through a gateway.

(xii) *Libpal*: This user-friendly packet assembly library provides utilities to build and send forged ethernet, IP, ICMP, TCP and UDP packets. It uses a struct to represent a packet.

(xiii) *Aicmpsend*: This ICMP packet sending tool supports several features including ICMP flooding and spoofing. It allows one to implement all the ICMP flags and codes.

Among these packet forging attack tools, Packeth, Packet excalibur and Nemesis are very effective due to (i) user-friendly interface, (ii) a large number of functionalities for various packet traffic activities as well as visualization support and (iii) provision for injecting custom packets. Although these tools usually support IP, TCP, ICMP and UDP packets, they mostly facilitate TCP/IP traffic related activities.

8.2.3.4   Application Layer Attack Tools

In an application layer attack, the attacker uses legitimate application layer HTTP requests from legitimately connected network machines to overwhelm a Web server [391]. The application layer attack may behave as a session flooding attack, a request flooding attack or an asymmetric attack [309], [410]. Application layer DDoS attacks are more subtle than network layer attacks and the detection of application layer attacks is challenging since they use legitimate protocols and legitimate connections. Application layer attacks, of four types, are discussed below.

(i) *HTTP-related attacks*: Some commonly used tools of this category are Code Red Worm and its mutations, Nimda Worm and its mutations, Cross Site Scripting (XSS) attacks, Malicious URLs and AppDDoS.

(ii) *SMTP-related attacks*: Some example attack tools of this category are SMTP Mail Flooding, SMTP worms and their mutations, Extended Relay attacks and Firewall Traversal attacks.

(iii) *FTP-related attacks*: These application layer attack tools facilitate creation of FTP bounch attacks, FTP port injection attacks, passive FTP attacks and TCP segmentation attacks.

(iv) *SNMP-related attacks*: Examples of this category of attacks include SNMP flooding attacks default community attacks and SNMP put attacks.

Among the four types of application layer attacks discussed above, HTTP-related attacks have gained significant importance among attackers and consequently also in the network research community. Several tools to launch such attacks at varied scales have been introduced. In addition, recently a few benchmark datasets (public and private) have been published, especially to support assessment of detection mechanisms for HTTP-related attacks. However, with increasing growth of specialized XSS attack types, support of adequate tool(s) for monitoring, analysis and detection, is still missing. Hence, the attention of researchers to study, analyze and develop appropriate tool(s) for this category of application layer attack is highly essential.

8.2.3.5 Fingerprinting Attack Tools

Fingerprinting tools are used to identify specific features of a network protocol implementation by analyzing its input and output behavior. The identified features include protocol version, vendor information and configurable parameters. Fingerprinting tools are used to identify the operating system running on a remote machine and can also be used for other purposes. Existing fingerprinting tools show that implementations of most key Internet protocols such as ICMP, TCP, Telnet and HTTP can all be targets of fingerprinting [42],[335],[401]. Network administrators can use remote fingerprinting to collect information to facilitate management and an intrusion detection system can capture the abnormal behavior of attackers or worms by analyzing their fingerprints.

(i) *Nmap*: Nmap is one of the best fringerprinting tools for both Unix and Windows operating systems. Using Nmap one can learn port entries, the operating system used, firewall methods employed and services running. In addition, a client can perform vulnerability detection, host detection and back door detection by writing a script supported by the Nmap Scripting Engine (NSE).

(ii) *P0f*: P0f is a passive OS fingerprinting tool that uses techniques such as active fingerprinting performed by Nmap. The only difference is that passive fingerprinting simply sniffs the network and classifies the host based on observed traffic. This is more difficult than active fingerprinting, since one has to accept whatever communication happens rather than designing custom probes.

(iii) *Xprobe*: This OS fingerprinting tool is used to find the operating system run by a remote machine. Xprobe is as simple as Nmap and it exploits the ICMP protocol in its fingerprinting approach.

(iv) *CronOS*: This fingerprinting tool is used to determine the operating system of a target machine. This tool is embedded in Nmap-CronOS and it has three options to perform different operations. The s option guesses the timeout of SYN_RCVD states, the i option determines the last ACK state timeout and the f option uses FIN_WAIT_1 state timeout for fingerprinting.

(v) *Queso*: This utility runs on Linux and Solaris operating systems. It is used to remotely determine the operating system's version and manufacturer information by analyzing network packets. This utility provides precise information about a network or system by scanning the network.

(vi) *AmapV4.8*: The Amap fingerprinting tool identifies applications and services by creating bogus communication without listening on default ports. It maintains a database of all the known applications, including non-ASCII-based applications and enterprise services.

(vii) *Disco*: The Disco fingerprinting tool is used to discover unique IP addresses on a network. In addition to IP discovery, it also fingerprints TCP SYN packets.

(viii) *Sprint*: This fingerprinting tool is used to identify the operating system running on a machine. In addition, Sprint also has the ability to calculate up-times and contains advanced banner grepping functionality. Sprint, when run with an *-n* switch, simulates netcraft.

Table 8.4 shows platforms used and sources for these tools. Almost all tools work in the Linux environment.

TABLE 8.4:   Fingerprinting Tools

Tool	Platform used	Source
Nmap	Linux, Windows	http://www.nmap.org
POf	Linux, Windows	http://www.lcamtuf.coredump.cx
Xprobe	Linux	http://www.sourceforge.net
CronOS		
Queso	Linux, Solaris	http://www.tools.l0t3k.net
AmapV4.8	Linux, Unix	http://www.linux.softpedia.com
Disco	Linux, BSD	http://www.tools.l0t3k.net
Sprint	Unix	http://www.safemode.org

Among these tools, the most commonly used fingerprinting tool is Nmap. The effectiveness of this tool has already been established in the context of information gathering and network mapping and scanning. To identify vulnerabilities of a host and for back door detection, the Nmap scripting facility is very useful from the network defender as well as an attacker's point of view.

8.2.3.6 User Attack Tools

In user attacks [229], either the attacker (i) attempts, as a normal legitimate user, to gain the privileges of a root or superuser or (ii) attempts to access a local machine by exploiting its vulnerabilities without having an account on that machine. Both types of attempts are very difficult to detect because their behavior resembles normal behavior.

We discuss these attacks by category along with tools that can be used to launch them.

(i) *U2R Attack*: In this attack, as shown in Figure 8.6, the attacker initially attempts to gain access to the local victim machine as a legitimate user by some means. The means may be a password sniffing attempt, dictionary attack or any social engineering approach. The attacker then explores the possible vulnerabilities or bugs associated with the operating system running in the victim machine to perform the transition from user to superuser or root level. Once the root privileges are acquired, the attacker possesses full control of the victim machine to install backdoor entries for future exploits, manipulate system files to gather information and to carry out other damaging actions. Two well-known U2R attack tools are given next.

(a) *Yaga*: This tool is used to create a new administrator account by hacking registry files. The attacker edits the registry file to crash some system services on the victim machine and create a new administrator account.

(b) *Sqlattack*: In this attack, the attacker creates a TCP connection with an SQL database server on a Unix machine. The database shell exits when a special escape sequence is issued and the root shell of the machine is started by running a Perlmagic script.

(ii) *R2L Attack*: In this attack, a remote attacker, without having an account on a local machine, attempts to send packets to that machine by gaining local access based on the vulnerabilities of that machine. To gain access to the local machine, the attacker attempts various ways shown in Figure 8.7. Two such ways are using online and offline dictionary attacks to acquire the password to access the machine and making repeated guesses at pos-

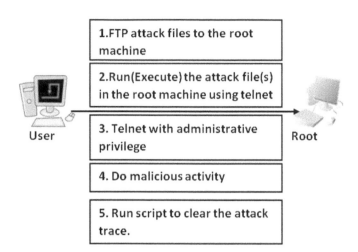

FIGURE 8.6:   U2R attack

sible usernames and passwords. The attacker also attempts to take advantage of those legitimate users who are often casual in choosing their passwords. Below are two R2L attack tools.

(a) *Netcat*: This R2L attack tool uses a Trojan program to install and run Netcat on the victim machine on port number 53. The Netcat program works as a back door to access the machine using Netcat port without any username and password.

(b) *ntfsdos*: The attacker gains the console of a WinNT machine by running ntfsdos. The program mounts the machine's disk drives. Thus, the attacker can copy secret files on the secondary media.

Among these user attacks, SQL attack is a more serious. Due to many possibilities of crafted SQL variants, it often becomes very difficult to handle with traditional statistical approaches. An adequate simulation tool that supports the generation of a large number of attack scenarios synthetically may be of great help to researchers in building appropriate defense mechanisms for this category of attack.

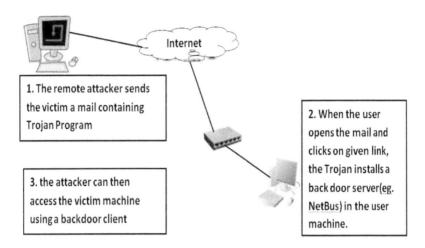

1. The remote attacker sends the victim a mail containing Trojan Program

2. When the user opens the mail and clicks on given link, the Trojan installs a back door server(eg. NetBus) in the user machine.

3. the attacker can then access the victim machine using a backdoor client

FIGURE 8.7:   R2L attack

8.2.3.7   Other Attack Tools

In addition to the tools discussed in the preceding sections, there are other tools which have direct or indirect use in the attack launching process. In this section, we introduce some of these tools to increase awareness of learners and security researchers.

(i) *Ping*: This tool is used to test network connectivity or reachability of a host on an IP network. Ping was a pioneering tool developed to check a computer, a router and Internet connectivity. The Ping request is sent to a particular host or to a network using a command prompt. As a reply, it displays the response of the destination and how long it takes to receive a reply. It uses the ICMP protocol, which has low priority and slower speed than regular network traffic.

(ii) *Hping2*: This is used to send custom TCP/IP packets and it displays reply messages received from the target. It handles fragmentation and arbitrary packet size and can also be used to transfer files. It performs firewall rule testing, port scanning, protocol-based network performance testing and path MTU discovery.

(iii) *Hping3*: This tool works almost like Hping2 and handles fragmentation and arbitrary packet size. It finds the sequence numbers for reply packets from the source port. It starts with a base source port number and increases this number for each packet sent. The default base source port is random. The source port number may be kept constant for each sent packet.

(iv) *Traceroute*: Traceroute is used to show the route between two systems in a network. It also lists all intermediate routers from the source end to the destination end. Using this tool, one determines how systems are connected to each other or how an ISP (Internet Service Provider) connects to the Internet to provide services. The traceroute program is available with most OSs such as Unix OS, Mac OS and Windows 95.

(v) *Tctrace*: Though tctrace is similar to traceroute, it uses TCP SYN packets to trace. This makes it possible for one to trace through firewalls if one knows a TCP service that is allowed to pass from the outside.

(vi) *Tcptraceroute*: Tcptraceroute sends either UDP or ICMP ECHO request packets using a TTL field which is incremented on each hop until the destination is reached. It shows the path that a packet has traversed to reach the destination. However, due to the widespread use of firewall filters, Tcptraceroute packets may not be able to complete the path to the destination.

(vii) *Traceproto*: Traceproto is similar to traceroute but this tool allows the user to choose protocols to be traced. It currently allows TCP, UDP and ICMP protocol traces. It can be used to test and bypass firewalls and packet filters and check if ports are open. Traceproto is actually a traceroute replacement written in C.

(viii) *Fping*: Fping uses the ICMP protocol to determine whether a host is active or not. Fping is more powerful than ping because it can scan any number of hosts or a file containing the list of hosts. Instead of trying one host until it times out or replies, fping sends out a ping packet and moves on to the next host in a round-robin fashion. If a host replies, it is noted and removed from the list of hosts to check. If a host does not respond within a certain time limit and/or retry limit, it is considered unreachable. Unlike ping, fping is meant to be used in scripts and its output is easy to parse.

(ix) *Arping*: The arping tool is used in the Linux platform to send an ARP request message to a destination host in a LAN. It is used to test whether an IP address is in use or not.

TABLE 8.5: Additional Attack Tools

Tool	Platform used	Source
Ping	Linux, Windows	http://www.download.cnet.com
Hping2	Linux, Mac	http://www.hping.org.
Hping3	Linux, Mac	http://www.hping.org.
Traceroute	Linux, Solaris, Windows	http://www.brothersoft.com
Tctrace	Linux, Solaris	http://www.tcptrace.org/
Tcptraceroute	Linux, Solaris	http://www.michael.toren.net/
Traceproto	Linux	http://www.traceproto.sourceforge.net
Fping	Linux, Windows	http://www.softpedia.com
Arping	Linux	http://www.linux.softpedia.com

8.2.4 Network Monitoring Tools

Monitoring of network traffic is an essential activity for network administrators to observe, analyze and finally identify any anomalies occuring in the network. To support such activities of network administrators as well as to assist in meaningful interpretation of the outcomes of their analysis, network monitoring and analysis tools have an important role to play. Frequent incidences of malicious attempts to compromise the confidentiality and integrity of and access control mechanisms of a system or to prevent legitimate users of a service from accessing the requested resources have led to an increased demand for developing useful tools to visualize network traffic in a meaningful manner to support subsequent analysis. We introduce some of these tools under two distinct categories, *visualization* and *analysis*.

8.2.4.1 Visualization Tools

An effective network traffic (for both packet traffic and network flows) visualization tool can be of significant help to the network administra-

TABLE 8.6:   Attacking Tools

Tool	Platform used	Source
Jolt	Windows 95/NT	
Burbonic	Linux, Windows	http://www.packetstormsecurity.org/
Targa	Linux	http://www.packetstormsecurity.org/
Blas20	Linux, Windows	
Crazy Pinger	Linux, Windows	http://www.softwaretopic.informer.com
UDPFllod	Windows	http://www.foundstone.com
FSMax	Windows	http://www.brothersoft.com
Nemsey	Windows	http://packetstormsecurity.org/
Panther	Windows	http://www.bestspywarescanner.net
Land & LaTierra	Windows	
Slowloris	Windows	http://www.ha.ckers.org/slowloris/
Blackenergy	Linux, Windows	http://www.airdemon.net
HOIC	Windows, Linux	https://www.rapidshare.com
Shaft	Linux, Windows	
Knight	Windows	http://www.cert.org
Kaiten	Windows	http://www.mcafee.com
RefRef	Windows	
Hgod	Windows	
LOIC	Linux, Windows	http://www.sourceforge.net
Trinoo	Linux, Windows	http://www.nanog.org
TFN	Linux, Windows	http://www.codeforge.com
TFN2K	Linux, Windows	http://www.goitworld.com
Stachaldraht	Linux, Windows	http://www.packetstormsecurity.org
Mstream	Linux, Windows	
Trinity	Linux, Windows	

tor in monitoring and in analyzing the traffic. Appropriate visualization not only supports meaningful interpretation of the analysis results, but also assists the system administrator in identifying anomalous patterns. It also helps in taking appropriate action to mitigate attacks before they propagate and infect other parts of the network. Some visualization tools are presented next.

(i) *Tnv*: This time-based traffic visualization tool presents packet details and links among local and remote hosts. Such a tool assists in learning the normal patterns in a network, investigating packet details and network troubleshooting. Tnv provides multiple services to support inspection and analysis activities, such as opening and reading libpcap files, capturing live packets and saving captured data in a MYSQL database.

(ii) *Network Traffic Monitor*: This tool supports presenting and scanning detailed traffic scenarios since the inception of an application process and also allows analyzing traffic details.

(iii) *Rumint*: This tool enables one to visualize live captured traffic as well as saved PCAP traffic data in the Windows environment.

(iv) *EtherApe*: EtherApe allows one to sniff live packet data and to monitor captured data in the Unix environment.

 (v) *NetGrok*: This is a real-time network visualization tool which aids in presenting a graphical layout and a tree map to support visual organization of the network data. It also supports live packet and trace capture and filtering activities.

(vi) *NetViewer*: This tool not only supports observing captured live traffic in aggregate, but also helps in identifying network anomalies. Additionally, NetViewer also supports presenting useful traffic characteristics to support tuning of defense mechanisms.

(vii) *VizNet*: This helps visualize the performance of a network based on bandwidth utilization.

TABLE 8.7: Visualization Tools

Tool	Platform used	Source
Tnv	Linux, Windows	http://www.tnv.sourceforge.net
Network Traffic Monitor 1.02	Windows	http://www.monitor-network-traffic.winsite.com
Rumint	Windows	http://www.rumint.org
EtherApe	Linux, Unix	http://www.brothersoft.com
Netgrok	Windows	http://www.softpedia.com
Netviewer	Windows	http://www.brothersoft.com
VizNet	Windows	http://www.viznet.ac.uk

Most of the above visualization tools also support analysis of network traffic. Among these, Tnv, NetGrok and NetViewer are very effective in terms of their user-friendly interface and support for a large number of functionalities, such as real-time visualization support. Additionally, Tnv is atttractive because it can interface with a MYSQL database.

TABLE 8.8: Various Attack Generation Tools

Category	Tool	Source
Trojans	NukeNabbler AIMSpy NetSpy	http://www.securitystronghold.com http://www.netspy-trojan-horse.downloads
Information gathering tools	ASS NMap p0f MingSweeper THC Amap Angry IP Scanner	http://www.manpages.ubuntu.com http://www.nmap.org http://www.lcamtuf.coredump.cx/p0f.shtml http://www.hoobie.net/ mingsweeper http://www.freeworld.thc.org/thc-amap http://www.angryziber.com/w/Download
DoS attack tools	Targa Burbonic Blast20	http://www.security-science.com/ http://www.softpedia.com
Spoofing attack tools	Engage Packet Builder Hping Nemesis Packet Excalibur Scapy	http://www.engage-packet-builder.software.informer.com/ http://www.hping.org http://www.nemesis.sourceforge. net http://www.linux.softpedia.com http://www.softpedia.com
TCP session Hijacking tools	Firesheep Hunt Juggernaut TTY Watcher IP Watcher Hjksuit-v0.1.99	http://www.codebutler.github.com/firesheep/ http://www.packetstormsecurity. org/sniffers/hunt http://www.tools.l0t3k.net/Hijacking/1.2.tar.gz http://www.security-science.com http://www.download.cnet.com http://www.tools.l0t3k.net/ Hijacking/hjksuite-0.1.99.tar.gz
Probe attack tools	Solarwind Network Probe NMap	http://www.solarwinds.com http://www.softpedia.com http://nmap.org
Spoofing attack tools in wireless	Kismet libpcap libnet libdnet libradiate	http://www.linux.die.ne http://www.sourceforge.net/projects/libpcap http://www.libnet.sourceforge.net http://www.libdnet.sourceforge.net/ http://www.packetfactory.net/projects/libradiate
Application layer attack tools	HOIC LOIC RefRef	https://www.rapidshare.com http://www.softpedia.com http://www.softpedia.com

8.3 Attack Detection Systems

We now briefly discuss some popular attack or intrusion detection systems which identify known as well as unknown attacks using statistical, data mining or soft computing approaches.

(i) Bro [288]: This Linux-based open source misuse detection system passively monitors network traffic and attempts to identify network intrusions in real time. To identify anomalies, it parses network traffic to extract semantics for application level information and uses a module to analyze and match the input traffic pattern against stored signatures. Bro is able to identify signature-based attacks, event-oriented attacks and some unusual attacks without dropping packets faster than its competitors. It also allows behavioral monitoring, multilayer analysis, policy enforcement and packet logging activities. It includes an extended set of scripts to support detection of known attacks with a minimum number of false alarms.

(ii) Snort [312]: This lightweight signature-based IDS inspects TCP/IP traffic to identify network intrusions based on feature rules and a content pattern matching procedure. It allows libpcap-based sniffing and logging of packet traffic for monitoring and detection of known attacks. It assists network administrators by providing enough data during the detection of different types of attacks such as buffer overflows, stealth port scans, CGI attacks and SMB probes. Snort is also able to detect any other data in the packet payload that can be characterized by a unique detection fingerprint. Once a packet matches a specified rule pattern, Snort offers three basic actions: *pass* rules to simply drop the packet, *log* rules to write the full packet selected by a user at runtime and *alert* rules to generate alarms based on the method specified by the command-line user.

(iii) Nessus [246]: This is an open source active detection plug-in for vulnerability identification. A Windows version of this system includes a large collection of database scripts to support identification of vulnerabilities. Generally, plug-ins are expected to be written very carefully so that they identify the known types of intrusions with a minimum number of false alarms. Nessus provides a user-friendly environment which interfaces to an HTTP server and a Web client. One only needs to install the Nessus server to make it work.

(iv) SHADOW [312]: The Secondary Heuristic Analysis for Defensive Online Warfare system is a cost-effective open source NIDS with a combination of tcpdump and Perl scripts. It exploits the flexibility and power of Perl to make the architecture attractive from a usability point of view. The two basic parts SHADOW are *Sensor station*, i.e., the server, which runs tcpdump to capture network traffic and store in a file and *Analysis station*, which accepts the stored output of the sensor station for analysis and identification of vulnerabilities. Based on the data collected by the sensor, a variety of external third party tools are used for postprocessing. A major limitation of this system is the lack of real-time alerts and an effective classification tool to support the activities of an analyst.

(v) STAT [182]: This is a misuse detection system that performs well in real time. STAT uses state transition analysis and provides a framework for developing a modular, stateful misuse detection system which can operate in multiple environments. Two major features of STAT are a detection tool for real-time attack identification using a knowledge-based approach and a facility to analyze audit trails of multi-user systems.

(vi) NID [1]: This open source IDS can work on multiple OSs including Linux. It is designed to serve in a limited manner and it is especially targeted for government organizations. It allows one to monitor IP traffic, speed and layouts that include FDDI (Fiber Distributed Data Interface). It supports auditing the network traffic in three modes: (a) to identify known anomalous patterns based on attack signatures, (b) to observe general safety parameters and (c) to identify unknown anomalous patterns.

(vii) ISS RealSecure [341]: This is an effective commercial purpose IDS developed for the Windows NT platform. Like other IDSs, ISS RealSecure also allows one (a) to monitor traffic, (b) to match against stored attack signatures, (c) to generate alarms while matched and (d) to implement possible countermeasures automatically. Once an attack is identified, along with the alarm information, it dynamically generates several useful pieces of information such as attack class, source and destination addresses and source and destination ports. It also allows one to monitor traffic based on the services used. ISS assumes that most attacks are from the inside. Hence, it maintains an appropriate data structure to store traffic information in addition to the traffic permitted by the perimeter security system. Additionally, it checks if the activities are permitted by the firewall.

In addition to the above IDSs available in the public domain, several other excellent IDSs also have come into existence as a result of the contributions of the network research community. Some of them are discussed in brief next.

(i) ADAM (*Automated Data Analysis and Mining*) [83]: This data mining-based system combines association rule mining and classification to discover attacks in tcpdump audit trail data. ADAM trains the classifier to classify suspicious connections as either a known type of attack or an unknown type or a false alarm with respect to the existing rules or profiles.

(ii) MINDS (*Minnesota Intrusion Detection System*) [110]: This is another popular data mining-based system for detecting network attacks or intrusions. It takes Netflow version 5 data collected through flow tools. Before entering into the anomaly detection module, a data filtering step is executed to remove noninteresting network traffic patterns. The anomaly detection engine uses an outlier detection algorithm to assign an anomaly score to each network connection. Finally, it reports alarms for any malicious activity based on the anomaly scores.

(iii) DNIDS (*Dependable Network Intrusion Detection System*) [208]: This NIDS uses a *combined strangeness and isolation* measure with the k-Nearest Neighbor (CSI-kNN) algorithm. DNIDS can detect network intrusions while providing continued service even under attacks. The intrusion detection algorithm analyzes characteristics of network data by employing two measures, strangeness and isolation. Based on these measures, a correlation unit raises intrusion alerts with associated confidence estimates. Multiple CSI-kNN classifiers work in parallel to deal with different types of network traffic and report an alarm for any abnormal traffic patterns.

(iv) HIDE [425]: This is a hierarchical anomaly-based system, developed using statistical modeling and neural networks. It consists of several tiers, each tier containing several Intrusion Detection Agents (IDAs), which are IDS components that monitor activities of a host or a network. The statistical processor maintains a reference model of typical network activities and compares reports from the event preprocessor with the reference model. It forms a stimulus vector to feed into the neural network classifier that analyzes the vector to decide whether the network traffic is normal or an attack. The post-processor generates reports for agents at higher tiers.

(v) NSOM (*Network Self-Organizing Maps*) [215]:   This Self-Organizing Map(SOM)-based IDS detects anomalies by quantifying the usual or acceptable behavior and flags irregular behavior as potentially intrusive. The structured SOM is used to classify real-time ethernet network traffic data. It collects network traffic data continuously from a network port and preprocesses and selects suitable features to classify them as an attack or normal.

(vi) FSAS (*Flow-Based Statistical Aggregation Scheme for Network Anomaly Detection*) [346]: This has a 2-layer architecture containing a feature generator and a flow-based detector. The feature generator collects network traffic data from a host or a network and the event time module periodically calls the feature extraction module to convert the flow statistic information into the format required by the model. The feature scoring metric calculates the probability scores of these features by comparing the features with the reference model generated by past normal and attack users. The higher the maliciousness of a flow, the higher is the possibility of the flow being an attack. FSAS provides 22 significant features relevant for DoS attack detection.

(vii) N@G (*Network at Guard*) [358]: This is a hybrid IDS that contains both network and host sensors. It analyzes the audit trail using statistical techniques as part of the host sensor. The system has a management console to aggregate alerts from various sensors using a user interface, a middle tier and a data management component. It provides real-time protection to client computers against malicious traffic, which can include unsolicited changes to Windows host files and Windows messenger service. It also provides Layered Service Provider (LSP) and Domain Name Server

(DNS) protection. The system can dynamically apply access controls to routers (Cisco) to actively block network attacks.

(viii) FIRE (*Fuzzy Intrusion Recognition Engine*) [98]: This fuzzy logic-based IDS combines simple network traffic metrics with fuzzy rules to determine the likelihood of specific or general network attacks. FIRE relies on fuzzy network traffic profiles as inputs to its rule set and uses simple data mining techniques to process the network input data for anomaly detection.

(ix) NFIDS [258]: This neuro-fuzzy-based hierarchical intrusion detection system is composed of several autonomous agents. It consists of three tiers. Tier-I contains several intrusion detection agents (IDAs). IDAs are IDS components that monitor activities of a host or a network and report abnormal behavior to Tier-II. Tier-II agents detect the network status of a LAN based on network traffic they observe as well as the reports received from the Tier-I agents within the LAN. Tier-III combines higher level reports, correlates data and sends alarms to the user interface for further action.

(x) D-WARD [253]: This adaptive source-end DDoS defense system detects attacks autonomously and gives surgically accurate responses using its traffic profiling techniques. D-WARD inflicts very low collateral damage to legitimate traffic, while quickly detecting and severely rate-limiting outgoing attacks.

(xi) LADS (*Large-Scale Automated DDoS Detection System*) [329]: This is a triggered, multistage detection system that addresses both scalability and accuracy in detecting DDoS attacks. LADS has been used Netflow data in detecting DDoS attacks in a Tier-1 ISP.

(xii) ANTID [217]: This IDS detects and filters DDoS attacks which use spoofed packets to circumvent conventional intrusion detection schemes. The anti-DDoS scheme intends to complement, rather than replace conventional schemes by embedding in each IP packet a unique path fingerprint that represents the route an IP packet has traversed. ANTID is able to distinguish IP packets that traverse different Internet paths. A server requires each of its communicating clients to map from the client's IP address to the corresponding path fingerprint. A spoofed DDoS attack can be detected by observing a surge of spoofed packets. It is lightweight and robust and is incrementally deployable.

(xiii) DCD [69]: This uses change aggregation trees (CAT) to detect distributed flooding attacks at flow level. The idea is to detect abrupt traffic changes across multiple network domains at the earliest time. The system is built over attack-transit routers, which work together. Each ISP domain has a CAT server to aggregate flooding alerts reported by routers. To resolve policy conflicts at different ISP domains, a new secure infrastructure protocol (SIP) is developed to establish mutual trust or consensus.

A comparison of the detection systems based on parameters such as detection type (host based, network based or both), class of detection approach (misuse, anomaly or both), nature of detection (online or offline), nature of processing (centralized or distributed), data gathering mechanism (centralized or distributed) and the technical approach for analysis is given in Table 8.9.

8.4   Discussion

Based on the detailed discussion of tools and systems available for network security research, we make the following observations.

- An integrated tool with support for capture, preprocessing, analysis and visualization of both flow and packet data is lacking. Existing tools (e.g., wireshark, Nfsen and Nfdump) can support either flow capture and presentation or packet analysis and presentation, not both.

- Existing feature extraction tools (such as tcptrace) are protocol centric (mostly for the TCP protocol), developed to extract basic features from raw packets. To derive attack specific complex features, specialized C or C++ programs or Perl scripts are needed.

- Existing DDoS attack tools cannot launch attacks at multiple layers. They support launching of only single layer attacks.

TABLE 8.9: Attack Detection Systems: A Comparative Study

System	H/ N/ Hy*	M/A/ B*	R/N*	C/D*	Source
Bro	N	M	R	C	www.bro-ids.org
Snort	N	M	R	C	www.snort.org
Nessus	N	M	R	C	www.nessus.org/plugins
SHADOW	N	M	R	C	www.nswc.navy.mil
STAT	N	M	R	C	sourceforge.net/project/stat
NID	N	M	R	C	ciac.llnl.gov/ctsc/nid/
ISS RealSecure	N	M	R	C	www.iss.net
FIRE	N	A	N	C	[98]
ADAM	N	A	R	C	[83]
HIDE	N	A	R	C	[425]
NSOM	N	A	R	C	[215]
MINDS	N	A	R	C	[110]
NFIDS	N	A	N	C	[258]
N@G	Hy	B	R	C	[358]
D-WARD	N	B	R	D	[253]
ANTID	N	A	R	C	[217]
FSAS	N	A	R	C	[346]
LADS	N	A	R	C	[329]
DNIDS	N	A	R	C	[208]
DCD	N	A	R	C	[69]

*H-Host/N-Network/Hy-Hybrid M-Misuse/A-Anomaly/B-Both R-Real time/N-Non real time C-Centralised/D-Distributed)

- Most existing DDoS attack tools are restricted to a limited number of attack scenarios. Such tools cannot be customized to develop additional attack scenarios.

- Most existing NIDSs are dependent on several user input parameters and their performance is highly sensitive to these parameters.

- Almost all anomaly-based NIDSs perform either near real time or offline. In addition, most suffer from a large number of false alarms.

- An effective tool to support correlation between flow traffic and packet traffic is still lacking.

Based on the above observations, we have identified the following list of research challenges for network defenders.

- It is a challenging task to develop an integrated tool to support capture, preprocessing (e.g., filtering and feature extraction), analysis and visualization of both flow and packet traffic.

- It is also a challenging task to develop a tool for fast capture, preprocessing and extraction of all types of features for network traffic, corresponding to all transport layer protocols.

- It is a nontrivial task to develope a GUI-based DDoS attack traffic generation tool capable of handling all possible attack scenarios for multiple network layers (e.g., application and transport layers).

- Development of an anomaly-based NIDS dependent on a minimum number of user parameters and capable of handling both known as well as unknown attacks in real time with a minimum number of false alarms is another challenging task.

- Development of a real-time detection system for both low rate and high rate DDoS attacks at the victim end without affecting legitimate users or normal service is another challenging task.

Chapter 9

Open Issues, Challenges and Concluding Remarks

Although in the last decade, a large number of methods and systems have been developed to counter network intrusions; there are still a number of open research issues and challenges. The suitability of performance metrics to evaluate a NIDS is a commonly identified unsolved issue in intrusion detection. In evaluating a NIDS, the four most important qualities that need to be measured are accuracy, performance, completeness and data quality.

A formal proof of correctness [283] in the intrusion detection domain in terms of all the known vulnerabilities is exceptionally challenging and expensive. Therefore, "pretty good assurance" presents a way in which systems can be measured allowing fuzzy decisions, trade-offs and priorities. Such a measure must take into consideration the amount of work required to discover a vulnerability or weakness to exploit for an attack and execute an attack on the system. Lack of reliable, valid and qualitative data is another major bottleneck in the classification accuracy and poor performance of most NIDSs. The current state-of-the-art in intrusion detection restricts evaluation of new systems to tests over incomplete datasets and micro-benchmarks that test narrowly defined components of the system. A number of anomaly-based systems have been tested using contrived datasets. This evaluation is limited by the quality of the dataset that the system is measured against. Construction of an unbiased, realistic and comprehensive dataset is an extremely difficult task. After a study of existing NIDSs, we find that it is still a challenge to design a new NIDS to ensure robustness, scalability and high performance. In particular, practitioners find it difficult to decide where to place the NIDS and how to best configure it for use within an environment with multiple stakeholders. We sort out some of the important issues as challenges and enumerate them below.

9.1   Runtime Limitations for Anomaly Detection Systems

Runtime limitations present an important challenge for a NIDS. Without losing any packets, a real-time NIDS should ideally capture and inspect each packet as per the current network scenario for appropriate analysis and accurate detection.

9.2   Reducing the False Alarm Rate

Ideally, a NIDS or detection method must avoid a high rate of false alarm. However, it is not possible in an anomaly-based intrusion detection system to totally escape false alarms, even though it needs to aim for no false alarm in any environment and also facilitate adaptability at runtime. This is another challenging task for the NIDS development community.

9.3   Issues in Dimensionality Reduction

Many network traffic features usually (i) have low variations or (ii) have correlations or functional dependencies among themselves, with reference to a given class of normal or anomalous instances. So, developing an appropriate method to select an optimal set of features for anomaly detection without compromising performance is yet another challenging task.

9.4 Computational Needs of Network Defense Mechanisms

To handle more sophisticated and complex layered attacks, defense mechanisms to protect from them are built on top of an existing system with associated computational modules. However, with continued development in high speed network technology, such incremental extensions may actually be counter-productive and may lead to bottlenecks in detection performance. Therefore, IDS developers need to be careful in incorporating such sophistications so that efficiency in performance is not compromised.

9.5 Designing Generic Anomaly Detection Systems

Most NIDSes and network intrusion detection methods depend on the environment. Ideally, a system or method should be independent of the environment. How to develop a NIDS so that it performs consistently in varied environments is another important issue.

9.6 Handling Sophisticated Anomalies

The nature of anomalies keeps changing over time as intruders adapt their network attacks to evade existing intrusion detection solutions. So the adaptability of a NIDS or detection method must be updated with the current anomalies encountered in the local network or on the Internet.

9.7   Adaptability to Unknown Attacks

Almost every day new vulnerabilities or exploits come into existence. Dynamically updating the profile or signature base as new exploits or vulnerabilities are identified, without causing conflicts with the existing signature base and without compromising real-time performance is yet another challenging task.

9.8   Detecting and Handling Large-Scale Attacks

Today's distributed attacks can compromise hundreds to thousands of machines very fast and can damage the network instantly. So, a NIDS should not only be able to detect the attack at an early stage, but also must be able to control the attack rate without compromising service to legitimate users, which is a challenging task.

9.9   Infrastructure Attacks

Currently predominant distributed attacks usually target a large number of hosts or servers or end machines. In addition to flooding network links and servers or end machines, such attacks may also attempt to make services unavailable for as many users as possible. One such example is a DDoS attack on a root DNS server. In addition, such attacks may target, more importantly, certificate servers, LDAP servers, key distribution servers, etc.

9.10   High Intensity Attacks

The present distributed attack scenarios may include thousands of compromised hosts when launching a denial of service attack. Such attacks spread instantly and are capable of damaging the whole network in a second. So, IDS designers must not only strive to detect such attacks, but also be able to control such high intensity attack traffic immediately.

9.11   More Inventive Attacks

Generally, most existing attacks are reflections of the hacker's desire to establish or demonstrate his or her ability [252]. However, recently sophisticated attacks with unknown motives are also being launched. The target of an attacker may not be merely to hack a few hosts or servers; rather it may have a more social, political or criminal motivation. Cell phone services, text messaging and other wireless devices that are increasingly using Internet services are providing another important victim for such attacks. The Internet has become an integral component of the law and order system in a developed or developing country. So sophisticated attacks in the Internet affects the criminal investigation process. The use of electronic voting machines (EVMs) in a country's election process is a common practice today. However, connecting these EVMs to the Internet can be dangerous. So developing a robust NIDS with the ability to counter any such inventive attacks with high accuracy is an important research issue.

9.12   Concluding Remarks

In this book, we have focused on the characterization of network anomalies which occur due to various malicious attempts and on detecting them using machine learning techniques. We have discussed the possible vulnerabilities a network faces at various layers due to weaknesses in protocols or other reasons. We have also introduced the reader to various types of layer-specific intrusions and their modes of operation. We have introduced machine learning methods, systems and techniques to counter network intrusion under categories such as supervised learning, unsupervised learning, probabilistic learning, soft computing and combination learners. We have also provided analysis of the pros and cons of these methods. We hope that such an analysis will help the reader in acquiring a clear understanding of the abilities of each method, system or technique. Often in the literature, the same class of attack is described by researchers in different ways. To avoid such inconsistency, this book has also provided a taxonomy of attacks to help readers in describing attacks in a consistent manner. The discussion in this book will also help beginners learn about anomalous or attack patterns and their characteristics, how one can look for such patterns in captured network traffic to unearth potential unauthorized attempts to damage a system or a network and to improve performance during attempts to locate such anomalous patterns. When looking for such patterns, researchers and practitioners can implement machine learning algorithms discussed in this book and can test their detection performance. A detailed technical description of these methods and algorithms and their applications is given in this book. By the end of the book, we hope that the reader has learned the specifics of most attacks, the available tools that intruders use to attack networks and also how network defenders can use the knowledge of such tools to protect their own networks from attacks. Finally, the authors believe addressing the issues and challenges discussed in this chapter will help build cost-effective strategies for better protection of networks from future trends that are producing complex and sophisticated attacks.

References

[1] http://www.softpanorama.org/security/intrusion_detection.shtml.

[2] A., H., NAVARRO, M., CORCHADO, E., AND JULIN, V. RT-MOVICAB-IDS: Addressing real-time intrusion detection. *Future Generation Computer Systems 29*, 1 (January 2013), 250–261.

[3] ADAM POCOCK. MIToolbox, 2012. MATLAB, http://mloss.org/software/view/325/.

[4] AGGARWAL, C., WOLF, J. L., YU, P. S., AND PROCOPIUE, C. M. Fast algorithms for projected clustering. In *ACM SIGMOD'99* (New York, USA, 1999), ACM, pp. 61–72.

[5] AGGARWAL, C., AND YU, P. S. Finding generalized projected clusters in high dimensional spaces. In *ACM SIGMOD Record* (2000), vol. 29, ACM, pp. 70–81.

[6] AGRAWAL, R., GEHRKE, J., GUNOPULOS, D., AND RAGHAVAN, P. Automatic subspace clustering of high dimensional data for data mining applications. In *ACM SIGMOD* (Seattle, 1998), ACM, pp. 94–105.

[7] AGRAWAL, R., IMIELIŃSKI, T., AND SWAMI, A. Mining association rules between sets of items in large databases. In *ACM SIGMOD Record* (1993), vol. 22, ACM, pp. 207–216.

[8] AGRAWAL, R., IMIELINSKI, T., AND SWAMI, A. Mining association rules between sets of items in large databases. In *Proc. of the ACM SIGMOD Conference* (Washington, DC, USA, May 1993), ACM, pp. 207–216.

[9] AGRAWAL, R., AND SRIKANT, R. Mining sequential patterns. In *Proc. of the 11th International Conference on Data Engineering* (USA, 1995), IEEE CS, pp. 3–14.

[10] AGYEMANG, M., BARKER, K., AND ALHAJJ, R. A comprehensive survey of numeric and symbolic outlier mining techniques. *Intelligence Data Analysis 10*, 6 (2006), 521–538.

[11] AHIRWAR, D. K., SAXENA, S. K., AND SISODIA, M. S. Anomaly detection by naive Bayes & RBF network. *International Journal of Advanced Research in Computer Science and Electronics Engineering 1*, 1 (2012), 14–18.

[12] ALI, A. G., LU, W., AND TAVALLAEE, M. *Network Intrusion Detection and Prevention: Concepts and Techniques.* Advances in Information Security. Springer, October 2009.

[13] ALMUALLIM, H., AND DIETTERICH, T. Learning with many irrelevant features. In *Proc. of the 9th National Conference on Artificial Intelligence* (1991), vol. 2, pp. 547–552.

[14] AMINI, M., JALILI, R., AND SHAHRIARI, H. R. RT-UNNID: a practical solution to real-time network-based intrusion detection using unsupervised neural networks. *Computers & Security 25*, 6 (2006), 459–468.

[15] AMIRI, F., YOUSEFI, M. M. R., LUCAS, C., SHAKERY, A., AND YAZDANI, N. Mutual information-based feature selection for intrusion detection systems. *Journal of Network and Computer Applications 34*, 4 (2011), 1184–1199.

[16] AMOR, N. B., BENFERHAT, S., AND ELOUEDI, Z. Naive Bayes vs. decision trees in intrusion detection systems. In *Proc. of the ACM Symposium on Applied Computing (SAC'04)* (Nicosia, Cyprus, March 14–17 2004), ACM, pp. 420–424.

[17] ANDERSON, D., LUNT, T. F., JAVITZ, H., TAMARU, A., AND VALDES, A. Detecting unusual program behavior using the statistical component of the next-generation intrusion detection expert system (nides). Tech. Rep. SRIO-CSL-95-06, Computer Science Laboratory, SRI International, USA, 1995.

[18] ANDERSON, J. P. Computer security threat monitoring and surveillance. Tech. rep., James P Anderson Co, Fort Washington, P. A., April 1980.

[19] ANKEREST, M., BREUING, M. M., KRIEGEL, H. P., AND SANDER, J. Optics: Ordering points to identify the clustering structure. In *ACM SIGMOD* (1999), ACM, pp. 49–60.

[20] APTE, C., HONG, S. J., HOSKING, J., LEPRE, J., PEDNAULT, E., AND ROSEN, B. Decomposition of heterogeneous classification problems. *Intelligent Data Analysis 2*, 1 (1998), 81–96.

[21] ARFKEN, G. Lagrange multipliers. In *Mathematical Methods for Physicists 3rd ed* (Orlando, 1985), Academic Press, pp. 945–950.

[22] ARIU, D., TRONCI, R., AND GIACINTO, G. HMMPayl: An intrusion detection system based on hidden Markov models. *Computers & Security 30*, 4 (2011), 221–241.

[23] ARUMUGAM, M., THANGARAJ, P., SIVAKUMAR, P., AND PRADEEPKUMAR, P. Implementation of two-class classifiers for hybrid intrusion detection. In *Proc. of the International Conference on Communication and Computational Intelligence* (December 2010), pp. 486–490.

[24] AXELSSON, S. The base-rate fallacy and its implications for the difficulty of intrusion detection. In *Proc. of the 6th ACM Conference on Computer and Communications Security* (New York, NY, USA, 1999), ACM, pp. 1–7.

[25] AXELSSON, S. The base-rate fallacy and the difficulty of intrusion detection. *ACM Transactions on Information and System Security 3*, 3 (August 2000), 186–205.

[26] AYAD, H., AND KAMEL, M. Finding natural clusters using multi-cluster combiner based shared nearest neighbours. In *Proc of Multi-classifier systems* (Berlin, Heidelberg, 2003), Springer Verlag, pp. 166–175.

[27] BAHROLOLUM, M., AND KHALEGHI, M. Anomaly intrusion detection system ssing Gaussian mixture model. In *Proc. of the 3rd International Conference on Convergence and Hybrid Information Technology* (Tehran, November 11–13 2008), vol. 1, IEEE Computer Society, pp. 1162–1167.

[28] BAHROLOLUM, M., SALAHI, E., AND KHALEGHI, M. Anomaly intrusion detection design using hybrid of unsupervised and supervised neural networks. *International Journal of Computer Networks & Communications (IJCNC) 1*, 2 (July 2009), 26–33.

[29] BAKAR, Z., MOHEMAD, R., AHMAD, A., AND ANDDERIS, M. A comparative study for outlier detection techniques in data mining. In *Proc. of the IEEE Conference on Cybernetics and Intelligent Systems* (2006), pp. 1–6.

[30] BALAJINATH, B., AND RAGHAVAN, S. V. Intrusion detection through learning behavior model. *Computer Communications 24*, 12 (July 2001), 1202–1212.

[31] BANDYOPADHYAY, S., MAULIK, U., AND MUKHOPADHYAY, A. Multiobjective genetic clustering for pixel classification in remote sensing imagery. *IEEE Transactions on Geoscience and Remote Sensing 45*, 2 (2007), 1506–1511.

[32] BANDYOPADHYAY, S., AND PAL, S. K. Pixel classification using variable string genetic algorithms with chromosomal differentiation. *IEEE Transactions on Geoscience and Remote Sensing 39*, 2 (2001), 303–308.

[33] BANKS, J. *Principles of Quality Control*. John Wiley & Sons, New York, USA, 1989.

[34] BARBARA, D., COUTO, J., JAJODIA, S., AND WU, N. Detecting novel network intrusions using Bayes estimators. In *Proc. of the 1st SIAM International Conference on Data Mining* (2001).

[35] BARNETT, V., AND LEWIS, T. *Outliers in statistical data*. John Wiley and Sons, 1994.

[36] BARRY, B. I. A., AND CHAN, H. A. A hybrid, stateful and cross-protocol intrusion detection system for converged applications. In *Proc. of the OTM Confederated International Conference on the Move to Meaningful Internet Systems, Part II*.

[37] BAUER, E., AND KOHAVI, R. An empirical comparison of voting classification algorithms: Bagging, boosting, and variants. *Machine learning 36*, 1 (1999), 105–139.

[38] BAYES, T. An essay towards solving a problem in the doctrine of chances. *Philosophical Transactions of the Royal Society of London 53*, 6 (1763), 370–418.

[39] BECKMAN, R. J., AND COOK, R. D. Outliers. *Technometrics 25*, 2 (1983), 119–149.

[40] BEN-DOR, A., SHAMIR, R., AND YAKHINI, Z. Clustering gene expression patterns. *Journal of Computational Biology 6*, 3-4 (1999), 281–297.

[41] BEN-HUR, A. Pyml-machine learning in python, 2009. *Software available at http://pyml.sourceforge.net*.

[42] BEVERLY, R. A robust classifier for passive tcp/ip fingerprinting. in passive and active network measurement. 5th International Workshop.

[43] BEZDEK, J., AND PAL, S. *Fuzzy Models for Pattern Recognition*, vol. 23. IEEE Press, New York, 1992.

[44] BHASKAR, T., KAMATH, B. N., AND MOITRA, S. D. A hybrid model for network security systems: Integrating intrusion detection system with survivability. *International Journal of Network Security 7*, 2 (2008), 249–260.

[45] BHUYAN, M. H., BHATTACHARYYA, D. K., AND KALITA, J. K. Surveying port scans and their detection methodologies. *The Computer Journal 54*, 4 (April 2011), 1–17.

[46] BILMES, J. A gentle tutorial on the EM algorithm and its application to parameter estimation for Gaussian mixture and hidden Markov models. Tech. Rep. ICSI-TR-97-021, University of Berkeley, 1997.

[47] BORAH, B., AND BHATTACHARYYA, D. K. A parallelization of density based clustering technique on distributed memory multicomputer. In *ADCOM'04* (Ahmedabad, 2004), pp. 536–541.

[48] BORIAH, S., CHANDOLA, V., AND KUMAR, V. Similarity measures for categorical data: A comparative evaluation. In *Proc. of the 8th SIAM International Conference on Data Mining* (2008), pp. 243–254.

[49] BORJI, A. Combining heterogeneous classifiers for network intrusion detection. In *Proc. of the 12th Asian Computing Science Conference on Advances in Computer Science: Computer and Network Security* (2007), Springer, pp. 254–260.

[50] BOUSQUET, O., AND ELISSEEFF, A. Algorithmic stability and generalization performance. *Advances in Neural Information Processing Systems 13* (2001), 196.

[51] BREIMAN, L. Random forests. *Machine Learning 45*, 1 (2001), 5–32.

[52] BREIMAN, L., FREIDMAN, J. H., OLSHEN, R. A., AND STONE, C. J. *Classification and Regression Trees*. Chapman and Hall, 1984.

[53] BREUNIG, M. M., KRIEGEL, H. P., NG, R. T., AND SANDER, J. LOF: Identifying density-based local outliers. *ACM SIGMOD 29*, 2 (June 2000), 93–104.

[54] BRIN, S., MOTWANI, R., ULLMAN, J. D., AND TSUR, S. Dynamic itemset counting and implication rules for market basket data. vol. 26, Proc. of ACM SIGMOD'97, pp. 255–268.

[55] BRODER, A. Z. Some applications of Rabin's fingerprinting method. In *Sequences II: Methods in Communications, Security, and Computer Science* (1993), Springer Verlag, pp. 143–152.

[56] BROWN, G., POCOCK, A., ZHAO, M., AND LUJÁN, M. Conditional likelihood maximisation: A unifying framework for information theoretic feature selection. *The Journal of Machine Learning Research 13* (2012), 27–66.

[57] BURBECK, K., AND NADJM-TEHRANI, S. ADWICE — Anomaly detection with real-time incremental clustering. In *Proc. of Information Security and Cryptology —ICISC 2004* (Berlin, Germany, May 2005), vol. 3506/2005, Springer, pp. 407–424.

[58] CAI, Z., GUAN, X., SHAO, P., PENG, Q., AND SUN, G. A rough set theory based method for anomaly intrusion detection in computer network systems. *Expert Systems 20*, 5 (November 2003), 251–259.

[59] CANNADY, J. Applying CMAC-based On-line Learning to Intrusion Detection. In *Proc. of the IEEE-INNS-ENNS International Joint Conference on Neural Networks* (2000), vol. 5, pp. 405–410.

[60] CASAS, P., MAZEL, J., AND OWEZARSKI, P. UNADA: Unsupervised network anomaly detection using sub-space outliers ranking. In *Proc. of the 10th Int'nl IFIP TC 6 Conference on Networking — Volume Part I (Networking'11)* (Heidelberg, 2011), Springer Verlag Berlin, pp. 40–51.

[61] CHA, S. H. Comprehensive survey on distance/similarity measures between probability density functions. *International Journal of Mathematical Models and Methods in Applied Science 1*, 4 (November 2007), 300–307.

[62] CHAN, P. K., MAHONEY, M. V., AND ARSHAD, M. H. A machine learning approach to anomaly detection. Tech. Rep.

CS-2003-06, Department of Computer Science, Florida Institute of Technology, 2003.

[63] CHANDOLA, V., BANERJEE, A., AND KUMAR, V. Anomaly detection: A survey. *ACM Computing Surveys 41*, 3 (September 2009), 15:1–15:58.

[64] CHATZIGIANNAKIS, V., ANDROULIDAKIS, G., PELECHRINIS, K., PAPAVASSILIOU, S., AND MAGLARIS, V. Data fusion algorithms for network anomaly detection: Classification and evaluation. In *Proc. of the 3rd Int'nl Conference on Networking and Services* (Greece, 2007), IEEE CS, pp. 50–57.

[65] CHEBROLU, S., ABRAHAM, A., AND THOMAS, J. P. Feature deduction and ensemble design of intrusion detection systems. *Computers & Security 24*, 4 (2005), 295–307.

[66] CHEESEMAN, P., KELLY, J., SELF, M., STUTZ, J., TAYLOR, W., AND FREEMAN, D. AutoClass: A Bayesian classification system. In *Proc. of the Fifth International Conference on Machine Learning (ML'88)* (1988), vol. 27, Morgan Kaufmann, pp. 54–64.

[67] CHEN, R. C., CHENG, K. F., CHEN, Y. H., AND HSIEH, C. F. Using rough set and support vector machine for network intrusion detection system. In *Proc. of the First Asian Conference on Intelligent Information and Database Systems* (2009), IEEE Computer Society, pp. 465–470.

[68] CHEN, W. H., HSU, S. H., AND SHEN, H. P. Application of SVM and ANN for intrusion detection. vol. 32, Computers & Operations Research, Elsevier, pp. 2617–2634.

[69] CHEN, Y., HWANG, K., AND KU., W.-S. Collaborative Detection of DDoS Attacks over Multiple Network Domains. *IEEE Transactions on Parallel Distrib. Syst. 18*, 12 (December 2007), 1649–1662.

[70] CHEN, Y., LI, Y., CHENG, X., AND GUO, L. Survey and taxonomy of feature selection algorithms in intrusion detection system. In *Information Security and Cryptology* (2006), Springer, pp. 153–167.

[71] CHENG, C., FU, A. W., AND ZHANG, Y. Entropy based subspace clustering for mining numerical data. In *SIGKDD'99* (New York, USA, 1999), vol. 3916, pp. 84–93.

[72] CHENG, J. C., AND JIN, D. S. A new cell based clustering method for large, high dimensional data in data mining applications. In *ACM Symposium on Applied Computing* (New York, USA, 2002), ACM, pp. 503–507.

[73] CHHABRA, P., SCOTT, C., KOLACZYK, E. D., AND CROVELLA, M. Distributed spatial anomaly detection. In *Proc. of the 27th IEEE International Conference on Computer Communications* (2008), pp. 1705–1713.

[74] CHIMPHLEE, W., ABDULLAH, A. H., NOOR, M., SAP, M., CHIMPHLEE, S., AND SRINOY, S. Unsupervised clustering methods for identifying rare events in anomaly detection. In *Proc. of World Academy of Science, Engineering and Technology (PWASET)* (Stankin, Moscow, October 2005), vol. 8, WASET, pp. 253–258.

[75] CHIMPHLEE, W., ABDULLAH, A. H., NOOR, M. S. M., SRINOY, S., AND CHIMPHLEE, S. Anomaly-based intrusion detection using fuzzy rough clustering. In *Proc. of the International Conference on Hybrid Information Technology* (Washington, DC, USA, 2006), vol. 01, IEEE Computer Society, pp. 329–334.

[76] CHOU, T. S., AND CHOU, T. N. Hybrid classifier systems for intrusion detection. In *Proc. of the 7th Annual Communication Networks and Services Research Conference* (2009), IEEE CS, pp. 286–291.

[77] CHRISTODORESCU, M., JHA, S., SESHIA, S. A., SONG, D., AND BRYANT, R. E. Semantics-aware malware detection. In *Proc. of the 2005 IEEE Symposium on Security and Privacy* (Washington, DC, USA, 2005), SP '05, IEEE Computer Society, pp. 32–46.

[78] CISCO.COM. Cisco IOS NetFlow Configuration Guide, Release 12.4. http://www.cisco.com, September, 2010.

[79] CLAISE, B. RFC 3954: Cisco Systems NetFlow Services Export Version 9. http://www.ietf.org/rfc/rfc3954.txt, 2004.

[80] COMBS, G. Wireshark. http://www.wireshark.org/, 2009.

[81] COMPTON, P., PRESTON, P., EDWARDS, G., AND B, K. Knowledge based systems that have some idea of their limits. In *Tenth Knowledge Acquisition for Knowledge Based Systems Workshop* (1996).

[82] CURK, T., DEMAR, J., XU, Q., LEBAN, G., PETROVIC, U., BRATKO, I., SHAULSKY, G., AND ZUPAN, B. Microarray data mining with visual programming. *Bioinformatics 21* (Feb. 2005), 396–398.

[83] DANIEL, B., JULIA, C., SUSHIL, J., AND NINGNING, W. ADAM: A testbed for exploring the use of data mining in intrusion detection. *ACM SIGMOD Record 30*, 4 (2001), 15–24.

[84] DANIELLE, L. Global information assurance certification paper: Introduction to dsniff. SANS Institute, USA.

[85] DANKE MIXTER. Attacks tools and information. http://packetstormsecurity.nl/index.html, 2003.

[86] DAS, K., SCHNEIDER, J., AND NEILL, D. B. Anomaly pattern detection in categorical datasets. In *Proc. of the 14th ACM SIGKDD International Conference on Knowledge Discovery and Data Mining* (USA, 2008), ACM, pp. 169–176.

[87] DAS, S. Filters, wrappers and a boosting-based hybrid methods for feature selection. In *Machine Learning— Int'nl Workshop* (2001), Citeseer, pp. 74–81.

[88] DASGUPTA, D., AND MAJUMDAR, N. S. Anomaly detection in multidimensional data using negative selection algorithm. In *Proc. of the IEEE Conference on Evolutionary Computation* (2002), IEEE, pp. 1039–1046.

[89] DASH, M., AND LIU, H. Feature selection for classification. *Intelligent Data Analysis 1*, 1-4 (1997), 131–156.

[90] DASH, M., AND LIU, H. Consistency-based search in feature selection. *Artificial Intelligence 151*, 1 (2003), 155–176.

[91] DAVIES, D. L., AND BOULDIN, D. W. A cluster separation measure. *IEEE Transactions on Pattern Analysis and Machine 1*, 2 (1979), 224–227.

[92] DE ARGAEZ, E. Internet world stats, http://www.internetworldstats. com.

304   *References*

[93] DEBAR, H., DACIER, M., AND WESPI, A. Towards a taxonomy of intrusion-detection systems. Computer Networks: Elsevier, pp. 805–822.

[94] DEMPSTER, A., LAIRD, N., AND RUBIN, D. Maximum likelihood from incomplete data via the EM algorithm. *Journal of the Royal Statistical Society 39*, 1 (1977), 1–38.

[95] DEMPSTER, A. P. Upper and lower probabilities induced by a multivalued mapping. *Ann. Math. Stat. 38* (1967), 325–339.

[96] DENNING, D. E., AND NEUMANN, P. G. Requirements and model for IDES, a real-time intrusion detection system. Tech. Rep. 83F83-01-00, Computer Science Laboratory, SRI International, USA, 1985.

[97] DHILON, I. S., AND MODHA, D. S. A data clustering algorithm on distributed memory multi-processors. In *SIGKDD'99* (San Diego, USA, 1999), vol. 3916.

[98] DICKERSON, J. E. Fuzzy network profiling for intrusion detection. In *Proc. of the 19th International Conference of the North American Fuzzy Information Processing Society* (Atlanta, July 2000), pp. 301–306.

[99] DIETTERICH, T. G. An experimental comparison of three methods for constructing ensembles of decision trees: Bagging, boosting, and randomization. *Machine Learning 40*, 2 (2000), 139–157.

[100] DING, C., AND PENG, H. Minimum redundancy feature selection from microarray gene expression data. *Journal of Bioinformatics and Computational Biology 3*, 2 (2005), 185–205.

[101] DOKAS, P., ERTOZ, L., LAZAREVIC, A., SRIVASTAVA, J., AND TAN, P. N. Data mining for network intrusion detection. In *Proc. of the NSF Workshop on Next Generation Data Mining* (November 2002).

[102] DONNET, B., GUEYE, B., AND KAAFAR, M. A. A survey on network coordinates systems, design, and security. *IEEE Communication Surveys & Tutorials 12*, 4 (October 2010), 488–503.

[103] DORIGO, M., MANIEZZO, V., AND COLORNI, A. Positive feedback as a search strategy. Tech. rep., Departmento di Elettronica, Politecnico di Milano, Italy, 1992.

[104] DORIGO, M., MANIEZZO, V., AND COLORNI, A. Ant system: Optimization by a colony of cooperating agents. *IEEE Transactions on Systems, Man and Cybernetics, Part B 26*, 1 (1996), 29–41.

[105] DUBOIA, D., AND PRADE, H. Rough-fuzzy sets and fuzzy-rough sets. *International Journal of General Systems 17* (1990), 191–209.

[106] DUFFIELD, N. G., HAFFNER, P., KRISHNAMURTHY, B., AND RINGBERG, H. Rule-based anomaly detection on IP flows. In *Proc. of the 28th IEEE International Conference on Computer Communications, Joint Conference of the IEEE Computer and Communications Societies* (Rio de Janeiro, Brazil, 2009), IEEE press, pp. 424–432.

[107] DUNN, J. Well separated clusters and optimal fuzzy partitions. *Journal of Cybernetics 4* (1974), 95–104.

[108] EATON, J., ET AL. *Gnu Octave*. Free Software Foundation, 1997.

[109] EDGEWORTH, F. Y. On discordant observations. *Philosophy Magazine 23*, 5 (1887), 364–375.

[110] ERTOZ, L., EILERTSON, E., LAZAREVIC, A., TAN, P., KUMAR, V., AND SRIVASTAVA, J. MINDS — Minnesota Intrusion Detection System, 2004.

[111] ERTOZ, L., STAINBACH, M., AND KUMAR, V. Finding clusters of different sizes, shapes and densities in noisy high dimensional data. In *SIAM'03* (2003).

[112] ESKIN, E. Anomaly detection over noisy data using learned probability distributions. In *Proc. of the 7th Int'nl Conference on Machine Learning* (2000), Morgan Kaufmann Publishers Inc., pp. 255–262.

[113] ESKIN, E., STOLFO, S. J., AND LEE, W. Modeling system call for intrusion detection using dynamic window sizes. In *Proc. of DARPA Information Survivability Conference and Exposition (DISCEX II'01)* (Anaheim, CA, 12 – 14 June 2001), vol. 1, IEEE Computer Society.

[114] ESTER, M., AND KRIEGEL, H. A density-based algorithm for discovering clusters in large spatial databases with noise. In *Proc.*

2nd Int'nl Conf. on Knowledge Discovery and Data Mining, Portland (Portland, Aug. 1996), AAAI Press, pp. 226–231.

[115] ESTER, M., KRIEGEL, H. P., SANDER, J., WIMMER, M., AND XU, X. An incremental clustering for mining in a data warehousing environment. In *Proc. of VLDB98* (New York, USA, 1998).

[116] ESTEVEZ-TAPIADOR, J. M., GARCA-TEODORO, P., AND DAZ-VERDEJO, J. E. Stochastic protocol modeling for anomaly based network intrusion detection. In *Proc. of the 1st International Workshop on Information Assurance* (2003), IEEE CS, pp. 3–12.

[117] ESTEVEZ-TAPIADOR, J. M., GARCIA-TEODORO, P., AND DIAZ-VERDEJO, J. E. Anomaly detection methods in wired networks: A survey and taxonomy. *Computers & Security 27* (2004), 1569–1584.

[118] FENG, C., PENG, J., QIAO, H., AND ROZENBLIT, J. W. Alert fusion for a computer host based intrusion detection system. In *Proc. of the 14th Annual IEEE International Conference and Workshops on the Engineering of Computer-Based Systems* (USA, 2007), IEEE CS, pp. 433–440.

[119] FLEURET, F. Fast binary feature selection with conditional mutual information. *The Journal of Machine Learning Research 5* (2004), 1531–1555.

[120] FOLINO, G., PIZZUTI, C., AND SPEZZANO, G. An ensemble-based evolutionary framework for coping with distributed intrusion detection. *Genetic Programming and Evolvable Machines 11*, 2 (June 2010), 131–146.

[121] FRED, A. L. N., AND JAIN, A. Data clustering using evidence accumulation. In *Proc of ICPR'02* (Washington, DC, USA, 2002), IEEE Press, pp. 276–280.

[122] FREUND, Y., AND SCHAPIRE, R. E. Experiments with a new boosting algorithm. In *Proc. of the 13th International Conference on Machine Learning* (1996), pp. 325–332.

[123] FRIEDMAN, J. Greedy function approximation: a gradient boosting machine (English summary). *The Annals of Statistics 29*, 5 (2001), 1189–1232.

[124] FRIEDMAN, J. H., AND MEULMAN, J. J. Clustering objects on subspace of attributes. *Journal of the Royal Statistical Society 66* (2004), 815–849.

[125] FUJIMAKI, R., YAIRI, T., AND MACHIDA, K. An approach to spacecraft anomaly detection problem using kernel feature space. In *Proc. of the 11th ACM SIGKDD International Conference on Knowledge Discovery in Data Mining* (USA, 2005), ACM, pp. 401–410.

[126] GADDAM, S. R., PHOHA, V. V., AND BALAGANI, K. S. K-Means+ID3: A novel method for supervised anomaly detection by cascading k-means clustering and ID3 decision tree learning methods. *IEEE Transactions on Knowledge and Data Engineering 19*, 3 (Mar 2007), 345–354.

[127] GAN, G., MA, C., AND WU, J. *Data Clustering – Theory, Algorithms and Applications.* SIAM, 2007.

[128] GANTI, V., RAMAKRISHNAN, R., AND GEHRKE, J. Clustering large datasets in arbitrary metric spaces. In *Fifteenth Int'nl Conference on Data Engineering* (1998), pp. 502–511.

[129] GAO, H. H., YANG, H. H., AND WANG, X. Y. Ant colony optimization based network intrusion feature selection and detection. In *Proc. of the International Conference on Machine Learning and Cybernetics* (August 2005), vol. 6, pp. 3871–3875.

[130] GASSER, T., MULLER, H., AND MAMMITZSCH, V. Kernels for non-parametric curve estimation. *Journal of the Royal Statistical Society Series B (Methodological)* (1985), 238–252.

[131] GELENBE, E. Dealing with software viruses: A biological paradigm. *Information Security Technical Report 12(4)* (2007), 242–250.

[132] GENG, L., AND JIA, H. A novel intrusion detection scheme for network-attached storage based on multisource information fusion. In *Proc. of the International Conference on Computational Intelligence and Security* (Washington, DC, USA, 2009), IEEE Computer Society, pp. 469–473.

[133] GHAHRAMANI, Z. An Introduction to hidden Markov models and Bayesian networks. *International Journal of Pattern Recognition and Artificial Intelligence 15*, 1 (2001), 9–42.

[134] GHOTING, A., OTEY, M. E., AND PARTHASARATHY, S. Loaded: Link-based outlier and anomaly detection in evolving data sets. In *Proc. of the 4th IEEE Int'nl Conference on Data Mining* (Brighton, UK, Nov. 2004), IEEE Computer Society, pp. 387–390.

[135] GIACINTO, G., PERDISCI, R., RIO, M. D., AND ROLI, F. Intrusion detection in computer networks by a modular ensemble of one-class classifiers. *Information Fusion 9*, 1 (January 2008), 69–82.

[136] GIACINTO, G., ROLI, F., AND DIDACI, L. Fusion of multiple classifiers for intrusion detection in computer networks. *Pattern Recognition Letters 24*, 12 (August 2003), 1795–1803.

[137] GILBERT, E. Pioneer maps of health and disease in England. *Geographical Journal 124* (1958), 172–183.

[138] GINI, C. Variabilita e mutabilita. *Journal of the Royal Statistical Society 76*, 3 (February 1913), 326–327.

[139] GOGOI, P., BHATTACHARYYA, D. K., BORAH, B., AND KALITA, J. K. A survey of outlier detection methods in network anomaly identification. *The Computer Journal 54*, 4 (2011), 570–588.

[140] GOGOI, P., BHUYAN, M. H., BHATTACHARYYA, D. K., AND KALITA, J. K. Packet and flow based network intrusion dataset. In *Proc. of the 5th Int'nl Conference on Contemporary Computing (IC3-2012)* (August 6–8 2012), vol. 306 of *CCIS*, Springer, pp. 322–334.

[141] GOGOI, P., BORAH, B., AND BHATTACHARYYA, D. K. Anomaly detection analysis of intrusion data using supervised and unsupervised approach. *Journal of Convergence Information Technology 5*, 1 (Feb. 2010), 95–110.

[142] GOGOI, P., BORAH, B., AND BHATTACHARYYA, D. K. Network anomaly detection using unsupervised model. *Int'nl Journal of Computer Applications (Special Issue on Network Security and Cryptography) NSC*, 1 (Dec. 2011), 19–30.

[143] GOIL, S., NAGESH, H., AND CHOUDHARY, A. Mafia: Efficient and scalable subspace clustering for very large data sets. Tech. rep., Northwestern University, 1999.

[144] GOLBERG, D. E. *Genetic Algorithms in Search, Optimization and Machine Learning.* Addison-Wesley, New York, 1989.

[145] GÓMEZ, C. *Engineering and Scientific Computing with SciLab.* Birkhauser, 1999.

[146] GÓMEZ, J., GIL, C., PADILLA, N., BAÑOS, R., AND JIMÉNEZ, C. Design of a Snort based Hybrid Intrusion Detection System. In *Proc of 10th Int'nl Work-Conference on Artificial Neural Networks: Part II:* (2009), Springer, pp. 515–522.

[147] GONG, W., FU, W., AND CAI, L. A neural network based intrusion detection data fusion model. In *Proc. of the 3rd Int'nl Joint Conference on Computational Science and Optimization - Volume 2* (USA, 2010), IEEE CS, pp. 410–414.

[148] GUHA, S., RASTOGI, R., AND SHIM, K. Cure: An efficient clustering algorithm for large databases. In *SIGMOD 1998* (1998), vol. 27, ACM, pp. 73–84.

[149] GUHA, S., RASTOGI, R., AND SHIM, K. Rock: A robust clustering algorithm for categorical attributes. In *Int'nl Conference on Data Engineering* (1999), pp. 512–521.

[150] GUYON, I., AND ELISSEEFF, A. An introduction to variable and feature selection. *The Journal of Machine Learning Research 3* (2003), 1157–1182.

[151] GUYON, I., WESTON, J., BARNHILL, S., AND VAPNIK, V. Gene selection for cancer classification using support vector machines. *Machine Learning 46*, 1 (2002), 389–422.

[152] GWADERA, R., ATALLAH, M. J., AND SZPANKOWSKI, W. Detection of significant sets of episodes in event sequences. In *Proc. of the 4th IEEE International Conference on Data Mining* (Washington, DC, USA, 2004), IEEE Computer Society, pp. 3–10.

[153] GWADERA, R., ATALLAH, M. J., AND SZPANKOWSKI, W. Reliable detection of episodes in event sequences. *Knowledge and Information Systems 7*, 4 (2005), 415–437.

[154] HAAG, P. Nfdump & nfsen. http://nfdump.sourceforge.net/, September, 2010.

[155] HALL, M. A., AND SMITH, L. A. Feature subset selection: a correlation based filter approach. In *Proc. of the International Conference on Neural Information Processing and Intelligent Information Systems* (1997), Springer, pp. 855–858.

[156] HAN, J., AND KAMBER, M. *Data Mining: Concepts and Techniques*. Morgan Kaufmann Publishers, 2000.

[157] HAN, J., PEI, J., YIN, Y., AND MAO, R. Mining frequent patterns without candidate generation: A frequent-pattern tree approach. Data Mining and Knowledge Discovery, vol 8, pp. 53–87.

[158] HANDL, J., AND KNOWLES, J. An evolutionary approach to multi-objective clustering. *IEEE Transactions on Evolutionary Computing 11*, 1 (2007), 56–76.

[159] HANDL, J., KNOWLES, J., AND KELL, D. B. Computational cluster validation in post-genomic data analysis. *Bioinformatics 21* (2005), 3201–3212.

[160] HANSELMAN, D., AND LITTLEFIELD, B. *Mastering MATLAB 5: A Comprehensive Tutorial and Reference*. Prentice Hall PTR, 1997.

[161] HANSMAN, S., AND HUNT, R. A taxonomy of network and computer attacks. *Computers & Security 24*, 1 (September 2005), 31–43.

[162] HARTIGAN, J. A., AND WONG, M. A. Algorithm AS 136: A k-means clustering algorithm. *Applied Statistics 28*, 1 (1979), 100–108.

[163] HAWKINS, D. *Identification of Outliers*. Chapman and Hall, New York, 1980.

[164] HAWKINS, S., HE, H., WILLIAMS, G., AND BAXTER, R. Outlier detection using replicator neural networks. In *Proc. of the 4th Int'nl Conference on Data Warehousing and Knowledge Discovery* (London, UK, Sep. 2002), Springer Verlag, pp. 170–180.

[165] HAYKIN, S. *Neural Networks*. Prentice Hall, NJ, 1999.

[166] HECKERMAN, D. A tutorial on learning with Bayesian networks. Tech. Rep. MSRTR-95-06, Microsoft Research, 1995.

[167] HINNEBURG, A., ER, H., AND KEIM, D. A. An efficient approach to clustering in large multimedia databases with noise. In *Proc. of Knowledge Discovery and Data Mining* (1998), AAAI Press, pp. 58–65.

[168] HIPP, J., GUNTZER, U., AND NAKHAEIZADEH, G. Algorithms for association rule mining — A general survey and comparison. In *Proc. of the ACM SIGKDD Int'nl Conference on Knowledge Discovery and Data Mining* (Boston, MA, USA, 2000), ACM, pp. 58–64.

[169] HODGE, V., AND AUSTIN, J. A survey of outlier detection methodologies. *Artificial Intellligence Review 22*, 2 (2004), 85–126.

[170] HOFMEYR, S. A., FORREST, S., AND SOMAYAJI, A. Intrusion detection using sequences of system calls. *Journal of Computer Security 6*, 3 (1998), 151–180.

[171] HOLLAND, J. H. *Adaptation in Natural and Artificial Systems.* MIT Press, Cambridge, MA, 1975.

[172] HOLMES, G., DONKIN, A., AND WITTEN, I. Weka: A machine learning workbench. In *Intelligent Information Systems, 1994* (1994), IEEE, pp. 357–361.

[173] HONG, S. Use of contextual information for feature ranking and discretization. *IEEE Transactions on Knowledge and Data Engineering 9*, 5 (1997), 718–730.

[174] HOUTSMA, M., AND SWAMI, A. Set oriented mining for association rules in relational databases. IEEE Conference on Data Engineering, pp. 25–34.

[175] HRUSCHKA, E. R., CAMPELLO, R. J., FREITAS, A. A., AND CARVALHO, A. C. A survey of evolutionary algorithms for clustering. *IEEE Transactions on Systems, Man and Cybernetics, Part C: Applications and Reviews 29* (1999), 433–439.

[176] HRUSCHKA, E. R., CAMPELLO, R. J., FREITAS, A. A., AND CARVALHO, A. C. A survey of evolutionary algorithms for clustering. *IEEE Transactions on Systems, Man and Cybernetics, Part C: Applications and Reviews 39*, 2 (2009).

[177] HSU, C. W., CHANG, C. C., AND LIN, C. J. A practical guide to support vector classification. Tech. rep., University of Freiburg, July 2003.

[178] HU, Q., YU, D., LIU, J., AND WU, C. Neighborhood rough set based heterogeneous feature subset selection. *Information Sciences 178*, 18 (2008), 3577–3594.

[179] HUANG, Z. Clustering large data sets with mixed numeric and categorical values. In *Proc. of the 1st Pacific-Asia Conference on Knowledge Discovery and Data Mining (PAKDD)* (1997), pp. 21–34.

[180] HUBERT, L., AND SCHULTZ, J. Quadratic assignment as a general data-analysis strategy. *British Journal of Mathematical and Statistical Psychology 29* (1976), 190–241.

[181] HUNG, S. S., AND LIU, D. S. M. A user-oriented ontology-based approach for network intrusion detection. *Computer Standards & Interfaces 30*, 1–2 (January 2008), 78–88.

[182] ILGUN, K., KEMMERER, R., AND PORRAS, P. State transition analysis: A rule-based intrusion detection approach. *IEEE Transactions on Software Engineering 21*, 3 (1995), 181–199.

[183] IZETTA, C., AND GRANITTO, P. Feature selection with simple ANN ensembles. In *XV Congreso Argentino de Ciencias de la Computación* (2009).

[184] JACOBSON, D. *Introduction to Network Security*. Chapman and Hall/CRC Press, 2011.

[185] JAIN, A. K., MURTY, M. N., AND FLYNN, P. J. Data clustering: A review. *ACM Computing Survey 31*, 3 (1999), 264–323.

[186] JANUZAJ, E., KRIEGEL, H. P., AND PFEIFLE, M. Towards effective and efficient distributed clustering. In *ICDM'03* (Melbourne, FL, 2003), pp. 49–58.

[187] JEMILI, F., ZAGHDOUD, M., AND AHMED, M. B. A framework for an adaptive intrusion detection system using Bayesian network. IEEE, pp. 66–70.

[188] JENSEN, F. V. *Introduction to Bayesian Networks*. Springer Verlag, New York, USA, 1996.

[189] JIANG, J., AND PAPAVASSILIOU, S. Enhancing network traffic prediction and anomaly detection via statistical network traffic separation and combination strategies. *Computer Communications 29*, 10 (June 2006), 1627–1638.

[190] JIANGAB, F., SUIA, Y., AND CAOA, C. A rough set approach to outlier detection. *International Journal of General Systems 37*, 5 (Oct. 2008), 519–536.

[191] JOSHI, M. V., AGARWAL, R. C., AND KUMAR, V. Mining Needle in a Haystack: Classifying Rare Classes via Two-phase Rule Induction. In *Proc. of the 7th ACM SIGKDD International Conference on Knowledge Discovery and Data Mining* (2001), ACM, pp. 293–298.

[192] KARYPSIS, G. AND HAN H. AND KUMAR V. Chameleon: A hierarchical clustering algorithm using dynamic modeling. *IEEE Computer 32*, 8 (1999), 68–75.

[193] KASAREKAR, V., AND RAMAMURTHY, B. Distributed hybrid agent based intrusion detection and real time response system. In *Proc. of the 1st International Conference on Broadband Networks* (USA, 2004), IEEE CS, pp. 739–741.

[194] KAUFMAN, L., AND ROUSSEEUW, P. *Clustering by Means of Medoids*. Reports of the Faculty of Mathematics and Informatics. Delft University of Technology, 1987.

[195] KDDCUP99. Knowledge discovery in databases DARPA archive. http://www.kdd.ics.uci.edu/databases/kddcup99, 1999.

[196] KHAN, L., AWAD, M., AND THURAISINGHAM, B. A new intrusion detection system using support vector machines and hierarchical clustering. *The VLDB Journal 16*, 4 (October 2007), 507–521.

[197] KHAN, M. S. A. Rule based network intrusion detection using genetic algorithm. *International Journal of Computer Applications 18*, 8 (March 2011), 26–29.

[198] KHANNA, R., AND LIU, H. Control theoretic approach to intrusion detection using a distributed hidden Markov model. *IEEE Wireless Communications 15*, 4 (August 2008), 24–33.

[199] KHOR, K.-C., TING, C.-Y., AND AMNUAISUK, S.-P. A feature selection approach for network intrusion detection. In *Proc. on Information Management and Engineering, ICIME'09* (April 2009), pp. 133–137.

[200] KIM, H., ROZOVSKII, B. L., AND TARTAKOVSKY, A. G. A nonparametric multi-chart CUSUM test for rapid detection of DoS attacks in computer networks. *International Journal of Computing and Information Sciences 2*, 3 (December 2004), 149–158.

[201] KIRA, K., AND RENDELL, L. The feature selection problem: Traditional methods and a new algorithm. In *Proc. of the National Conference on Artificial Intelligence* (1992), John Wiley & Sons Ltd., pp. 129–129.

[202] KNORR, E. M., AND NG, R. T. Algorithms for mining distance-based outliers in large datasets. In *Proc. of the 24th Int. Conf. on Very Large Databases* (New York, USA, Sep. 1998), Morgan Kaufmann, pp. 392–403.

[203] KNORR, E. M., AND NG, R. T. Finding intentional knowledge of distance-based outliers. In *Proc. of the 25th International Conference on Very Large Data Bases* (Edinburgh, Scotland, UK, Sep. 1999), Morgan Kaufmann, pp. 211–222.

[204] KOHAVI, R., AND JOHN, G. Wrappers for feature subset selection. *Artificial Intelligence 97*, 1 (1997), 273–324.

[205] KOHONEN, T. *Self-Organizing Maps*. Springer, Berlin, 2000.

[206] KOUFAKOU, A., AND GEORGIOPOULOS, M. A fast outlier detection strategy for distributed high-dimensional data sets with mixed attributes. *Data Mining and Knowledge Discovery 20*, 2 (Mar. 2010), 259–289.

[207] KRUEGEL, C., MUTZ, D., ROBERTSON, W., AND VALEUR, F. Bayesian event classification for intrusion detection. In *Proc. of the 19th Annual Computer Security Applications Conference* (2003).

[208] KUANG, L. V. DNIDS: A dependable network intrusion detection system using the CSI-KNN algorithm. Master's thesis, Queen's University, Kingston, Ontario, Canada, September 2007.

[209] KUHN, M. Building predictive models in R using the caret package. *Journal of Statistical Software 28*, 5 (2008), 1–26.

[210] KUKIELKA, P., AND KOTULSKI, Z. Adaptation of the neural network-based IDS to new attacks detection. *Computing Research Repository abs/1009.2406* (2010).

[211] KUMAR, V., SRIVASTAVA, J., AND LAZAREVIC, A. *Managing Cyber Threats—Issues, Approaches and Challenges*, vol. 5. Springer, June 7, 2006.

[212] KUNCHEVA, L. Combining pattern classifiers: Methods and algorithms. *IEEE Transactions on Neural Networks 18*, 3 (2007), 964–964.

[213] KUNCHEVA, L. I., AND RODRIGUEZ, J. J. Classifier ensembles with a random linear oracle. *IEEE Transactions on Knowledge and Data Engineering 19*, 4 (April 2007), 500–508.

[214] KURSA, M. B., AND RUDNICKI, W. R. Feature selection with the boruta package. *Journal of Statistical Software 36*, 11 (September 2010), 1–13.

[215] LABIB, K., AND VEMURI, R. NSOM: A tool to detect DoS attacks using Self-Organizing Maps. Tech. rep., Department of Applied Science University of California, Davis, 2002.

[216] LANGLEY, P., IBA, W., AND THOMAS, K. An analysis of Bayesian classifiers. In *Proc. of the Tenth National Conference of Artificial Intelligence* (1992), AAAI Press, pp. 223–228.

[217] LEE, F.-Y., AND SHIEH, S.-P. Defending against spoofed DDoS attacks with path fingerprint. *Computers & Security 24* (2005), 571–586.

[218] LEE, H., CHEN, C., CHEN, J., AND JOU, Y. An efficient fuzzy classifier with feature selection based on fuzzy entropy. *IEEE Transactions on Systems, Man, and Cybernetics, Part B: Cybernetics 31*, 3 (2001), 426–432.

[219] LEE, I., AND ESTIVIL-CASTRO, V. Autoclust: Automatic clustering via boundary extraction for mining point dataset. In *Proc. of the 5th Int'nl Conference on Geocomputation* (2000), Citeseer.

[220] LEE, S. C., AND HEINBUCH, D. V. Training a neural-network based intrusion detector to recognize novel attacks. *IEEE Trans-*

actions on Systems, Man, and Cybernetics: Part A 31, 4 (2001), 294–299.

[221] LEE, W., AND STOLFO, S. J. Data mining approaches for intrusion detection. In *Proc. of the 7th USENIX Security Symposium* (USA, 1998), vol. 7, USENIX Association, pp. 79–94.

[222] LEE, W., STOLFO, S. J., AND MOK, K. W. A data mining framework for building intrusion detection models. In *Proc. of the IEEE Symposium on Security and Privacy* (Oakland, CA, USA, 1999), IEEE, pp. 120–132.

[223] LEE, W., STOLFO, S. J., AND MOK, K. W. Adaptive intrusion detection—a data mining approach. *Artificial Intelligence Review 14* (2000), 533–567.

[224] LEON, E., NASRAOUI, O., AND GOMEZ, J. Anomaly detection based on unsupervised niche clustering with application to network intrusion detection. *IEEE Congress on Evolutionary Computation 1* (2004), 502–508.

[225] LEUNG, K., AND LECKIE, C. Unsupervised anomaly detection in network intrusion detection using clusters. In *Proc. of 28th Australasian Conference on Computer Science - Volume 38* (Newcastle, NSW, Australia, January/February 2005), Australian Computer Society, Inc., Darlinghurst, pp. 333–342.

[226] LI, Y., AND FANG, B. X. A lightweight online network anomaly detection scheme based on data mining methods. In *Proc. of the IEEE International Conference on Network Protocols* (USA, 2007), IEEE CS, pp. 340–341.

[227] LI, Y.-Z., ZHAO, B., XU, J., AND YANG, G. Anomaly intrusion detection method based on rough set theory. In *Proc. of the International Conference on Wavelet Analysis and Pattern Recognition* (Hong Kong, August 30–31 2008), IEEE Computer Society.

[228] LINDQVIST, U., AND JONSSON, E. How to systematically classify computer security intrusions. *IEEE Security and Privacy* (1997), 154–163.

[229] LIPPMANN, R. P., AND CUNNINGHAM, R. K. Improving intrusion detection performance using keyword selection and neural networks. MIT Lincoln Laboratory, Rm S4-121.

[230] LIPPMANN, R. P., FRIED, D. J., GRAF, I., HAINES, J., KENDALL, K., MCCLUNG, D., WEBER, D., WYSCHOGORD, S. W. D., CUNNINGHAM, R. K., AND ZISSMAN, M. A. Evaluating intrusion detection systems: The 1998 DARPA offline intrusion detection evaluation. In *Proc. of the DARPA Information Survivability Conference and Exposition* (January 2000), pp. 12–26.

[231] LIU, G., YI, Z., AND YANG, S. A hierarchical intrusion detection model based on the PCA neural networks. *Neurocomputing 70*, 7-9 (2007), 1561–1568.

[232] LIU, H., AND SETIONO, R. Feature selection via discretization. *IEEE Transactions on Knowledge and Data Engineering 9*, 4 (1997), 642–645.

[233] LIU, H., SETIONO, R., ET AL. A probabilistic approach to feature selection — A filter solution. In *Machine Learning —Int'nl Workshop* (1996), Citeseer, pp. 319–327.

[234] LIU, H., AND YU, L. Toward integrating feature selection algorithms for classification and clustering. *IEEE Transactions on Knowledge and Data Engineering 17*, 4 (2005), 491–502.

[235] LOCASTO, M. E., WANG, K., KEROMYTIS, A. D., AND STOLFO, S. J. FLIPS: Hybrid adaptive intrusion prevention. In *Recent Advances in Intrusion Detection, Lecture Notes in Computer Science* (2006), vol. 3858, Springer, pp. 82–101.

[236] LU, W., AND GHORBANI, A. A. Network anomaly detection based on wavelet analysis. *EURASIP Journal on Advances in Signal Processing 2009*, 837601 (January 2009).

[237] LU, W., AND TONG, H. Detecting network anomalies using CUSUM and EM clustering. In *Proc. of the 4th International Symposium on Advances in Computation and Intelligence* (2009), Springer, pp. 297–308.

[238] MA, J., AND PERKINGS, S. Online novelty detection on temporal sequences. In *Proc. of the 9th ACM SIGKDD International Conference on Knowledge Discovery and Data Mining* (2003), ACM, pp. 613–618.

[239] MA, J., AND PERKINGS, S. Time-series novelty detection using one-class support vector machines. In *Proc. of the International*

Joint Conference on Neural Networks (2003), vol. 3, pp. 1741–1745.

[240] MABU, S., CHEN, C., LU, N., SHIMADA, K., AND HIRASAWA, K. An intrusion-detection model based on fuzzy class-association-rule mining using genetic network programming. *IEEE Transactions on Systems, Man, and Cybernetics, Part C: Applications and Reviews 41*, 1 (2011), 130–139.

[241] MAHONEY, M. V., AND CHAN, P. K. Learning non-stationary models of normal network traffic for detecting novel attacks. In *Proc. of the 8th ACM SIGKDD Int'nl Conference on Knowledge Discovery and Data Mining* (2002), ACM Press, pp. 376–385.

[242] MAHONEY, M. V., AND CHAN, P. K. Learning rules for anomaly detection of hostile network traffic. In *Proc. of the 3rd IEEE International Conference on Data Mining* (Washington, DC, 2003), IEEE CS.

[243] MANIKOPOULOS, C., AND PAPAVASSILIOU, S. Network intrusion and fault detection: A statistical anomaly approach. *IEEE Communications Magazine 40*, 10 (October 2002), 76–82.

[244] MANNILA, H. Methods and problems in data mining. Proc. of the Int'nl Conference on Database Theory, pp. 41–55.

[245] MARINOVA-BONCHEVA, V. A short survey of intrusion detection systems. *Problems of Engineering Cybernetics and Robotics, Institute of Information Technologies, 1113 Sofia 58* (2007), 23–30.

[246] MASSICOTTE, F., COUTURE, M., BRIAND, L., AND LABICHE, Y. Context-based intrusion detection using Snort, Nessus and Bugtraq databases. In *Proc. of the Third Annual Conference on Privacy, Security and Trust* (2005), New Brunswick, Canada, pp. 1–12.

[247] MAULIK, U., AND BANDYOPADHYAY, S. Fuzzy partitioning using real-coded variable-length genetic algorithm for pixel classification. *IEEE Transactions on Geoscience and Remote Sensing 41*, 5 (2003), 1075–1081.

[248] MAXION, R. A., AND ROBERTS, R. R. Proper use of ROC curves in intrusion/anomaly detection. Tech. Rep. CS-TR-871, School of Computing Science, University of Newcastle upon Tyne, November 2004.

[249] MEYER, P., SCHRETTER, C., AND BONTEMPI, G. Information-theoretic feature selection in microarray data using variable complementarity. *IEEE Journal of Selected Topics in Signal Processing 2*, 3 (2008), 261–274.

[250] MI, A., AND HAI, L. A clustering-based classifier selection method for network intrusion detection. In *Proc. of the 5th International Conference on Computer Science & Education* (Hefei, China, August 2010), IEEE, pp. 1001–1004.

[251] MIERSWA, I., WURST, M., KLINKENBERG, R., SCHOLZ, M., AND EULER, T. Yale: Rapid prototyping for complex data mining tasks. In *Proc. of the 12th ACM SIGKDD Int'nl Conference on Knowledge Discovery and Data Mining* (2006), ACM, pp. 935–940.

[252] MIRKOVIC, J., AND REIHER, P. A taxonomy of DDoS attack and DDoS defense mechanisms. vol. 34, ACM SIGCOMM Computer Communication Review, pp. 39–53.

[253] MIRKOVIC, J., AND REIHER, P. D-ward: A source-end defense against flooding denial-of-service attacks. *IEEE Transactions Dependable and Secure Computing 2*, 3 (July 2005), 216–232.

[254] MIT LINCOLN LAB., I. S. T. G. The 1998 intrusion detection off-line evaluation plan, Mar. 1998.

[255] MITCHELL, T. M. *Machine Learning*. McGraw-Hill, Inc., New York, USA, 1997.

[256] MITRA, P., AND MAJUMDER, D. D. Feature selection and gene clustering from gene expression data. In *Proc. of the 17th Int'nl Conference on Pattern Recognition (ICPR'04), Volume 2* (Washington, DC, 2004), IEEE Computer Society, pp. 343–346.

[257] MITRA, P., MURTHY, C., AND PAL, S. Unsupervised feature selection using feature similarity. *IEEE Transactions on Pattern Analysis and Machine Intelligence 24*, 3 (2002), 301–312.

[258] MOHAJERANI, M., MOEINI, A., AND KIANIE, M. NFIDS: A Neuro-Fuzzy Intrusion Detection System. In *Proc. of the 10th IEEE International Conference on Electronics, Circuits and Systems* (December 2003), vol. 1, pp. 348–351.

[259] MOHAMMAD, E., AND ZAINE, O. R. Inverted matrix: Efficient discovery of frequent items in large datsets in the context of interactive mining. vol. 26, Proc. of the ACM SIGKDD'03, pp. 255–268.

[260] MOLINA, L., BELANCHE, L., AND NEBOT, À. Feature selection algorithms: A survey and experimental evaluation. In *IEEE International Conference on Data Mining* (2002), IEEE CS Press, pp. 306–313.

[261] MONTGOMERY, D. C. *Introduction to Statistical Quality Control*. John Wiley & Sons, New York, USA, 2000.

[262] MORIN, B., MÉ, L., DEBAR, H., AND DUCASSÉ, M. A logic-based model to support alert correlation in intrusion detection. *Information Fusion 10*, 4 (October 2009), 285–299.

[263] MUDA, Z., YASSIN, W., SULAIMAN, M. N., AND UDZIR, N. I. A K-means and naive Bayes learning approach for better intrusion detection. *Information Technology Journal 10* (2011), 648–655.

[264] MUNSON, A., AND CARUANA, R. Cluster ensembles for network anomaly detection. Tech. Rep. 2006-2047, Cornell University, September 2006.

[265] NADARAYA, E. On estimating regression. *Theory of Probability & Its Applications 9*, 1 (1964), 141–142.

[266] NALDURG, P., SEN, K., AND THATI, P. A temporal logic based framework for intrusion detection. In *Proc. of the 24th IFIP WG 6.1 International Conference on Formal Techniques for Networked and Distributed Systems* (2004), pp. 359–376.

[267] NEUMANN, P. G., AND PARKER, D. B. A summary of computer misuse techniques. In *Proc. of the 12th National Computer Security Conference* (Baltimore, MD, 1989), pp. 396–407.

[268] NGUYEN, H. H., HARBI, N., AND DARMONT, J. An efficient local region and clustering-based ensemble system for intrusion detection. In *Proc. of the 15th Symposium on International Database Engineering & Applications* (USA, 2011), ACM, pp. 185–191.

[269] NING, P., AND JAJODIA, S. *Intrusion Detection Techniques*. H Bidgoli (Ed.), The Internet Encyclopedia, 2003.

[270] NOEL, S., WIJESEKERA, D., AND YOUMAN, C. Modern intrusion detection, data mining, and degrees of attack guilt. In *Proc. of the International Conference on Applications of Data Mining in Computer Security* (2002), Springer.

[271] NORTON, D. An ettercap primer. SANS Institute InfoSec Reading Room.

[272] NOTO, K., BRODLEY, C., AND SLONIM, D. Anomaly detection using an ensemble of feature models. In *Proc. of the IEEE International Conference on Data Mining* (USA, 2010), IEEE CS, pp. 953–958.

[273] NSL-KDD. NSL-KDD data set for network-based intrusion detection systems. http://iscx.cs.unb.ca/NSL-KDD/, March 2009.

[274] OTEY, M. E., GHOTING, A., AND PARTHASARATHY, S. Fast distributed outlier detection in mixed-attribute data sets. *Data Mining and Knowledge Discovery 12*, 2-3 (2006), 203–228.

[275] OTEY, M. E., PARTHASARATHY, S., AND GHOTING, A. Fast lightweight outlier detection in mixed-attribute data. In *ACM SIGKDD Workshop on Data Mining Methods for Anomaly Detection* (2005).

[276] OWEZARSKI, P., MAZEL, J., AND LABIT, Y. 0 day anomaly detection made possible thanks to machine learning. In *Wired/Wireless Internet Communications*, vol. 6074 of *LNCS*. Springer, 2010, pp. 327–338.

[277] PAPADOPOULOS, C., TARTAKOVSKY, A. G., AND POLUNCHENKO, A. S. A hybrid approach to efficient detection of distributed denial-of-service attacks. Tech. rep., Department of Computer Science, Colorado State University, June, 2008.

[278] PARIKH, D., AND CHEN, T. Data fusion and cost minimization for intrusion detection. *IEEE Transactions on Information Forensics and Security 3*, 3 (2008), 381–389.

[279] PARK, J., AND SANDBERG, J. W. Universal approximation using radial basis functions network. *Neural Computation 3* (1991), 246–257.

[280] PARK, J. S., CHEN, M. S., AND YU, P. S. An efficient hash

based algorithm for mining association rules. ACM SIGMOD'95, pp. 175–186.

[281] PARLOS, A., CHONG, K., AND ATIYA, A. Application of the recurrent multilayer perceptron in modeling complex process dynamics. *IEEE Transactions on Neural Networks 5*, 2 (1994), 255–266.

[282] PASCHALIDIS, I. C., AND CHEN, Y. Statistical anomaly detection with sensor networks. *ACM Transactions on Sensor Networks 7*, 2 (August 2010), 17–23.

[283] PATCHA, A., AND PARK, J.-M. Detecting denial-of-service attacks with incomplete audit data. In *Proc. of the 14th Int'nl Conference on Computer Communications and Networks (ICCCN 2005)* (October 2005), IEEE Computer Society, pp. 263–268.

[284] PATCHA, A., AND PARK, J. M. An overview of anomaly detection techniques: Existing solutions and latest technological trends. *Computer Networks 51*, 12 (2007), 3448–3470.

[285] PAWLAK, Z. Rough sets. In *Proc. of the ACM 23rd Annual Conference on Computer Science* (1995), ACM, pp. 262–264.

[286] PAWLAK, Z. Rough set approach to knowledge-based decision support. *European Journal of Operational Research 99*, 1 (1997), 48–57.

[287] PAWLAK, Z., GRZYMALA-BUSSE, J., AND ZIARKO, W. Rough sets. *Communications of the ACM 38*, 11 (November 1995), 88–95.

[288] PAXSON, V. Bro: A system for detecting network intruders in real-time. *Computer networks 31*, 23 (1999), 2435–2463.

[289] PEDDABACHIGARI, S., ABRAHAM, A., GROSAN, C., AND THOMAS, J. Modeling intrusion detection system using hybrid intelligent systems. *Journal of Network and Computer Applications 30*, 1 (January 2007), 114–132.

[290] PENG, H., LONG, F., AND DING, C. Feature selection based on mutual information criteria of max-dependency, max-relevance, and min-redundancy. *IEEE Transactions on Pattern Analysis and Machine Intelligence 27*, 8 (2005), 1226–1238.

[291] PENG, T., LECKIE, C., AND RAMAMOHANARAO, K. Survey of network-based defense mechanisms countering the DoS and DDoS problems. *ACM Computing Surveys 39*, 1 (April 2007), 1–42.

[292] PERDISCI, R., ARIU, D., FOGLA, P., GIACINTO, G., AND LEE, W. McPAD: A multiple classifier system for accurate payload-based anomaly detection. *Computer Networks 53*, 6 (April 2009), 864–881.

[293] PERDISCI, R., GU, G., AND LEE, W. Using an ensemble of one-class SVM classifiers to harden payload-based anomaly detection systems. In *Proc. of the 6th International Conference on Data Mining* (USA, 2006), IEEE CS, pp. 488–498.

[294] PETROVSKIY, M. I. Outlier detection algorithms in data mining systems. *Programming and Computer Software 29*, 4 (2003), 228–237.

[295] POLIKAR, R. Ensemble based systems in decision making. *IEEE Circuits System Magazine 6*, 3 (2006), 21–45.

[296] PORRAS, P. A., AND NEUMANN, P. G. EMERALD: Event monitoring enabling response to anomalous live disturbances. In *Proc. of the 20th National Information Systems Security Conference* (1997), pp. 353–365.

[297] PORTNOY, L., ESKIN, E., AND STOLFO, S. J. Intrusion detection with unlabeled data using clustering. In *Proc. of ACM Workshop on Data Mining Applied to Security* (2001).

[298] PRAS, A., SPEROTTO, A., MOURA, G. C. M., DRAGO, I., BARBOSA, R., SADRE, R., SCHMIDT, R., AND HOFSTEDE, R. Attacks by anonymous? wikileaks proponents not anonymous. Design and Analysis of Communication Systems Group (DACS) CTIT Technical Report, pp. 1–10.

[299] PRAYOTE, A. *Knowledge Based Anomaly Detection*. PhD thesis, School of Computer Science and Egineering, University of New South Wales, November 2007.

[300] PRIESTLEY, M., AND CHAO, M. Non-parametric function fitting. *Journal of the Royal Statistical Society. Series B (Methodological)* (1972), 385–392.

[301] PROCOPIUE, C. M., JONES, M., AGARWAL, P. K., AND MU-RALI, T. M. A Monte Carlo algorithm for fast projective clustering. In *ACM SIGMOD'02* (New York, USA, 2002), ACM, pp. 418–427.

[302] PROVOST, F. J., AND FAWCETT, T. Robust classification for imprecise environments. *Machine Learning 42*, 3 (2001), 203–231.

[303] PUURONEN, S., TSYMBAL, A., AND SKRYPNYK, I. Correlation-based and contextual merit-based ensemble feature selection. *Advances in Intelligent Data Analysis* (2001), 135–144.

[304] QUINLAN, J. R. *C4. 5: Programs for Machine Learning*, vol. 1. Morgan Kaufmann, 1993.

[305] QUITTEK, J., ZSEBY, T., CLAISE, B., AND ZENDER, S. RFC 3917: Requirements for IP Flow Information Export: IPFIX, Hawthorn Victoria. http://www.ietf.org/rfc/rfc3917.txt, 2004.

[306] R DEVELOPMENT CORE TEAM. *R: A Language and Environment for Statistical Computing*. R Foundation for Statistical Computing, Vienna, Austria, 2012.

[307] RABIN, M. *Fingerprinting by Random Polynomials*. TR // Center for Research in Computing Technology, Harvard University. 1981.

[308] RAMASWAMY, S., RASTOGI, R., AND SHIM, K. Effcient algorithms for mining outliers from large data sets. In *Proc. of the ACM SIGMOD International Conference on Management of Data* (2000), ACM, pp. 427–438.

[309] RANJAN, S., SWAMINATHAN, R., UYSAL, M., AND KNIGHTLY, E. DDoS-resilient scheduling to counter application layer attacks under imperfect detection. Proc. of IEEE INFOCOM, 2006, Barcelona, Spain, pp. 1–13.

[310] RAUBER, T. TOOLDIAG Pattern Recognition Toolbox.

[311] REYNOLDS, D. A., QUATIERI, T. F., AND DUNN, R. B. Speaker verification using adapted Gaussian mixture models. *Digital Signal Processing 10*, 1-3 (2000), 19–41.

[312] ROESCH, M. Snort — Lightweight intrusion detection for networks. In *Proc. of the 13th USENIX Conference on System Administration* (Washington, DC, 1999), pp. 229–238.

[313] ROKACH, L. Ensemble-based classifiers. *Artificial Intelligence Review 33*, 1-2 (February 2010), 1–39.

[314] ROMANSKI, P., AND ROMANSKI, M. Package fselector. *http://cran.r-project.org/web/packages/FSelector/* (2009).

[315] ROSENBLATT, F. Two theorems of statistical separability in the perceptron. In *Proc. of the Symposium of Mechanization of Thought Processes* (HM Stationary Office, London, 1959), National Physical Laboratory, pp. 421–456.

[316] ROUSSEEUW, P. J. Silhouettes: A graphical aid to the interpretation and validation of cluster analysis. *Journal of Computational and Applied Mathematics 20*, 1 (1987), 53–65.

[317] ROUSSEEUW, P. J., AND LEROY, A. M. *Robust Regression and Outlier Detection.* John Wiley & Sons, 1987.

[318] SAEYS, Y., INZA, I., AND LARRAÑAGA, P. A review of feature selection techniques in bioinformatics. *Bioinformatics 23*, 19 (2007), 2507–2517.

[319] SANDER, J., ESTER, M., KRIEGEL, H. P., AND XU, X. Density based clustering in spatial databases: The algorithm gdbscan and its applications. *Data Mining and Knowledge Discovery 2*, 2 (1998), 169–194.

[320] SANNER, M., ET AL. Python: a programming language for software integration and development. *Journal of Molecular Graph Model 17*, 1 (1999), 57–61.

[321] SARKAR, M., AND YEGNANARAYANA, B. Fuzzy-rough membership functions. In *Proc. of the IEEE Int'nl Conference on Systems, Man and Cybernetics* (San Diego, CA, USA, October 1998), vol. 2, pp. 2028–2033.

[322] SATTEN, C. Lossless gigabit remote packet capture with Linux. University of Washington Network Systems, http://staff.washington.edu/corey/gulp/, March, 2008.

[323] SAVESERE, A., OMIECINSKI, E., AND NAVATHE, S. An effective algorithm for mining asociation rules in large database. In *Proc. of Int'nl Conference on VLDB95* (1995), pp. 432–443.

[324] SCHAPIRE, R. E. A brief introduction to boosting. In *Proc. of the 16th International Joint Conference on Artificial Intelligence* (Morgan Kaufmann, 1999), pp. 1401–1406.

[325] SCHEIRER, W., AND CHUAH, M. C. Syntax vs. semantics: Competing approaches to dynamic network intrusion detection. *Int'nl Journal Security and Networks 3*, 1 (December 2008), 24–35.

[326] SCHIFFMAN, M. D. Libnet 101, part 1: The primer. In *Guardent security digital infrastructure* (2000).

[327] SEKAR, R., GUANG, Y., VERMA, S., AND SHANBHAG, T. A high-performance network intrusion detection system. In *Proc. of the 6th ACM Conference on Computer and Communications Security* (USA, 1999), ACM, pp. 8–17.

[328] SEKAR, R., GUPTA, A., FRULLO, J., SHANBHAG, T., TIWARI, A., AND YANG, H. Specification-based anomaly detection: A new approach for detecting network intrusions. In *Proc. of the 9th ACM Conference on Computer and Communications Security* (2002), pp. 265–274.

[329] SEKAR, V., DUFFIELD, N., SPATSCHECK, O., VAN DER MERWE, J., AND ZHANG, H. LADS: Large-scale automated DDoS detection system. In *Proc. of the Annual Conference on USENIX, 2006* (Berkeley, CA), USENIX Association, pp. 16–16.

[330] SELIM, S., HASHEM, M., AND NAZMY, T. M. Hybrid multi-level intrusion detection system. *International Journal of Computer Science and Information Security 9*, 5 (2011), 23–29.

[331] SEQUEIRA, K., AND ZAKI, M. ADMIT: Anomaly-based data mining for intrusions. In *Proc. of the Eighth ACM SIGKDD Int'nl Conference on Knowledge Discovery and Data Mining* (New York, NY, USA, 2002), ACM, pp. 386–395.

[332] SETIONO, R., AND LIU, H. Neural-network feature selector. *IEEE Transactions on Neural Networks 8*, 3 (1997), 654–662.

[333] SHABTAI, A., KANONOV, U., AND ELOVICI, Y. Intrusion detection for mobile devices using the knowledge-based, temporal

abstraction method. *Journal of System Software 83*, 8 (August 2010), 1524–1537.

[334] SHAFER, G. A Mathematical Theory of Evidence. Princeton University Press, Princeton, NJ, 1976.

[335] SHAH, S. An introduction to HTTP fingerprinting. http://net-square.com/httprint/httprint paper.html, 2004.

[336] SHARAN, R., AND SHAMIR, R. Click: A clustering algorithm with applications to gene expression analysis. In *Proc. of Intelligent System for Molecular Biology* (2000), AAAI Press, pp. 307–316.

[337] SHARKEY, A. *Combining Artificial Neural Nets: Ensemble and Modular Multi-net Systems*. Springer Verlag, New York, 1999.

[338] SHAWN OSTERMANN. Tcptrace. Ohio University, Athens, http://www.tcptrace.org, 2009.

[339] SHEIKHOLESLAMI, G., CHATTERJEE, S., AND ZHANG, A. Wavecluster: A multi-resolution clustering approach for very large spatial database. In *Proc. of the int'nl conference on Very Large Data Bases* (Seattle, 1998), ACM, pp. 428–439.

[340] SHIFFLET, J. A technique independent fusion model for network intrusion detection. In *Proc. of the Midstates Conference on Undergraduate Research in Computer Science and Mathematics* (2005), vol. 3, pp. 13–19.

[341] SHIPLEY, G. ISS RealSecure pushes past newer IDS players. *Network Computing 10*, 10 (1999), 95–111.

[342] SHON, T., HAN, K., PARK, J., AND CHANG, H. A novel approach to detect network attacks using G-HMM-based temporal relations between internet protocol packets. *EURASIP Journal on Wireless Communications and Networking* (2011), 1–14.

[343] SHON, T., AND MOON, J. A hybrid machine learning approach to network anomaly detection. *Information Science 177* (2007), 3799–3821.

[344] SNYDER, D. Online intrusion detection using sequences of system calls. Master's thesis, Department of Computer Science, Florida State University, 2001.

[345] SOMMER, R., AND PAXSON, V. Outside the closed world: On using machine learning for network intrusion detection. In *Proc. of the IEEE Symposium on Security and Privacy* (2010), pp. 305–316.

[346] SONG, S., LING, L., AND MANIKOPOULO, C. N. Flow-based statistical aggregation schemes for network anomaly detection. In *Proc. of the IEEE International Conference on Networking, Sensing* (2006), pp. 786–791.

[347] SONG, X., WU, M., JERMAINE, C., AND RANKA, S. Conditional anomaly detection. *IEEE Transactions on Knowledge and Data Engineering 19*, 5 (2007), 631–645.

[348] SORENSEN, S. *Competitive Overview of Statistical Anomaly Detection*. Juniper Networks, USA, 2004.

[349] SOULE, A., SALAMATIAN, K., AND TAFT, N. Combining filtering and statistical methods for anomaly detection. In *Proc. of the 5th ACM SIGCOMM Conference on Internet Measurement* (USA, 2005), ACM, pp. 1–14.

[350] SPEROTTO, A., SCHAFFRATH, G., SADRE, R., MORARIU, C., PRAS, A., AND STILLER, B. An overview of IP flow-based intrusion detection. *IEEE Communications Surveys & Tutorials 12*, 3 (2010), 343–356.

[351] SRIKANT, R. *Fast algorithms for mining association rules and sequential patterns*. PhD thesis, University of Wisconsin, 1996.

[352] SRIKANT, R., AND AGRAWALA, R. Mining generalized association rules. In *Proc. of the 21st VLDB Conference, Zurich, Switzerland* (1995), pp. 407–419.

[353] STALLINGS, W. *Data and Computer Communication*, eighth ed. Pearson Prentice Hall, 2007.

[354] STIBOR, T., TIMMIS, J., AND ECKERT, C. A comparative study of real-valued negative selection to statistical anomaly detection techniques. In *Proc. of the 4th International Conference on Artificial Immune Systems* (2005), vol. LNCS-3627, pp. 262–275.

[355] STORLOKKEN, R. Labelling clusters in an anomaly based IDS by means of clustering quality indexes. Master's thesis, Faculty

of Computer Science and Media Technology, Gjovik University College, Norway, 2007.

[356] STOUFFER, K. A., FALCO, J. A., AND SCARFONE, K. A. Guide to industrial control systems (ICS) security. Tech. Rep. SP 800-82, National Institute of Standards & Technology, Gaithersburg, MD, United States, 2011.

[357] STREHL, A., AND GHOSH, J. Cluster ensembles — A knowledge reuse framework for combining multiple partitions , journal = Journal of Machine Learning Research, volume = 3, number = , month = , year = 2003, pages = 583–617, doi = , publisher = , address = ,.

[358] SUBRAMONIAM, N., PAWAR, P. S., BHATNAGAR, M., KHEDEKAR, N. S., GUNTUPALLI, S., SATYANARAYANA, N., VIJAYAKUMAR, V. A., AMPATT, P. K., RANJAN, R., AND PANDIT, P. S. Development of a comprehensive intrusion detection system — Challenges and approaches. In *Proc. of the 1st International Conference on Information Systems Security* (Kolkata, India, 2005), pp. 332–335.

[359] SUGUMARAN, V., MURALIDHARAN, V., AND RAMACHANDRAN, K. Feature selection using decision tree and classification through proximal support vector machine for fault diagnostics of roller bearing. *Mechanical Systems and Signal Processing 21*, 2 (2007), 930–942.

[360] SUN, J., YANG, H., TIAN, J., AND WU, F. Intrusion detection method based on wavelet neural network. In *Proc. of the 2nd International Workshop on Knowledge Discovery and Data Mining* (USA, 2009), IEEE CS, pp. 851–854.

[361] SUTTON, S., AND BARTO, A. G. *Reinforcement Learning: An Introduction*. The MIT Press, USA, 2011.

[362] TAJBAKHSH, A., RAHMATI, M., AND MIRZAEI, A. Intrusion detection using fuzzy association rules. *Applied Soft Computing 9*, 2 (March 2009), 462–469.

[363] TAN, P. N., STEINBACH, M., AND KUMAR, V. *Introduction to Data Mining*. Addison-Wesley, 2005.

[364] TANENBAUM, A. S. *Computer Networks*, fourth ed. Pearson Prentice Hall, 2003.

[365] TAPIADOR, J. M. E., TEODORO, P. G., AND DIAZ-VERDEJO, J. E. Detection of web-based attacks through Markovian protocol parsing. In *Proc. of the 10th IEEE Symposium on Computers and Communications* (USA, June 2005), IEEE CS, pp. 457–462.

[366] THEILER, J., AND CAI, D. M. Resampling approach for anomaly detection in multispectral images. In *Proc. of SPIE* (2003), vol. 5093, SPIE, pp. 230–240.

[367] THOTTAN, M., AND JI, C. Anomaly detection in IP networks. *IEEE Transactions on Signal Processing 51*, 8 (August 2003), 2191–2204.

[368] TOMIDA, S., HANAI, T., HONDA, H., AND KOBAYASHI, T. Analysis of expression profile using fuzzy adaptive resonance theory. *Bioinformatics 18*, 8 (2002), 1073–1083.

[369] TONG, H., LI, C., HE, J., CHEN, J., TRAN, Q. A., DUAN, H. X., AND LI, X. Anomaly Internet Network Traffic Detection by Kernel Principle Component Classifier. In *Proc. of the 2nd International Symposium on Neural Networks* (2005), vol. LNCS. 3498, pp. 476–481.

[370] TONG, X., WANG, Z., AND YU, H. A research using hybrid RBF/Elman neural networks for intrusion detection system secure model. *Computer Physics Communications 180*, 10 (2009), 1795–1801.

[371] TRIER, O. D., JAIN, A., AND TAXT, T. Feature extraction methods for character recognition — A survey. *Pattern Recognition 29*, 4 (1996), 641–662.

[372] TUV, E., BORISOV, A., AND TORKKOLA, K. Feature selection using ensemble based ranking against artificial contrasts. In *IJCNN'06, International Joint Conference on Neural Networks* (2006), IEEE, pp. 2181–2186.

[373] VALDES, A., AND SKINNER, K. Adaptive model-based monitoring for cyber attack detection. In *Proc. of the Recent Advances in Intrusion Detection* (Toulouse, France, 2000), pp. 80–92.

[374] VANDERLOOY, S. MATLAB toolbox for machine learning. Tech. Rep. MICC 08-03, Universiteit Maastricht, 2008.

[375] VAPNIK, V. N. *The Nature of Statistical Learning Theory.* Springer Verlag, New York, USA, 1995.

[376] VISCONTI, A., AND TAHAYORI, H. Artificial immune system based on interval type-2 fuzzy set paradigm. *Applied Soft Computing 11*, 6 (September 2011), 4055–4063.

[377] VISWANATH, P., AND BABU, V. S. A fast hybrid density based clustering method for large datasets. *Pattern Recognition Letters 30* (2009), 1477–1488.

[378] WANG, K., AND STOLFO, S. J. Anomalous payload-based network intrusion detection. In *Proc. of the Recent Advances in Intrusion Detection* (2004), Springer, pp. 203–222.

[379] WANG, W., YANG, J., AND MUNZ, R. R. Sting: A statistical information grid approach to spatial data mining. In *Proc. of VLDB97* (Athens, Greece, 1997), pp. 186–195.

[380] WANG, Y. *Statistical Technique for Network Security.* Information Science Reference (IGI Global), 2009.

[381] WATTENBERG, F. S., PEREZ, J. I. A., HIGUERA, P. C., FERNANDEZ, M. M., AND DIMITRIADIS, I. A. Anomaly detection in network traffic based on statistical inference and α-stable modeling. *IEEE Transactions on Dependable and Secure Computing 8*, 4 (July/August 2011), 494–509.

[382] WEISS, S. M., AND ZHANG, T. *The Handbook of Data Mining.* Lawrence Erlbaum Assoc. Inc., 2003, pp. 426–439.

[383] WERBOS, P. *Beyond Regression: New Tools for Predictions and Analysis in the Behavioral Science.* PhD thesis, Harvard University, Cambridge, MA, 1974.

[384] WIDROW, B., AND HOFF, M. E. Two theorems of statistical separability in the perceptron. In *Proc. of IRE Western Electric Show and Convention Record, Part 4* (1960), pp. 96–104.

[385] WIKIMEDIA, FOUNDATION. Intrusion detection system. http://en.wikipedia.org/wiki/Intrusion-detection_system, February 2009.

[386] WU, S. X., AND BANZHAF, W. The use of computational intelligence in intrusion detection systems: A review. *Applied Soft Computing 10*, 1 (January 2010), 1–35.

[387] WU, Z., OU, Y., AND LIU, Y. A taxonomy of network and computer attacks based on responses. In *Proc. of the International Conference of Information Technology, Computer Engineering and Management Sciences* (China, 2011), IEEE Computer Society, pp. 26–29.

[388] XIAN, J. Q., LANG, F. H., AND TANG, X. L. A novel intrusion detection method based on clonal selection clustering algorithm. In *Proc. of the International Conference on Machine Learning and Cybernetics*, vol. 6. IEEE Press, USA, 2005.

[389] XIAO, Z., DELLANDREA, E., DOU, W., AND CHEN, L. Esfs: A new embedded feature selection method based on sfs. *Rapports de Recherché* (2008).

[390] XIE, X. L., AND BENI, G. A validity measure for fuzzy clustering. *IEEE Transactions on Pattern Analysis and Machine Intelligence 13*, 4 (1991), 841–847.

[391] XIE, Y., AND YU, S.-Z. Monitoring the application-layer DDoS attacks for popular websites. *IEEE/ACM Transactions on Networking 17*, 1 (2009), 15–25.

[392] XU, X. Sequential anomaly detection based on temporal-difference learning: Principles, models and case studies. *Applied Soft Computing 10*, 3 (2010), 859–867.

[393] XU, X., ESTER, M., KRIEGEL, H. P., AND SANDER, J. A nonparametric clustering algorithm for knowledge discovery in large spatial datasets. In *Proc. on Data Engineering* (1998), IEEE Press.

[394] XU, X., JAGER, J., AND KRIEGEL, H. P. A fast parallel clustering algorithm for large spatial databases. *Data Mining and Knowledge Discovery 3*, 3 (1999), 263–290.

[395] YAMANISHI, K., AND ICHI TAKEUCHI, J. Discovering outlier filtering rules from unlabeled data: Combining a supervised learner with an unsupervised learner. In *Proc. of the 7th ACM SIGKDD Int'nl Conference on Knowledge Discovery and Data Mining* (2001), ACM Press, pp. 389–394.

[396] YAMANISHI, K., TAKEUCHI, J. I., WILLIAMS, G., AND MILNE, P. On-line unsupervised outlier detection using finite mixtures

with discounting learning algorithms. *Data Mining and Knowledge Discovery 8* (2004), 275–300.

[397] YANG, H., XIE, F., AND LU, Y. Clustering and classification based anomaly detection. *Fuzzy Systems and Knowledge Discovery 4223/2006* (2006), 1082–1091.

[398] YANG, J., AND HONAVAR, V. Feature subset selection using a genetic algorithm. *Intelligent Systems and Their Applications, IEEE 13*, 2 (1998), 44–49.

[399] YANG, J., WANG, W., AND YU, P. δ-clusters: Capturing subspace correlation in a large dataset. In *Int'nl Conference on Data Engineering* (2002), pp. 517–528.

[400] YAO, Y., WEI, Y., GAO, F. X., AND YU, G. Anomaly intrusion detection approach using hybrid MLP/CNN neural network. In *Proc. of the 6th Int'nl Conference on Intelligent Systems Design and Applications (ISDA'06)* (Washington, DC, USA, 2006), IEEE Computer Society, pp. 1095–1102.

[401] YAROCHKIN, F. Remote OS detection via TCP/IP stack fingerprinting. http://www.insecure.org, 1998.

[402] YE, N. A Markov chain model of temporal behavior for anomaly detection. In *Proc. of the 2000 IEEE Workshop on Information Assurance and Security United States Military Academy* (West Point, NY, USA), IEEE, pp. 171–174.

[403] YE, N., EHIABOR, T., AND ZHANG, Y. First-order versus high-order stochastic models for computer intrusion detection. *Quality and Reliability Engineering International 18*, 3 (2002), 243–250.

[404] YE, T., KALYANARAMAN, S., HARRISON, D., SIKDAR, B., MO, B., KAUR, H. T., VASTOLA, K., AND SZYMANSKI, B. Network management and control using collaborative on-line simulation. In *Proc. of IEEE Int'nl Conference on Communications (ICC 2001)* (Helsinki, Finland, June 2001), IEEE Computer Society Press, Los Alamintos, CA.

[405] YEUNG, D. Y. Host-based intrusion detection using dynamic and static behavioral models. *Pattern Recognition 36* (2003), 229–243.

[406] YEUNG, K. H., FUNG, D., AND WONG, K. Y. Tools for attacking layer 2 network infrastructure. In *Proc. of the Int'nl Multi-Conference of Engineers and Computer Scientists, vol 2* (2008).

[407] YIU-MING, C. k*-means: A new generalized k-means clustering algorithm. *Pattern Recognition Letters 24*, 15 (2003), 2883–2893.

[408] YONG, H., AND FENG, Z. X. Expert system based intrusion detection system. In *Proc. of the Int'nl Conference on Information Management, Innovation Management and Industrial Engineering* (November 2010), vol. 4, pp. 404–407.

[409] YOON, H. S., AHN, S. Y., LEE, S. H., CHO, S. B., AND KIM, J. H. Heterogenous clustering ensemble method for combining different cluster results. In *LNCS Proc BioDM'06* (Berlin, 2006), vol. 3916, Springer Verlag, pp. 82–92.

[410] YU, J., LI, Z., CHEN, H., AND CHEN, X. A detection and offense mechanism to defend against application layer DDoS attacks. Third Int'nl Conference on Networking and Services, IEEE.

[411] YU, L., AND LIU, H. Feature selection for high-dimensional data: A fast correlation-based filter solution. In *Machine Learning - Int'nl Workshop* (2003), vol. 20, p. 856.

[412] YU, M. A nonparametric adaptive CUSUM method and its application in network anomaly detection. *Int'nl Journal of Advancements in Computing Technology 4*, 1 (2012), 280–288.

[413] YU, X. A new model of intelligent hybrid network intrusion detection system. In *Proc. of the International Conference on Bioinformatics and Biomedical Technology* (2010), IEEE CS, pp. 386–389.

[414] YU, Z., AND TSAI, J. J. P. *Intrusion Detection– A Machine Learning Approach*. Imperial College Press, 2011.

[415] ZADEH, L. A. Fuzzy logic, neural networks, and soft computing. *Communications, ACM 37*, 3 (March 1994), 77–84.

[416] ZADEH, L. A. Role of soft computing and fuzzy logic in the conception, design and development of information/intelligent systems. *Lecture Notes in Computer Science 695* (1998), 1–9.

[417] ZANERO, S., AND SAVARESI, S. M. Unsupervised learning techniques for an intrusion detection system. In *Proc. of the 2004 ACM Symposium on Applied Computing* (2004), pp. 412–419.

[418] ZHANG, C., JIANG, J., AND KAMEL, M. Intrusion detection using hierarchical neural networks. *Pattern Recognition Letters 26*, 6 (May 2005), 779–791.

[419] ZHANG, C., ZHANG, G., AND SUN, S. A mixed unsupervised clustering-based intrusion detection. In *Proc. of 3rd Int'nl Conference on Genetic and Evolutionary Computing* (Gulin, China, October 2009), IEEE Computer Society.

[420] ZHANG, J., AND ZULKERNINE, M. A hybrid network intrusion detection technique using random forests. In *Proc. of 1st Int'nl Conference on Availability, Reliability and Security (ARES 2006)* (Vienna, Austria, April 2006), IEEE Computer Society, pp. 262–269.

[421] ZHANG, J., ZULKERNINE, M., AND HAQUE, A. Random-forests-based network intrusion detection systems. *IEEE Transactions on Systems, Man, and Cybernetics: Part C 38*, 5 (2008), 649–659.

[422] ZHANG, T., RAMAKRISHNAN, R., AND LIVNY, M. BIRCH: An effective data clustering method for very large databases. *SIGMOID Record 1996 ACM SIGMOID Int'nl Conference on Management of Data 25* (1996), 103–114.

[423] ZHANG, W., YANG, Q., AND GENG, Y. A survey of anomaly detection methods in networks. In *Proc. of the International Symposium on Computer Network and Multimedia Technology* (January 2009), pp. 1–3.

[424] ZHANG, Y. F., XIONG, Z. Y., AND WANG, X. Q. Distributed intrusion detection based on clustering. In *Proc. of the International Conference on Machine Learning and Cybernetics* (August 2005), vol. 4, pp. 2379–2383.

[425] ZHANG, Z., LI, J., MANIKOPOULOS, C. N., JORGENSON, J., AND UCLES, J. HIDE: A hierarchical network intrusion detection system using statistical preprocessing and neural network classification. In *Proc. of IEEE Man Systems and Cybernetics Information Assurance Workshop* (2001).

[426] ZHAO, M., AND SALIGRAMA, V. Anomaly detection with score functions based on nearest neighbor graphs. In *Proc. of the 23rd Annual Conference on Neural Information Processing Systems (NIPS)* (Vancouver, British Columbia, Canada, December 2009), vol. 22, Curran Associates, Inc., pp. 2250–2258.

[427] ZHI-DONG, L., WU, Y., WEI, W., AND DA-PENG, M. Decision-level fusion model of multi-source intrusion detection alerts. *Journal on Communications 32*, 5 (2011), 121–128.

[428] ZHONG, N., DONG, J., AND OHSUGA, S. Using rough sets with heuristics for feature selection. *Journal of Intelligent Information Systems 16*, 3 (2001), 199–214.

[429] ZHONG, S., KHOSHGOFTAAR, T., AND SELIYA, N. Clustering-based network intrusion detection. *International Journal of Reliability, Quality and Safety Engineering 14*, 2 (2007), 169–187.

[430] ZHOU, B., CHEUNG, D. W., AND KAO, B. A fast algorithm for density based clustering in large database. In *Proc. of 3rd PAKDD* (1999), Springer Verlag, pp. 338–349.

[431] ZHUOWEI, L., DAS, A., AND NANDI, S. Utilizing statistical characteristics of N-grams for intrusion detection. In *Proc. of the International Conference on Cyberworlds* (USA, 2003), IEEE CS, pp. 486–494.

Index

Milton Keynes UK
Ingram Content Group UK Ltd.
UKHW031126141024
449569UK00006B/399